BLOODY HAND!

WILLS AND CRIME

BLOODY HAND!

WILLS AND CRIME

De bloedige hand erft niet
(The bloody hand inherits nothing): Old Dutch legal maxim

BY

ELLISON KAHN

Professor Emeritus of Law and
Honorary Professorial Research Fellow,
University of the Witwatersrand, Johannesburg

2003

Siber Ink

First published September 2003

by

Siber Ink

Siber Ink CC
PO Box 44754
Claremont 7735
Cape Town
SOUTH AFRICA

subs@siberink.co.za
www.siberink.co.za

ISBN 0-9584540-5-1

Set in 11 on 13 pt New Baskerville by Wyvern, Cape Town
Printed and bound by Creda Communications (Pty) Ltd, Cape Town

About the author

Ellison Kahn needs no introduction, at least not to lawyers and to readers interested in the law. The doyen of writers on the law in South Africa, he is the author, co-author or editor of 14 books on the law, and he has published many articles in books and legal periodicals in South Africa and abroad. While he has previously compiled books on legal humour to leaven his more scholarly writing, this is his first book on real-life crime.

Professor Kahn is Professor Emeritus of Law in and Honorary Professorial Research Fellow of the University of the Witwatersrand, where he was a member of staff from 1948 and a professor of law from 1954 to 1989, and of which he was a Deputy Vice-Chancellor from 1972 to 1981. From 1967 to 1972 he was Dean of the Faculty of Law, and from 1987 to 1988 Dean of the Faculty of Commerce. He is a Senior Counsel of the Republic of South Africa and a Barrister of the Middle Temple, London. Professor Kahn holds the degrees of BCom LLB (Witwatersrand) and LLM LLD (Natal). The honorary degree of LLD has been conferred on him by the Universities of Cape Town, the Witwatersrand and Natal, and by the Rand Afrikaans University. In 1987 he was elected an Associate Member of the International Academy of International Law of Paris/New York. The Society of University Teachers of Law presented him in 1989 with its gold medallion for services to academic excellence, law teaching and legal publications.

He was associated with the editing of the *South African Law Journal* for 50 years (surely a record that is unequalled in the world, and will perhaps remain unequalled), having been associate editor from 1950 to 1958, joint editor from 1959 to 1967, and editor from 1968 to 1999.

Bloody Hand! — Wills and Crime is Professor Kahn's first book of its kind, having been written for the general reader not just for the lawyer.

Preface

This little book has its origin, I feel sure, in my work as general editor and co-author of M M Corbett, Gys Hofmeyr and Ellison Kahn *The Law of Succession in South Africa*, second edition, which was published in Cape Town by Juta & Co in 2001. After three years' hard labour at this task I must have felt the need for some light relief. It found its expression in what Graham Greene, if I dare mention the name of this great author in the same breath as mine, used to call 'an entertainment'. That description appears macabre in the context of this work. But then several of Greene's 'entertainments' involved murders and other unpleasantnesses.

I do hope that the title and subtitle of this book are not misleading. A will is not the only inducement to murder someone with the object of receiving a benefit from the estate of the deceased; the prospect of a benefit on the death of someone intestate may be equally attractive to the bloedige hand of the Roman-Dutch legal authorities. But I could not find a wording, both accurate and euphonious, that would embrace succession ab intestato. So please read 'wills' so as to cover succession of this type. Perhaps I can derive some consolation from the fact that the literature at my disposal has very few instances of homicide intended to lead to succession on the intestacy of the deceased. It may be that criminals are seldom aware of the rules of intestate succession.

Another difficulty also soon emerged. In South Africa, the home of this essay, in which many of the incidents related in it occurred, the person charged with having committed a crime is called the 'accused'. The word is also used in Scotland and in many common-law countries, among them Australia (in all courts), New Zealand and Canada. In England and the United States of America (both common-law countries), where, too, many of the incidents related in this essay occurred, nowadays such a person is usually called the 'defendant'. This term was used in the law of England of a person charged with having committed a misdemeanour, the person charged with having committed a felony (normally a more serious crime) being called the 'prisoner', a truly misleading term. The distinction between misdemeanour and felony was abolished in England in 1967 and the use of the term 'prisoner' was abandoned. In England and the United States the term 'accused' is occasionally used, but leading writers on criminal law and procedure tend to regard 'defendant' as preferable in being neutral.[1] The objection to this view may be raised, first, that 'accused' is neutral as well, and is more descriptive in criminal law and procedure, and, secondly, that a 'defendant' is, in addition, a person sued in an action in private law and it is advisable not to use the term, too, in criminal law and procedure. In order to avoid variation in the mode of description in this essay of a person charged with having committed a crime, the word 'accused' will be used throughout.

A would-be beneficiary from a deceased estate is not confined to ending the life of the intended distributor of largess in order to attain the desired end. There is the will itself. If need be, it can be forged or doctored; if there be one that a malefactor considers to be undesirable, it could be destroyed or hidden, or a later one could be forged.

Murders — some of the most celebrated ones — have often taken place in order to benefit from an insurance policy on the life of the victim. While that reason for ending someone's life really falls outside the scope of this work, I cannot refrain from giving a few examples of its operation.

In this book there are only twelve footnotes, strictly speaking. Eight are biographical in content and four are explanatory of something mentioned in the text. Each footnote is indicated by one of two signs: * and †. The rest of the notes are endnotes and indicated by consecutive arabic numerals. Almost all of them are simply references to relevant sources.

I would like to express my deep gratitude to my friends of many years in the world of legal publishing, Simon Sephton (whose firm bravely undertook publishing this effort of mine) and his colleague Richard Cooke. My prentice hand in writing this type of work sorely needed guidance, and how fortunate I have been that Simon and Richard gave it in assuming the role of manuscript editors. Of the deficiencies in the text and make-up that remain, I am the sole begetter.

My deep thanks go to Mrs Marian Fynn of the secretariat of the School of Law of the University of the Witwatersrand for her valuable help so cheerfully and efficiently rendered.

As always, I have been blessed with the assistance of my wife in the checking and proofreading of the text and notes.

EK
July 2003

Contents

DIRTY WORK WITH A WILL

List of illustrations

MURDER MOST FOUL

Uxoricide, matricide, patricide, parricide, fratricide and the maritic idal wife

DAISY DE MELKER[2] — *no time for men*

Daisy will never be forgotten. She was Daisy Louise de Melker, born Hancorn-Smith, formerly Cowle, formerly Sproat. Her trial for the murder of two husbands and a son before Mr Justice Leopold Greenberg* ran for thirty court days, within the period 17 October to 25 November 1932, and aroused enormous public interest.

The large courtroom was crowded every day, many of the spectators joining a queue long before the start of each day's hearing at 9:30 am. As the trial wore on, particularly when it came to the alleged murder of the son, the hostility of the spectators to the accused woman, muted as it had to be, was patent. In typically humorous vein, Harry Morris,† recalling his conducting of the defence, wrote: 'Daisy was not popular. Neither was I. During her trial she received threatening letters. So did I. She was told that if she were not hanged she would die. So was I. Her conviction appeared to be our only escape from death.'[3]

---

* Leopold Greenberg was born in Calvinia on 23 March 1885. His schooling was at Grey College, Bloemfontein. From there he went to the South African College, Cape Town, which taught for the degrees of the University of the Cape of Good Hope (CGH), to read for the degree of BA (Hons), which he obtained in 1904. He then proceeded to Johannesburg, where he took up articles with a firm of attorneys and studied privately for the degree of LLB (CGH), which he obtained in 1907. Greenberg then practised as an attorney until 3 October 1911, when he was admitted to the Johannesburg Bar. There he built up a substantial practice. On 17 July 1924 he was appointed a KC, and on 1 November the same year he was elevated to the Transvaal Bench. Greenberg proved to be one of the greatest judges in the history of South Africa. On 1 March 1938 he became Judge President of the Transvaal Provincial Division. He was appointed a judge of appeal on 1 August 1943, in which position he remained until he attained the then statutory age of retirement for judges of seventy years. He died in Johannesburg on 12 September 1964.

† Henry Harris (Harry) Morris was born in Beaufort West on 14 April 1878. After schooling at Marist Brothers College, Johannesburg, and the South African College School, Cape Town, he served in the Anglo-Boer War on the British side from the start until his discharge on 14 May 1901. Then he took articles with a firm of attorneys and qualified as an attorney, notary and conveyancer. Wishing to practise as an advocate, he proceeded to London, where he passed the Bar examinations and was admitted as a barrister by Gray's Inn on 26 January 1906. He was admitted to the Johannesburg Bar on 21 March 1906. There he attained great success, mainly as defence counsel in criminal cases. In 1924 he was appointed a KC. Morris died in Johannesburg on 6 October 1954.

I would say that it is the most famous criminal trial in the history of our country, more famous even than that of Von Veltheim in 1898 for the murder of Woolf Joel. The renowned author, Sarah Gertrude Millin, wrote: 'Her two husbands and [her son] Rhodes died, under her eyes, in terrible agony. She was one of the world's great poisoners: a classic who, because her stage was remote, has not had fair recognition in the annals of crime.'[4]

Daisy Hancorn-Smith was born near Grahamstown on 1 June 1886 of a family of seven daughters and four sons. When she was twelve, she and the other members of the family joined their father in Bulawayo, Southern Rhodesia. In 1901 she became a boarder at Good Hope Seminary in Cape Town, remaining there for two years. Then she returned to Bulawayo, where she reached an understanding with Bert Fuller, a Native Commissioner at Broken Hill. After eight months, she entered the Berea Nursing Home in Durban to qualify as a nurse. Mr Justice Greenberg concluded that after three years she did qualify, but Harry Morris KC, who defended her at her trial (and whom the judge in his judgment complimented for 'his very able and efficient conduct of the defence case'), doubted it, and believed that she never practised the profession of nursing. But he felt that it was then that she acquired some acquaintance with poisons — powders of inheritance, as they were called in seventeenth-century France. It must have been only a slight acquaintance, wrote Morris, for otherwise she would not have used arsenic to kill human beings, as its disadvantages for this purpose had long been very well known. While arsenic has the advantage of being tasteless and odorless, and the symptoms of its administration closely resemble the symptoms of other conditions, its persistence in a corpse has led to the conviction of many a murderer.

In 1907 Daisy saw Fuller in Bulawayo, and her engagement to him was announced. She returned to Johannesburg, where she had begun work, intending to marry Fuller in March 1908. Towards the end of February 1908, so she said, she received a telegram saying that Fuller was dangerously ill in Bulawayo Hospital, and she went there from Johannesburg to see him. Another account, wrote Morris, was that she was with Fuller a week before he went to hospital. One thing is clear, according to Morris: she was with him in hospital and at his bedside when he died, apparently of blackwater fever. In his last moments, so Morris stated, he made a will under which Daisy and his mother benefited. The prosecution had documents showing that she had obtained £236 5s 9d, but they were not admissible, and Greenberg J, in his superb, very careful, judgment said that was no reason to disbelieve her statement that she received only £95; and that there was not the slightest justification for thinking there was anything sinister about Fuller's will or death. My impression on reading Morris's memoirs is that he was most suspicious.[5]

A few months after the death of Fuller, Daisy became engaged to William Alfred Cowle, a plumber employed by the Johannesburg City Council, earning £7 4s a week, and being a member of the municipal provident and pension fund. Daisy and Cowle had been living in the same boarding house; and there Cowle had fallen in love with her. They were married out of community of property. Why men were attracted by this very plain woman, afflicted with a cleft palate, is a mystery, one to which I shall return.

On 5 June 1909, three months after the marriage, Cowle made a will instituting Daisy as sole heir. She also became the beneficiary of an insurance policy on his life.

Of the marriage, five children were born, all sons. First came twins, who survived only a few months. Daisy claimed they were premature and delicate. Next came Rhodes Cecil, named after the Cape politician and financial magnate. He was to survive from 21 June 1911 to 5 March 1932. Then Lester was born in June 1913. He lasted until October 1917. Daisy stated that he died of an abscess on the liver and convulsions. Eric was the last child, living from October 1915 to January 1917. His death, according to Daisy, was from convulsions and internal ailments. They had all been healthy children. In each case Daisy, as was her wont, summoned a doctor. It was said that she always wanted a daughter. No suspicion was aroused at the time by these regular deaths. The eminent forensic pathologist Professor Keith Simpson believed that deaths by poisoning at times escape doctors, the possibility of which simply doesn't cross their minds.[6] Daisy sensed this. If she poisoned her four children, which seems very possible, why did she spare Rhodes? Perhaps she realized that someone might then begin raising questions: indeed, the death of Rhodes years later caused this. Bear in mind that bodies had to be buried in those days; the crematorium for whites in the Braamfontein cemetery in Johannesburg was opened only in 1932.

Cowle died on 11 January 1923. He had been rather ill on and off for some time before then. Earlier that morning he had taken some Epsom salts, which is used to relieve constipation. He died in terrible agony, his body at times rigid and at other times arched backwards, resting on his head and heels. The symptoms are the result of poisoning with strychnine. In the four-part TV series on Daisy de Melker shown on SATV in 1993 (the far too attractive Susan Coetzer playing Daisy) the exquisite agony of the dying man was depicted with horrifying accuracy. Dr E A H Parkes, who was called by Daisy, suspected that Cowle had died of poisoning by strychnine — the only doctor, of the six who were called in to attend Cowle and Daisy's next husband and her son when they were dying, to suspect poisoning. He did not think that Daisy had administered it, and asked her to submit the Epsom salts to the police for analysis. She didn't do so. Naturally Parkes would not give a death certificate, so there was a postmortem examination. Parkes took it that the police had cleared the salts. He did not conduct the postmortem. The doctor who did decided that Cowle had died from chronic nephritis (kidney disease) and cerebral haemorrhage. No effort was made to see if he had suffered from poisoning. Daisy had had a narrow escape.

William Cowle was buried in Brixton cemetery in Johannesburg.

Cowle's death resulted in Daisy's inheriting from his estate £1 245 13s 2d and obtaining £553 0s 8d from the municipal provident fund.

To supplement her income, Daisy from November 1923 to June 1926 took up employment as a portress and general assistant at the Johannesburg children's hospital. An efficient person, her work was found to be perfectly satisfactory.

Towards the end of this period she attracted Robert Sproat, another Johannesburg municipal plumber. He was a healthy bachelor, aged forty-six, who had gold-mine shares, money in a building society and bank and municipal stock, making him in all worth an attractive some £4 000. Sproat married her on 1 June 1926 out of community of property.

Daisy was very unhappy with Sproat's will, which left all to his mother in England. But he was in no hurry to change it. On 10 October the following year, after Sproat had drunk a beer, he collapsed in agony, in a partial spasm and with severe abdominal pain. The nearest doctor was called, who felt he was suffering from a gastric ulcer. Sproat then completed a printed will form that Daisy had purchased some time before, leaving everything to her. After a few days he recovered fully. I have no doubt that she had given him a small, non-fatal, dose of strychnine. The full dose would have to be given later, to avoid talk of its coinciding with the change of Sproat's will.

Well, it was given the following month. The same doctor was called, and arrived when Sproat was in extremis. He died in great agony. At times he was rigid, at other times doubled up, unable to bear being touched. The TV programme on Daisy de Melker showed the anguish of Sproat with the same accuracy as it had with the anguish of Cowle. It appears that once again shortly before his collapse he had drunk a glass of beer. The attending doctor was very puzzled about the cause of Sproat's death, but finally signed a certificate attributing the death to arteriosclerosis (hardening of the arteries) through lead poisoning and to cerebral haemorrhage. There was no autopsy.

Robert Sproat died on 6 November 1927. Two days later he was buried in Brixton cemetery, his coffin being placed on top of the coffin of William Cowle.

Daisy inherited £4 174 0s 4d from Sproat's estate and obtained £563 5s 4d from the municipal provident fund. After she received these benefits her assets were a house in a working-class suburb and a healthy bank balance. It was only shortly before her execution in 1932 that Sproat's will was found to be invalid; but of that later.

For a few years Daisy was husbandless. Then, on 21 January 1931, she married a widower, Sidney Clarence de Melker (called Sid), a plumber on the New State Areas gold mine, who had been a member of Paul Roos's triumphant Springbok rugby team that toured Britain in 1906–7.

Daisy then moved from her house at 67 Terrace Road in Bertrams, Johanesburg to live with Sid de Melker and his daughter Eileen at 19 Simmer East Cottages in Germiston, some fifteen kilometres away.

By now Daisy's son, Rhodes Cecil Cowle, had become a problem to her. Born on 21 June 1911, he had been cared for tenderly by his mother through every form of childhood illness, his accidents and his attacks of malaria. She had sent him for periods to expensive private schools, to Hilton College in Natal and then Marist Brothers College in Johannesburg, although there were good free government schools. And she had spoilt him in many ways: taken him on a trip through Britain, Ireland and Holland; bought him a motor cycle and later, as it did not satisfy his mania for speed, a more expensive one; then a motor car and later, as he complained that it was too small, a larger one; and a pianola. Rhodes was a poor student and generally workshy, leaving one job after another. All he was interested in, and then to a limited extent, was working with motor cars. The last job he had was that of a greaser, earning between twenty and thirty shillings a week. He was always financially dependent on his mother.

But it was not her disappointment with her son's career that made Daisy decide to take drastic action. It was his behaviour towards her. Not only was he surly and unpleasant but he began assaulting her. Worse still, he started saying that she had kept him out of his rightful inheritance from his father's estate. Possibly he thought that all his mother's wealth came from Cowle, whereas four-fifths came from Sproat. When he turned twenty-one, he said, he had to get his due. Daisy may have been afraid that if Rhodes started suing her, the truth about the deaths of her first two husbands might emerge. That is what Harry Morris believed caused her to add Rhodes to her list of victims.

On Wednesday 2 March 1932 Rhodes set off on his motorbike to work, perfectly healthy. He took with him sandwiches Daisy had prepared and a thermos flask of coffee that Daisy had laced with arsenic. During the morning break he offered a fellow employee, James Henry Webster, a drink from the flask in its screw cap. Rhodes then drank some, finishing the flask at lunch.

In the afternoon Webster felt a severe pain in his stomach; on reaching home he was lame. His mother gave him pills to alleviate the pain and salts to flush out his system. By the following morning he was fit again. Later an investigation showed arsenic in his hair and nails.

Rhodes in the afternoon complained of a burning pain in his stomach and lameness. He believed it was a result of a recurrence of malaria. To cover herself, Daisy called in the doctor who had treated Rhodes for this illness in the past. He felt it was an attack of the influenza that was rife.

By Saturday morning Rhodes seemed fairly well again. Clearly the dose of arsenic he had drunk was not enough. Daisy was alone with him in the house. At nine o'clock she went to the house of a neighbour to call a doctor. Rhodes was vomiting badly, foaming at the mouth, turning blue. Dr Ferguson, who was called at eleven, found Rhodes unconscious and in a spasm. He administered chloroform to relieve the spasm. At twelve Dr Mackenzie called, to find Rhodes dying of asphyxia. Injections did not help. At fifteen minutes past one in the afternoon he died. Dr Mackenzie was baffled by the cause of death and was unable to give a death certificate. A postmortem examination revealed an enlarged spleen, a congested liver and brain, and inflamed stomach walls. The doctor who performed the postmortem knew nothing of the effects of poisoning by arsenic. Daisy's mention of malaria caused him to attribute Rhodes's death to cerebral malaria.

Daisy spent no time grieving over the death of her son. Two days later she called at the garage at which he had worked for the wages owing to him; and she wrote to the insurance company at which she had insured his life for £100 for payment of that sum. On the day of his death she arranged for death and funeral notices to be inserted in the *Sunday Times*. The death notice simply described Rhodes as the 'son of Mrs de Melker and stepson of S. C. de Melker'. The funeral notice called him 'son of Mrs D. L. de Melker [Sproat]'. The notices were calculated not to associate the Rhodes referred to with Rhodes Cowle, son of Daisy Cowle (as she had been).

The funeral took place on Sunday, the day after Rhodes died. He was buried in the same grave as his father and Robert Sproat, his coffin on top of that of Sproat.

A sibling of one of Daisy's former husbands (almost certainly William Sproat, brother of the late Robert) was now struck by the regularity of death visiting Daisy's spouses and kin. He informed the police. The police were then also struck by the same thing. With some difficulty they secured official permission to examine the bodies buried in the same grave in Brixton cemetery. The police performed the process on 19 April 1932 in the presence of two medical practitioners and a number of medical students. Rhodes's body, his coffin being on the top, was the first to be removed. The viscera — the large internal organs — were taken to the South African Institute for Medical Research. The following day the public prosecutor at Germiston was told that arsenic had been found in the viscera. There were 1.3 grains of pure arsenic and 1.7 grains of arsenious oxide, an exceptional amount for the weight of viscera examined — 4.5 pounds. In the spinal column of Cowle and Sproat minute quantities of strychnine were present. This poison is an alkaloid that eventually disappears; a small amount found in a corpse after a number of years points to a far greater amount taken before death.

Proceedings were set afoot to secure the arrest of Daisy.

On 20 April two detectives, a wardress and a doctor went to Daisy's house to arrest her and to try to find poisons. They found her but no poison.

The police particularly wanted to locate the source of Daisy's possession of arsenic, but queries at numerous pharmacies produced no result. Meanwhile the press were trying to obtain a photograph of Daisy, who was in custody. Eventually someone handed a photograph of her to a newspaper reporter. It was published in the newspaper. Abraham Spilkin, a pharmacist in Kenilworth, in the southern suburbs of Johannesburg, saw the photograph and went to the police. He told them that on 25 February a woman had telephoned him at his pharmacy, saying she was Mrs Cowle of Bertrams, a former cash customer. She wanted poison to kill a cat; as the animal was too heavy for her to bring it to him for him to administer the poison, she would call for it. She arrived after two hours. Spilkin recognized her. She signed the poison register 'D. L. Sproat', giving her old Bertrams address, saying that she had remarried. He sold her sixty grains of white arsenic.

In fact Daisy had been living for months at Simmer East Cottages in Germiston, a long journey from Kenilworth. There was a nearby pharmacy of which she was a customer.

Now the prosecution decided to start the criminal process by a preparatory examination before a magistrate in Germiston. It was a procedure then used. The prosecutor, Sylvester Quinlan, knew that Spilkin's evidence was damning. He decided to watch Daisy's reaction when Spilkin was called to the witness box. It was one of fury, horror and fear; her face was ashen. She must have realized that his evidence would mean the end of the road.

Daisy was in custody for six months as an awaiting-trial prisoner. The trial began on 17 October 1932. The prosecution was conducted by Cyril C Jarvis KC, Crown Prosecutor, who later became Attorney-General of Natal. Jarvis was assisted by Quinlan. Harry Morris KC was briefed for the defence, with him I A Maisels, who was to become a leading silk at the Johannesburg Bar.

The defence chose not to have a trial by jury. A jury in those days was composed of nine white males, at least seven of whom had to agree on the verdict. Public opinion was so hostile to Daisy de Melker that a trial of her by a judge was far preferable. The judge who presided was the eminent Mr Justice Leopold Greenberg. He decided to use his right to summon two assessors. They were Mr J M Graham, magistrate of Lichtenburg, and Mr A A Stanford, magistrate of Heidelberg. Both were most experienced and competent judicial officers. Though in those days assessors acted simply in an advisory capacity, the two who sat in the trial of Daisy actively participated in the proceedings, occasionally putting questions to counsel and witnesses.

Jarvis spent a month at the Medical School of the University of the Witwatersrand being schooled in the nature of poisons and their effects. Morris and Maisels, they later said, relied on literature referred to them by a pathologist and a general medical practitioner. As will appear, though, they seem to have received further help.

The Crown had the considerable benefit of having Professor John Mitchell Watt as an expert witness. He was Professor of Pharmacology at the University of the Witwatersrand. Watt, who was born in Port Elizabeth in 1892, had qualified in medicine at the University of Edinburgh and, after service in the Great War, was appointed Professor of Pharmacology at Wits in 1921. There he remained until his retirement in 1957.[7] Watt achieved a high reputation for research publications. In addition he had an extensive practice as a physician.

From the point of view of the prosecution, Professor Watt proved the ideal expert witness not only for his qualifications but for the way in which he equipped himself by reading all the available relevant literature to meet the examination in chief and cross-examination.* Many an expert witness in many a discipline has been trapped by failing

* In August 1972, at the golden jubilee dinner of Wits, Emeritus Professor Watt told me that, even though he was to be a prosecution witness, he helped Maisels to do research for the defence case at the Wits Medical School library.

to ensure that he or she is completely at home in his or her discipline and to realize that cross-examining counsel has tried to be fully acquainted with all its technical detail. Watt did not fall into this trap. He knew the facts; he was careful to make a concession when he believed it was necessary; he could not be moved in his conclusions. In his nine hours of relentless cross-examination of Watt, Morris was at his brilliant best, showing an amazing grasp of toxicology and the literature. But Watt did too, and was imperturbable throughout.

The Crown pinned its case for the alleged murder of Cowle and Sproat on the administration of strychnine to them by Daisy, and for the alleged murder of Rhodes on the administration of arsenic to him by Daisy. Its major problem with the cases of murder of the husbands was its inability to show possession of strychnine by the accused.

The Crown led evidence to show that from 1901 to 1908 the poison was freely available in Rhodesia, and contended that the accused could have stored it until 1923 and thereafter until 1927, when she could have used it initially to dispatch Cowle and then Sproat. The judge found the possibility too remote for serious consideration. If the accused did poison her husbands with strychnine, she must have obtained it from a pharmacist or some other local source. Morris in his memoirs[8] raised the possibility that Daisy had obtained the poison from someone connected with the racing stables at Turffontein racecourse, near which the Cowles once lived. Strychnine is used by some trainers to animate racehorses.

Professor Watt concluded that Cowle had died from strychnine poisoning. He relied on Cowle's life history, the onset and symptoms of his fatal illness, and the finding of the poison in his body. Watt was not quite so adamant in reaching the same conclusions, on similar facts, as to the cause of the death of Sproat.

In court, Morris contended that, on the symptoms described by witnesses and reflected in the death certificates, there was a reasonable possibility that Cowle had died of chronic nephritis and cerebral haemorrhage, Sproat of artereosclerosis, and Rhodes of cerebral malaria.

Jarvis was generously complimented by Morris in his memoirs[9] for 'the facile, painstaking and impartial way in which he conducted an arduous and difficult trial'. His cross-examination of Daisy, whose evidence in chief was led admirably by Morris, was devastating. She came out of it very poorly. But Jarvis was grievously hampered in presenting the case for the murder of Cowle and Sproat not only by the absence of evidence of possession of the poison by Daisy but also by the naïveté, ineptness and lack of certain medical knowledge of a number of the medical practitioners who were called by Daisy to attend to her dying husbands.

On the morning of 25 November 1932 Mr Justice Greenberg delivered a judgment that was almost entirely extempore, was in admirable detail, and took three and a half hours to complete.

He found that the Crown had failed to prove beyond a reasonable doubt that either Cowle or Sproat had died of strychnine poisoning. Then he dealt with the Crown's argument that the evidence in each one of these counts could fill in the gaps in the other — the 'similar-fact' argument. It had to be rejected, said the judge, because in neither case was the cause of death proved. And the third count, the alleged murder of Rhodes, was too dissimilar to the others to be of help.[10]

Thus he held that the accused had to be found not guilty of the murder of Cowle and that of Sproat. But the case of the Crown against Daisy for the murder of her son was found to be established beyond a reasonable doubt. Dr Watt was convinced that Rhodes had died through arsenical poisoning, and there was no conflicting medical evidence. The arsenic could only have been in the coffee to cause the Wednesday attack in Rhodes and Webster. There was no escaping the conclusion on the evidence that the accused had put the arsenic in that coffee. If it was a fatal dose, she was responsible; if it was not, subsequent doses could only have been given by her. The suggestion that he had committed suicide was untenable. Thus she was guilty of the murder of Rhodes. Daisy was sentenced to death. Morris saw Oswald Pirow KC, the Minister of Justice, to ask for commutation of the sentence. It was futile. The death sentence for poisoning, he wrote, was never commuted.[11] She was executed at the Pretoria Central Prison on 30 December 1932.

Morris revealed[12] that Daisy was suspected of having murdered seven others. Rhodesian police remained in Johannesburg until the end of the trial, intending to secure her arrest for the murder of Bert Fuller, and of an uncle of hers, and of another person.

It is of interest to note that Harry Morris believed that Sproat did not die of strychnine poisoning.[13] The strychnine found in his body was that used on the first occasion. Whoever administered it could not risk administering it again. On the second occasion, he wrote, one of the cyanides was used. No expert at the trial mentioned the word.

In August 1972 I asked Emeritus Professor John Watt at the golden jubilee dinner of Wits what he thought of this view. He totally disagreed with it. In his opinion Daisy de Melker had murdered six persons before her son Rhodes by administering strychnine to them. The two of these murders she had been charged with, those of Cowle and Sproat, Mr Justice Greenberg had rightly found not proved: there had not been enough evidence. When it came to Rhodes's turn, she had run out of strychnine, so she used arsenic.

Before she was executed, Daisy de Melker suffered another blow, though not as serious as the death sentence. The story was told in the *Rand Daily Mail* and retold by Joel Mervis in his book *The Fourth Estate.*[14] Cast your mind back to Robert Sproat's will, leaving all to Daisy. In terms of the Transvaal Wills Ordinance of 1903[15] such a will would have to be signed by the testator in the presence of two witnesses, who would have to sign in the presence of the testator and of each other. Daisy, clearly unaware of these critical formalities, asked a stranger, Edward Osborne, who was constructing a nearby building, to witness the will already signed by Sproat in bed. After Osborne had departed, Daisy asked Mrs Emily Stricker, her neighbour, to sign as the second witness. This was in the kitchen, in the presence of Daisy and William Sproat, brother of Robert Sproat. The will was clearly invalid, and the executors of the estate of Jane Sproat, who had died after her son Robert, successfully applied from Carlisle, England, to the Transvaal Provincial Division of the Supreme Court for an order to this effect. Daisy de Melker had to return the £4 174 0s 4d odd which she had inherited.

What did Sid de Melker do during this time? Well, at the trial he gave evidence that if his wife had bought arsenic, he did not know of any need for it, nor what her intentions were. Throughout the trial he stood by Daisy. According to a report in the newspaper *Die Burger* on 31 December 1932, De Melker was present at a service at the grave of Daisy, and placed a bunch of white carnations on the coffin as it was lowered into the grave. But, as Harry Morris wrote,[16] 'her next victim was to have gone about the time of the trial'. De Melker's impending demise was foreshadowed in a letter she wrote in January of the fateful year to a sister in whom she confided frequently. There she said that 'if anything should happen to Sid' she would sell up and go to Ireland with his daughter Eileen, and leave her with her aunts there, and return. 'Why should anything happen to Sid?' asked the sister, to which the reply was that he had a weak heart. In fact his heart was in perfect condition.

According to Harry Morris,[17] 'the balance of the arsenic not used for Rhodes was, considerably later, found hidden in the wireless — no doubt for future use'. It shows he was satisfied that Daisy had murdered Rhodes; no one could have thought otherwise. A more elaborate account is given in Izak Nortje's most amusing work, *Stilte in die Hof!*[18] He tells us that Sylvester Quinlan used to say that De Melker would not accept the decision of the trial court until the subsequent sale of some of the personal possessions of Daisy. Among them was a radiogram. The buyer found the machine faulty. At the repair shop the workman discovered, well hidden, an envelope on which was written 'For dear old Sid'. Inside was a white powder. It was taken to the police. Analysis revealed that the powder consisted of — arsenic.

What sort of a person was Daisy de Melker? Sarah Gertrude Millin spent several days watching the trial with her friend, the judge's wife. Later she produced a novel, *Three Men Die*, based on Daisy de Melker's life and misdeeds, on death and destruction. Sarah Millin 'thought the judge's summing-up an expression of eternal justice — beautiful'.[19]

'What chiefly interested me about this woman', she continued, 'was the attraction that, despite her apparent unattraction, she seemed to have. She was really ugly. She was small, thin, with tousled grey hair, claw-like fingers, a faded skin, large spectacles, a mouth like a fish, and a cleft palate. She was forty-six. She made no attempt to look beautiful. Her lips were not reddened, nor her cheeks painted. She wore, every day for six weeks, the same black dress with the same lace front. After a time, I looked at the stale lace front with nausea.

'Yet this woman had had a lover and three husbands. I could see that even the policeman who stood beside the dock liked her; all the people connected with the case quite liked her; she used to wave at the crowd as if she were a cinema star; a bishop protested to the end that she was innocent; and, after she was hanged, her third husband put white violets on her coffin.'

Mrs Millin concluded with these memorable words: 'I thought of all the meritorious, agreeable women who, in their lives, had never found a man to love them, and I asked myself why this ugly, cruel, avaricious, death-dealing woman had so easily engaged the interest of men.'

Isie Maisels described Daisy de Melker as 'probably the most unattractive woman I have ever seen in my life; she was revolting'.

In his memoirs, published well before Mrs Millin's book, Harry Morris said much the same of the appearance of Daisy and her effect on others, but went further. She had 'enormous vitality. She was a prodigious worker and could turn her hand to almost anything from delicate needlework to hard spade work.' And 'she was of a very sociable disposition — always bright and chatty. . . . She had a strong sense of humour. She complained one morning during the trial that she had had a bad night owing to neuralgia. In a moment of abstraction I advised her to take arsenic, meaning aspirin. She, more than anyone, enjoyed the *faux pas*.'

Morris, who had simply done his duty for Daisy de Melker as her counsel, and had no illusions as to the murders she had actually committed, summed up her character in two passages:

'Daisy was a paradox. She was an over-sexed woman who "had no time for men". All her victims were males. Her intimate friends were women. Not only did she like them, but they liked her.'[20]

And then the damning conclusion from the evidence in the case 'that she was ruthless, remorseless and pitiless and that she was a person who would, without hesitation or compunction, remove from her path even those who were merely inconvenient to her. She seemed almost incapable of emotion.'[21]

DOROTHY STRYDOM — *anoxia in Rhodesia*

After the fascinating details of the trial of Daisy de Melker, the details of the trial of Dorothy Dolores Strydom, another mariticidal wife (Daisy, everyone knew, really was one), may appear to be small beer. Still, they are intriguing, and the trial had been aptly described as a famous Rhodesian one,[22] and it calls for some attention.

Once again one encounters people with limited education and many who worked hard to better themselves materially. But this time there was a husband who was a harsh and cruel person. He was Johannes Adrian Strydom, of whose murder his wife Dorothy, her lover Pedro Concalves Sequiero, their hired assassin Finga Ngwenya and his accomplice John Ncube were found guilty by Mr Justice Gubbay and his assessors in the High Court of Rhodesia in a trial extending over March and early April 1980.

Strydom was a hard, quick-tempered man, given to violent and brutal behaviour to his African servants. His three children by Dorothy disliked him; the eldest had left home because of him and the other two helped their mother conceal from him her affair with Sequiero.

Why Dorothy and Sequiero decided to murder Strydom is far from clear. Sequiero, who had become Dorothy's lover in 1976 after the death of his wife, was resentful of her continuing to have sexual relations with her husband, and in mid-1979 told her that unless she left Strydom by the end of the year the affair would be over. Dorothy, who was terrified of and hated her husband, and in love with Sequiero, said she would leave her husband as Sequiero demanded. Indeed, she started moving possessions surreptitiously to Sequiero's house in the town of Gwelo, where he was stationed by the railways, by which he had been employed for twenty years.

The obvious solution to the problem seemed to be just that: for Dorothy to leave Strydom and join her lover. Strydom would have ample grounds to divorce her. If he would not, she could simply carry on being Sequiero's paramour. But there may have been at least two reasons for the pair not to choose to take this course. The one was fear of physical revenge by Strydom. The other was the financial benefit Dorothy, who had little private means, would derive from the death of Strydom. Under their joint will she was his sole heir provided she survived him for thirty days. And she would in addition receive $40 230 (Rhodesian) from insurance policies and Strydom's pension scheme operated by his employers, where he worked as a fitter and turner.

Certainly she tried almost immediately after his death to claim the insurance moneys and she did obtain $22 464 from the pension scheme.

Strydom's body, clad in pyjamas, was found on 26 October 1979 in a dam close by the homestead of the Strydoms. In an autopsy the same day a consultant pathologist found death due to anoxia (deprivation of oxygen). It could have been caused by a blow to the head of the deceased, causing him to be stunned, and then the inhalation of fluid obstructing the air passages.

The evidence in the case, largely based on admissions by Dorothy and Sequiero, revealed that all four accused had been party to a plan to drown Strydom in his bath. This had taken place, Ngwenya, a complete stranger, having been paid a considerable sum to participate. He had hit the deceased several times on the head with a piece of wood, in the presence of Dorothy and Sequiero. Ncube was not in the house at the time of the actual murder, but he had been a party to the plan to murder and had procured the services of Ngwenya.

After the three were satisfied that Strydom was dead, Dorothy let Ncube into the house. The two Africans then dried the body, clad it in pyjamas, and carried it to the dam. Dorothy cleaned up the bathroom.

There had been two previous attempts to kill Strydom. A year earlier, Dorothy, Sequiero and Ncube agreed that the latter two would try to drown Strydom in his bath. But he proved too strong for them, and they fled unrecognized. A previous African employee of the Strydoms, one Themba, was arrested for the crime, confessed (I imagine 'persuaded' by the police), then convicted, sentenced to imprisonment, and later released when the authorities realized he was absolutely innocent. At the murder trial Sequiero was questioned by the judge:

'You must have known that the wrong person had been arrested and convicted?'

'Correct, my lord.'

'What did you do about it then?'

'Mrs Strydom and I, my lord, did nothing about it whatever.'

The second attempt at killing Strydom — it seems to have really been a series of attempts — was to poison him with drugs of sorts obtained from African herbalists and others. The drugs were apparently put in Strydom's tea and other drinks, but all they did was to make him ill and vomit.

Sequiero made a complete confession after an initial denial of guilt and attempts to raise an alibi on the fatal night. In his evidence he made no effort whatever to exculpate Dorothy.

Dorothy denied complicity in the murder, contending that Sequiero, who knew she was going to come to live with him, must have killed her husband thinking of the money that would come her way. The court found her evidence completely unconvincing and her guilt established beyond a reasonable doubt.

In the event, she, Sequiero, Ngwenya and Ncube were found guilty of murder. With the first three extenuating circumstances were found not to exist, and they were sentenced to death. With Ncube they were found to exist, and he was sentenced to twelve years' imprisonment.

Good fortune, however, was to comc the way of those sentenced to death, though even one, such as I, opposed to capital punishment would wonder whether it should have. For on 24 April 1981 their sentences were commuted to life imprisonment as an act of clemency to mark the first anniversary of independent Zimbabwe.

COUNT HENRY DE TOURVILLE — *a slave in the salt mines*

Count Henry de Tourville, a man of means, was well known in London society. He owned a house in Craven Hill, Hyde Park, where, when he resided in London, he gave dinner parties that were much appreciated by the upper classes. A handsome Frenchman, fluent in several languages, he was originally a waiter in Paris, by name Henri Perreau. After the strange disappearance of William Cotton, a wealthy Englishman who had employed him as a travelling companion, Perreau assumed the name of Count Henry de Tourville.

On a day in November 1876 the Count was arrested on a request by the government of Austria for his extradition on several charges, one being that of murdering his wife Madeleine the previous July by pushing her over a precipice in the Stelvio Pass of the Austrian Tyrol. The account of De Tourville that follows is based to a considerable extent on Montagu Williams's *Leaves of a Life*;[23] it seems that Williams appeared for the Count at the extradition proceedings.

The accused, of an indeterminate age between forty and sixty, whose suspiciously glossy black hair and moustache could have disguised his actual years, had married a Mrs Madeleine Miller in London on 11 November 1875. She was very stout, but she was very wealthy.

After their marriage the couple travelled abroad, accompanied by a lady's maid, Sarah Clappinson. On Saturday 15 July 1876 they reached Spondinig in Austria, and put up at a hotel there. The following day the Count and his wife went alone to Ferdinandhöhe. At eleven that evening De Tourville returned to the hotel, and told this story. His wife had fallen down the side of a mountain, injuring her forehead, which was bleeding. He had left her, conscious, leaning against a tree, telling her that he was going off to obtain help. He had lost his way, finding himself eventually in the place he had left. But by then his wife had rolled far down the slope, and was dead. He finally returned with assistance.

Before leaving Austria, the Count wrote to a Mr Wilding, a friend of Madeleine's and a trustee of the marriage settlement, expressing great sorrow at the death of his 'dear wife' and explaining that on the mountain pass she had become very frightened whenever the horses turned a sharp corner, causing her to insist on proceeding on foot, and then she went too near a ravine and fell over, losing her life.

There was an interrogation of De Tourville in Austria by the district judge. On the evidence then presented, the judge discharged him. On further evidence becoming available, the Austrian authorities wanted to extradite him from England to try him.

The new evidence showed that when the Count returned with assistance, he remained in the carriage until all the jewellery of Madeleine had been given to him. Her bonnet, picked up twelve feet below the roadway, was found covered in blood, as was her blue silk collar. Near the body was one of her ear pendants. A track of blood was traced down to the valley, where the body was found. Across the grass there was a track eighteen inches wide, indicating that the deceased had been dragged along. All pointed to the Count's having assaulted his wife with great violence.

There was evidence that when De Tourville returned to the hotel in Spondinig there was blood on his fingers, and his one hand was so swollen that he could not pull his glove on.

To add to this additional evidence, there was an extraordinarily different account of the tragic incident given to Wilding by De Tourville when he returned to London. She had committed suicide, he said, by throwing herself down the slope.

Wilding said that the bequest to De Tourville in the will of his wife came to around £38 000, a considerable amount in those days.

De Tourville was extradited to Austria. At his trial in Bötzen before two judges, according to the account by Williams he was charged not only with the murder of Madeleine but with several other crimes. Among them was that of poisoning his first wife by putting powdered glass in her food and drink; shooting his mother-in-law; and setting fire to his house in order to kill his only child, whose death would result in a large sum of money coming to him.

De Tourville was convicted of murdering Madeleine. His original sentence of death, wrote Williams, 'was subsequently commuted to one of penal servitude, which meant, in that country, working as a slave in the salt mines'.[24] 'A slave in the salt mines', well, se non è vero, è molto ben trovato (if it is not true, it is very well invented).

George Joseph Smith — *and the 'bodies in the bath'*

Most people would classify George Joseph Smith as the world's worst murderer guilty of uxoricide. In fact none of the three women he murdered was actually his wife, though each believed that she was. What was the nature of his trial and what sort of a man was he? These words by Eric R Watson in the book he edited, *Trial of George Joseph Smith*, published in 1922,[25] give a startling picture: 'The trial of George Joseph Smith', he wrote, 'is without a parallel in the history of crime in any age or country. The singularly revolting means by which the murderer accomplished the destruction of his victims, the spectacle of Justice, in all its pomp and circumstance, solemnly deciding whether one transparently worthless man should live or die at a time when the war claimed a daily holocaust from among the youngest and bravest of manhood of Britain, the novelty of the questions of forensic medicine, the complexity of the evidence given by some 120 witnesses, twice as many as were needed to establish the guilt of Palmer[26] — all combine to make this a notable trial indeed.' He considered that Smith was 'the most atrocious English criminal since Palmer'. Long after these words were written Christie, Haigh, Heath and Sutcliffe performed their dreadful deeds, and vied with Smith for the accolade. Some years later Harold Shipman without a shadow of a doubt bore the palm.

Smith was born of a respectable family in 1872. It appears that at the age of nine he was sent to a reformatory, and remained there until sixteen. Whether this traumatic experience made him a confirmed dangerous criminal or whether he was born one is a matter of difference of opinion. His curriculum vitae makes depressing reading. Here is a bare outline which omits many of his crimes: In 1896 he was given a year's imprisonment for receiving stolen property. Two years later he married Caroline Thornhill, aged eighteen or nineteen, calling himself cynically George Oliver Love. This woman remained his wife. For two years they lived together. He induced her to steal from her employer — he seldom worked. On her arrest she gave him away, and he went to gaol in January 1901 for two years for receiving. On his release he looked for 'Mrs Love', but, fearing for her life, she fled to Canada. During his two years with Caroline, Smith started his career as a 'marriage swindler' by 'marrying' a middle-aged boarding house keeper and disappearing with her possessions entrusted to him. By 1908 Smith had made out that he was an antique dealer in Bristol. In that city he married in his own name his housekeeper, Edith Mabel Pegler. He seemed to have been fond of her, and she, never suspecting his real occupation, remained loyal to him.

August 1910 witnessed Smith's 'marriage' to Beatrice (Bessie) Constance Annie Mundy, aged thirty-one, he calling himself Henry Williams. (The literature is unclear as to her surname; it is sometimes spelled Munday.) Shortly before then he had 'married' a woman whom he deserted after taking all her money (£350) and clothes.

Miss Mundy was possessed of £2 500 in gilt-edged securities, but it was tied up. After he swindled her of all he could — £135 — he disappeared. Eighteen months later he met her in the street, and she fell for him again. They recommenced living as man and wife. Now Smith got her to sign a joint will in which each made the other heir. Then he bought a zinc bath for £1 17s 6d, having beaten the seller down from £2. In their house in Herne Bay on 13 July 1912 she was found drowned in the bath. The inquest determined that she had had an epileptic fit. Smith had duped an inexperienced doctor who had attended Beatrice. Smith, a shockingly mean person, refused to pay for a grave, and she was buried in a common grave. He inherited her estate.

Smith's next victim was Alice Burnham, aged twenty-five, a good-looking, healthy, semi-trained nurse, who had £104 in cash. They were 'married' on 31 October 1913. He then insured Alice's life for £500. The couple took lodgings in a boarding house in Blackpool, once Smith had been assured it had a bath. On 11 December that year Alice was found dead in it by the landlady, Mrs Crossley, and by Smith, who had summoned Mrs Crossley saying he could not make his wife hear. At the inquest a verdict of drowning by misadventure was returned. Smith refused to order anything other than the cheapest deal coffin, and on Mr Joseph Crossley saying it was not the way to bury a wife, Smith replied

'When they are dead they are done with'. As soon as he could, Smith sold Alice's clothes and jewellery. From Alice's death he made £600.

Smith returned to Miss Pegler in Bristol. In September the following year he 'married' Alice Reavil, a domestic servant. Then he disappeared, with all her savings (around a hundred pounds), all her clothes and all her jewellery. But she survived. His next and last victim did not. She was Miss Margaret Elizabeth Lofty, aged thirty-eight, whose father had been a clergyman. Her occupation was that of a lady's companion. Smith, going under the name of John Lloyd, a land agent, swept this lady, disappointed by a previous suitor turning out to be married, off her feet. They were 'married' on 17 December 1914 in — of all places — Bath. She made a will leaving all to 'John'. In fact she possessed virtually nothing — only £19 in a savings bank. But Smith ensured that she took out a life policy for £700. She made a will leaving her estate to John Lloyd.

The couple then moved to London to a boarding house in Highgate, Smith being satisfied that there was a bath. At 7:30 that very night the landlady, in the kitchen, heard splashing in the bathroom upstairs, a sound as if wet hands were drawn down the side of the bath, and then a sigh. At 8:15 a police constable was called in, to discover 'Mrs Lloyd' dead. At the inquest a finding of death by suffocation from drowning was returned. Smith took steps to get his inheritance.

But now the game was up. The inquest on Margaret Lofty was reported in the press, with details. Charles Burnham, brother of the murdered Alice, read it, was struck by the similarity of the death with that of his sister, and contacted the police. The report also struck Joseph Crossley, who had remonstrated with Smith for his meanness with the coffin of Alice. The upshot was an extended police investigation, the exhumation of the bodies of the three women, and postmortem examination of them by one of the leading forensic pathologists, Dr (later Sir) Bernard Spilsbury. He and Dr (later Sir) William Willcox, then an even more eminent forensic pathologist, were to give damning evidence at the subsequent trial of Smith for the murder of Bessie Mundy. Originally he was charged with three murders, but until the death sentence was abolished in England by the Homicide Act of 1986 there was a rule of practice (clearly unknown to almost all writers on murder trials) that only one count of murder could be tried at a time. (It was both disadvantageous and advantageous to the Crown — advantageous in that an acquittal would allow for a subsequent charge of another murder.)

The case of the 'brides in the bath', as it came to be known, extended at the Old Bailey (the Central Criminal Court in London) from 22 June to 1 July 1915, the longest murder trial in England since that of Dr Palmer sixty years before. The presiding judge was Mr Justice Scrutton, one of the great members of the English Bench, who controlled his customary bad temper admirably and ran the trial impeccably. The leader of the prosecuting team was Mr (later Sir) Archibald Bodkin and the leader of the defence team was the famed defence counsel Mr (later Sir) Edward Marshall Hall KC. It is of interest to note that in the prosecuting team was the future Mr Justice Travers Humphreys, a highly regarded judge in criminal trials.

For the prosecution it was crucial that evidence be allowed to be given of the similar drowning of the three victims. Naturally, Marshall Hall objected to it on the 'similar-fact' exclusionary rule aimed at protecting an accused from a jury inferring guilt from his bad character. It had been most clearly set out in the leading decision of the Privy Council in the case of *Makin v Attorney-General for New South Wales.*[27] But Mr Justice Scrutton did allow such evidence, on a ground allowed by *Makin's* case, such coincidence of happenings showing design by the accused. It was clearly a correct holding, there being an improbability to the highest degree of three such deaths taking place through natural causes.

After that the defence was forlorn of hope. The jury took only twenty minutes to find the accused guilty of murdering Beatrice Mundy. An appeal was made to the Court of Criminal Appeal on the ground that evidence as to the deaths of Alice Burnham and Margaret Lofty should not have been admitted. The Lord Chief Justice (Lord Reading), Mr Justice Darling and Mr Justice Lush rejected the appeal, holding that there had been prima facie evidence that Smith had murdered Beatrice Mundy, which allowed the evidence to be given of the deaths of the other two women.[28]

On 13 August 1915 Smith was executed at Maidstone. It was the penalty he paid for drowning three women in their baths through the exercise of his considerable strength. In a note[29] Willcox wrote that the procedure Smith used was probably to place his right hand on the head of his victim and his left forearm under both her knees, and then suddenly to raise his left forearm and press his right hand on her head. Her trunk would then slide down towards the end of the bath, her head being submerged in the water. Bodkin, at the commencement of his brilliant opening speech for the prosecution, mentioned the 'simple and terribly effective way in which a person in a bath can be drowned' — lifting that person's legs. In cross-examination Dr Spilsbury endorsed this view. The three baths were displayed in the courtroom, affecting witnesses greatly.

There was no possibility of epilepsy or fainting being the cause of any of the deaths. In the case of Bessie Mundy there was also evidence of strangling.

What has mystified commentators is how a person with the character and qualities of Smith imposed his will on so many women: usually, but far from always, of the class of servant. He was vulgar, clearly uneducated, unable to write a sentence grammatically or spell the most common words, without means, far from handsome. He could, though, put on the airs of a cultivated gentleman, likely to deceive many. He had a quality that a number of men have which attracts a certain type of woman, and such men can 'read' that woman almost on sight. With diabolic skill, Smith would pick up a simple and impressionable girl, court and flatter her, and by promises mislead her into revealing her savings and hand them over to him; and then, on a visit usually to a park or the National Gallery or other attractive place, would disappear, sometimes collecting her belongings en route to his next destination. How many poor creatures he duped in this way will never be known; the police believed many never responded to their invitation to tell them their story. This fraud and theft was Smith's main source of income for fifteen years. He was not a sadist, however, though he was not averse to beating an 'inamorata' if he thought she deserved it.

Why did Smith graduate to murder? The answer is: the attraction of money. Once he had killed Beatrice Mundy, he believed he had found the route that led to wealth.

But how did he attract the three women he murdered in their baths, and several others too, who were so far above him in breeding, upbringing and education that they could be expected to shudder at his very approach? And attract them in an extraordinarily short time after meeting them, and almost immediately cause them to agree to marry him, without inquiry, let alone investigation, as to his antecedents and the truth of his representations of his name, finances and occupation? And cause them to surrender their bodies and souls with abandon? To Eric Watson, 'the simple explanation that the unhappy women were in love with Smith explains all'. Love, stressed Watson, can make certain women do the most extraordinary things. He cited a divorce case of the eighteen-eighties, which had important political repercussions. The defendant wife said of the co-respondent, 'If Charles had asked me to stand on my head in the middle of Piccadilly, I would have done it'. I knew of an infatuated young woman who did something even more bizarre at the request of her beloved. Edward Marjoribanks in his highly praised *The Life of Sir Edward Marshall Hall* put 'the miserable tragedies of these three confiding and simple ladies' graphically. 'Theirs were horrible lives, which would normally have been spent in quiet, uneventful surroundings. That seemed to make their tragedies the more poignant. For these women asked so little of life; until Smith came along they did not even claim love. Some strange fascination in him called them from their quiet homes and employment. They learnt what love was; they became adventurous and passionate, and paid for it with their lives.'[30]

Smith was one of those depraved but plausible rogues who exercise an attraction for some women far above them in station. But why?

H R ARMSTRONG — *determined to have his way*

Major Herbert Rouse Armstrong MA (Cantab), Solicitor of the Supreme Court of England and Wales, as these words will immediately convey, was not of the ordinary run of men who commit uxoricide — indeed, murder of any type. But, as will emerge from what follows, it was not only his background and qualifications that place him in the front rank of murderers.[31]

He was a very small man, scarcely five feet tall and under a hundred pounds in weight. But his size did not diminish his determination to have his way; perhaps it spurred it on.

Born in 1870 of parents in modest financial circumstances, he was supported by relatives to enable him to read law at the University of Cambridge. He thereafter qualified as a solicitor in 1895, and after practising in his home town of Newton Abbot in Devonshire and then in Liverpool, in 1906 he accepted the position of managing clerk to an elderly solicitor by the name of Cheese in the small town of Hay, in Wales, on the border of England. Soon Armstrong became Cheese's partner. Within a very short time after that Cheese died with odd suddenness, and his wife the next day. Armstrong took over the practice. He then married an acquaintance of his Devonshire days, Katherine Mary Friend. Their union, solemnized in 1907, produced three offspring. Armstrong's practice expanded despite the competition of the other solicitor in the town, Mr Griffiths. The family moved to a larger house, Mayfield, in a nearby village. It had a big garden, in which Armstrong could indulge in his hobby of tending to flowers, and in particular of eradicating weeds by using a weed killer composed of pure arsenic.

Katherine Armstrong proved a devoted wife and parent, but a martinet. Her husband was forbidden to imbibe intoxicating liquor without her permission or to smoke anywhere except in a particular room in the house; he was publicly rebuked for the slightest infraction of the rules of behaviour she laid down. This galling experience the henpecked Armstrong apparently tolerated with equanimity, always treating his wife with consideration and not losing his excellent manners (he never did so anywhere). But his frequent visits to London gave expression to his need for consolations of the flesh. At the time of his trial he was suffering from a venereal disease.

Despite his diminutive size, Armstrong was a member of the volunteer Territorial Force of the army. On the outbreak of the Great War he was called up, soon to become a major, a rank he insisted on using after demobilization. After some service in France, he was located in England, and could keep his practice going to a degree.

When the war was over, old Griffiths took in Oswald Norman Martin as a partner. Martin was married to the daughter of the local pharmacist, Davies. In 1920 the senior partner died. Martin was now in sole charge of the practice.

By then Armstrong was also holding the honourable position of clerk to the Hay justices of the peace, in effect legal adviser to the magistrates' court. He drew up a new will for his wife in 1920. Her earlier will of 1917 in her handwriting had made provision for her children out of her estate of some £2 500; the new one made her husband sole heir. The witnessing of Katherine's signature, however, was not in compliance with the law.

Soon afterwards Katherine became alarmingly ill, displaying symptoms of delusion. The family doctor, Dr Thomas Hincks, had her admitted for observation at a lunatic asylum. Soon she began recovering and after five months returned home. Probably her husband had begun trying out the white arsenic he possessed. His wife had become an encumbrance. There was a woman resident in London who had attracted his fancy; possibly his apparent prospective modest inheritance on her death was a further inducement to cause Katherine's departure, but there is broad agreement that it was not a major one. Certainly that was the opinion of Edgar Wallace, who had followed the trial very carefully.

Katherine came home on 22 January 1921. Eleven days before, her husband had bought another quarter of a pound of arsenic from the local pharmacist, Davies. Shortly after her return Katherine became violently ill following a meal. Dr Hincks was summoned, thought the cause was her old peripheral neuritis, prescribed certain medicine and summoned a nurse, and Katherine recovered. Within a couple of days, however, she became violently ill again shortly after having, contrary to her objection to intoxicating liquors, drunk a glass of champagne offered by her husband, into which he had dropped five or six grains of white arsenic, a tasteless and colourless alkaloid. On 22 February, for all the devoted attention of Dr Hincks and a nurse, she died. Hincks, not suspecting the administration of arsenic, certified the cause of her death as disease of the heart, a consequence of rheumatism and nephritis; in addition she was suffering from acute gastritis.

Armstrong was now a free man, well circumstanced. Katherine's will was proved and not yet questioned, though Armstrong did not touch the capital, which was in the hands of the executor of her will. The only financial concern was £500 he held as a deposit arising from the sale of fixed property, which Martin was urging him to repay, and which he could not easily do.

Now he set about putting an end to the life of Martin. It could not have been because of the £500, for the death of Martin would not end the debt. It may have been to eliminate a competitor; it may have been only from bitter annoyance with him.

At all events, while Martin was pressing Armstrong for the return of the deposit, a box of chocolates from an unknown source was delivered to Martin's house. A few days later a visitor to dinner was invited to take a chocolate from the box. He did so, and became violently ill. The box was kept, and when it was examined later some of the chocolates were found to contain arsenic inserted through a hole, the size of which fitted the nozzle of Armstrong's weed-eradicator.

Negotiations about the sale of land and the deposit continued, and Martin agreed to discuss the matter with Armstrong at the latter's house on 26 October 1921. At tea Armstrong offered his guest a scone selected from a number on a plate, taking it with his fingers, saying politely 'Please excuse my fingers'. Martin accepted the offering.

That evening he fell ill. Dr Hincks was called. He noticed a very rapid pulse rate. When it did not subside, he sent a urine sample for professional analysis. A week later the report came: a thirty-third of a grain of arsenic had been found.

Dr Hincks knew of Martin's visit to Armstrong's house. He was also struck by the similarity of the symptoms of Katherine; inquiries of the doctors at the lunatic asylum where she had been lodged revealed that they thought the cause of her ailments might have been misjudged by them. Hincks's suspicions were conveyed to Davies, the local pharmacist, who was convinced that his son-in-law had been given arsenic. Consequently the doctor conveyed his suspicions to the Home Office.

The Director of Public Prosecutions decided to move very cautiously. By a remarkable coincidence, not long before, on 9 November 1920, at the Carmarthen Assizes in Wales, fifty miles away, another solicitor, Harold Greenwood, aged forty-five, was found not guilty by a jury in a historic trial of murdering his first wife on 16 June the previous year by the administration of arsenic. The body was exhumed and an autopsy revealed between a quarter and a half of a grain of arsenic. Greenwood was charged with murder. Two years before he had bought a couple of lots of Coopers' Weedicide, which contained 60 per cent arsenic. Contradictory evidence on when the poison would have been administered, coupled with evidence of the presence of Fowler's solution of arsenic in the dispensary of the attending doctor, gave Sir Edward Marshall Hall KC for the defence an excellent opportunity to display his skills in cross-examination and at addressing the jury.[32] This time the authorities were adamant the prosecution must not fail. The investigation of the case against Armstrong would have to be done with the utmost circumspection, they decided. He must not be put on his guard and then destroy incriminating evidence.

For several weeks Armstrong besieged Martin with invitations to tea and to a meal. Martin, aware of his danger, had been warned by the authorities not to accept any invitation but also not to allow Armstrong to conclude that he was under suspicion. The constant excuses by Martin for being unable to accept an invitation fortunately did not cause Armstrong any concern, for his overweening vanity convinced him that he had hoodwinked everybody and that his actions were not being investigated. On 31 December 1921 Martin's tribulations came to an end. After exhaustive inquiries the police had enough evidence to justify the arrest of Armstrong on a charge of attempted murder. In one of his pockets the police found a small packet of arsenic, doubtless meant for his intended guest, Martin. Armstrong had acted most foolishly. Later a two-ounce packet of arsenic was located in a bureau in his office.

The police now obtained an order permitting the exhumation of the body of Katherine Armstrong. Dr Bernard Spilsbury found three and a half grains of arsenic in certain organs. It was the greatest amount the prosecution experts had ever known in a case of alleged poisoning. On 19 January 1922 Armstrong was charged with the murder of his wife.

The trial commenced at Hereford Assizes on 3 April. As was customary in allegations of murder by poisoning, the prosecution was led by the Attorney-General. He was Sir Ernest Pollock KC, who later became Viscount Hanworth MR. The team for the accused was led by one of the finest of defence counsel, Sir Henry Curtis Bennett KC.

It so often happens in charges of murder by poisoning that the Crown is unable to adduce evidence showing the actual administration of the substance by the accused. Once more this was the case, though it could and did argue that the accused had opportunity, motive and means.

The presiding judge was Mr Justice Darling, hearing his last murder case at the age of seventy-three after almost twenty-five years on the Bench. His appointment as a High Court judge by Lord Halsbury LC had been an undeserved political one and had led to unprecedented criticism by the media and the legal profession. While he was a clever man, he proved in general a most unsatisfactory judge — except that, in murder trials, Judge Neville Laski was to write in the *Dictionary of National Biography*, he was good.

The prosecution, as in the trial of George Joseph Smith, regarded it as crucial to prove design by the accused. It proposed doing this by adding evidence of the attempted poisoning of Martin. Mr Justice Darling rejected the objections by Curtis Bennett, saying that if he were wrong in allowing the evidence the Court of Appeal could say so. In the event that tribunal decided that Darling was correct, holding that 'similar-fact' evidence could be used to show that the accused's possession of incriminating material was for a guilty purpose.[33]

The defence was constrained to argue that Katherine could have committed suicide; she had occasionally spoken of it in the past. The Crown, however, put an end to that contention. Katherine had been bedridden for several days before she died; Dr Hincks testified that she was in no condition to help herself then to medicine, indeed, even lift a cup to her lips. The medical evidence was that arsenic could not have caused her death if it was taken a week before she died. Most significant of all, Katherine had said to her nurse on the day she died: 'I am not going to die, am I? Because I have everything to live for — my children and my husband.'

Armstrong was called to the witness box by Curtis Bennett. In examination in chief he seemed a smooth, well-spoken, courteous gentleman. In cross-examination he did not fare so well. And Mr Justice Darling asked him some very awkward questions. 'Wait a minute, Major Armstrong', he intervened again, just as the accused was to return to the dock. Why had he, a solicitor, forgotten to mention to the police his purchase of the only white arsenic he had ever had? Why had he made it up into twenty little packets, each containing a lethal dose, instead of pouring all the contents straight into holes in the ground in order to kill the weeds? Why didn't he tell the police about the two lethal ounces in his bureau? These were but a few of the questions posed by the judge, to which there could be no satisfactory replies.

The summing-up by Mr Justice Darling must have fortified the members of the jury in the conclusion that the accused was guilty beyond a reasonable doubt. Strangely enough, popular belief was that he would be acquitted. The Greenwood acquittal was not to be repeated, though. The fifty minutes the jury took to return its verdict, so the story goes, were largely consumed by its members deciding to have a quiet smoke before returning to the court.

On 31 May 1922, shortly after the Court of Appeal had rejected his appeal, Armstrong was hanged at Gloucester prison. The only mystery he left behind was whether he had caused any others to die by poisoning. According to Filson Young, who edited the trial of Armstrong in the Notable British Trials Series, had the exhumation of Katherine Armstrong's body not revealed arsenic in it and led to the conviction of her husband, 'other graves would have been disturbed and other tragedies, now mercifully hidden for ever, would have been brought to light'.[34]

JOHN GILBERT GRAHAM — *and Flight 629*[35]

This case of matricide is the most ghastly one of all. On 1 November 1955 flight 629 of United Airlines left Stapelton Airport, Denver, Colorado en route to Alaska. Eleven minutes later the DC-6B exploded in the air, resulting in the death of all thirty-nine passengers and the five members of the crew. Debris spread over eight miles. In it were found strands of yellow wire that gave the clue to the source of the explosion: material that had been placed on board in No 4 baggage compartment, which contained the luggage of passengers who had caught the aircraft in Denver. Police investigation for a motive pointed to its being found with John Gilbert Graham, a twenty-three-year-old dissolute criminal who had served time for forgery of insurance policies and bootlegging. His mother, Mrs Daisy King, had boarded the plane in order to visit her daughter in Alaska. Graham, married with two children, had seen his mother off at the airport, having told his wife that he had put a 'Christmas present' for his mother in her suitcase. He was a beneficiary in her substantial estate and had taken out an insurance policy of $37 500 on her life. The 'present' was a time bomb that he had made of fourteen pounds of dynamite linked to an alarm-clock detonating mechanism. Graham confessed to having committed the crime. At a very early age his mother had been widowed and, being impoverished, had to place her son in an orphanage. When he was eight his mother married the well-to-do John Earl King, took her son out of the orphanage, and lavished affection on him. Nevertheless, John Graham maintained an overwhelming hatred of his mother. Never did he show remorse for having also caused the death of forty-four other people. Graham was tried only for the murder of his mother. His trial, witnessed by millions on the television screen, resulted in his conviction of first-degree murder, for which he was put to death in a gas chamber in 1957.

ATTORNEY-GENERAL v EDWARD BALL — danse macabre

The trial of Edward Ball in 1936 in Ireland understandably aroused enormous interest in that country. It is the subject of a gripping analysis in a chapter headed 'Danse Macabre' by Kenneth E L Deale SC, Judge of the Circuit Court of Eire, in his book *Memorable Irish Trials*.[36]

Early in the morning of Tuesday 18 February 1936 James Rafferty was delivering newspapers in Corbawn Lane, Shankill, a village on the east coast of Ireland, some ten miles from Dublin. The road, which leads to the sea, had a barrier about a hundred and fifty yards from the shore to prevent the passage of cars. Rafferty noticed at the barrier a two-door 'baby Austin' motor car. He spoke to a Mr Margetson, who occupied the nearest house, who had seen the vehicle shortly after midnight. When the two examined the car, they saw that the front was jammed against the right-hand side of the barrier; the sunshine roof was open; the driver's door was ajar; on the floor there was a bloodstained towel and a piece of bloodstained blotting paper; and on the back seat were drops of blood. In the pocket of the door were an envelope and some papers bearing the name of Mrs Vera Ball of Booterstown, a South Dublin suburb on the coast.

Margetson reported what he had seen to the Civic Guards (the Irish police) at Shankill. They arrived almost immediately. Their search showed further blood: on a wheel, a tyre, and the ground below. Off they went to Booterstown, where they ascertained that Mrs Ball lived in a small semidetached modern house, 23 St Helen's Road. Mrs Lavinia (Vera) Ball was fifty-five years old. She had lived since 1927 apart from her husband, a well-known Dublin physician. There were two children of the marriage, both sons. The younger son was Edward, nineteen and a half years old, who normally lived in a flat in Dublin but had been staying in his mother's house from the thirteenth of the month. He was a well-liked person, but had no occupation. His interest lay in the stage.

The house had a front and a back garden. On the ground floor were two living rooms, a kitchen and offices. Upstairs were three bedrooms off a small landing at the top of a narrow flight of stairs from the hall. The living rooms were off the hall. There was a door from the hall into the kitchen. Attached to the side of the house was a small garage.

The house was comfortably furnished. Vera Ball had private means and a considerable income which she supplemented by part-time work.

When the Guards arrived it was just after noon. Edward Ball was not in; nor was Mrs Ball, who, it appeared, had not slept in the house the previous evening. The dining table had been set for three by the maid. Mrs Ball, said the maid, Lily Kelly, was expecting two friends for lunch. Ball had arrived by now. At half-past six the Guards returned, led by Chief Superintendent Reynolds. There was no trace of Vera Ball's whereabouts. To questions by Reynolds, Ball answered all calmly. He had last seen his mother at about seven forty-five the previous evening. She had then left alone in her car, saying that she would probably stay the night with her sister or with a woman friend, both of whom lived nearby. It was quite common for his mother to stay the night away from home. He had opened the garage door and the front garden gate and closed them when his mother had gone.

His father had told him that afternoon that the car had been found near Shankill with bloodstains in it. He asked Reynolds where the car had been found, and was told where. He asked whether his mother had stayed with either lady and was told she had not.

In answer to questions, Ball said that he had been at home all night on Monday the seventeenth, going to bed around ten-thirty or eleven. His mother had left in a dark red dress, a blue-and-white check belted coat, a blue hat and brown shoes. At this stage Reynolds went alone into the kitchen, where he found a pair of man's brown shoes, sodden with water and covered with wet mud; then alone to Ball's bedroom, where he found a wet newspaper of the previous day wrapped around wet bloodstained linen.

On returning to Ball, Reynolds suggested that they force the door of Mrs Ball's locked bedroom, as she could be inside. Ball explained that his mother when she went out usually locked the door and took the key.

The door was forced. The room was in darkness. A portable electric fire was on near the bed, drying a large wet stain on the carpet. The bed had not been slept in. There was dirty water in the washbasin. The wardrobe was open. The maid disagreed with Ball's description of the clothes his mother had been wearing. The bedclothes were arranged differently from the way she had left them. The blue-and-white check coat described by Ball was used by Mrs Ball as a cushion in her car.

Ball told Reynolds that the previous day he had been in Dublin on his mother's business, returning at about five-fifteen. He had supper with his mother. She was highly strung and was frequently depressed, but definitely did not have suicidal tendencies. She and he were fond of each other.

The next day, Wednesday the nineteenth, interviewed by Superintendent Dunleary, Ball now said his mother had left the house at eight-thirty on the Monday night. On Tuesday the eighteenth he had gone after breakfast to Dublin for an interview for a job; then he did some business for his mother; had lunch at a café; called at the flat he had previously occupied for letters; went to a theatre where he had acted in small parts; knocked about between five and six, when he called at his father's house; then went home. The Guards discovered he had failed to mention two important calls, as will appear.

Ball falsely denied that he had left the house on Tuesday morning with a suitcase. Dunleary saw Ball keeping his hands folded or in his pocket, and that there were cuts on them. He explained the wound on his right thumb as a result of his cutting bread, clearly a lie, for he was right-handed. He did not even try to explain a cut on his left finger.

They then went to Ball's bedroom, where there were a vest, coat, socks and trousers, all very wet and bloodstained. Eventually Ball agreed he could have worn them on the Monday. No explanation was forthcoming for the bloodstains and mud; or the contents of the newspaper parcel — a towel, a handkerchief and collar of his, and a tablecloth — all bloodstained. Asked what shoes he had worn on the Monday, he finally produced a wet pair containing sand mixed with mud.

In the bedroom there were three other important items: a bottle of patent stain remover; a visiting card of a Mr Tanham; and the following note from his mother: 'If you stay here tonight I am going to Mrs Allen. You did the usual dirty trick, coming in at 12 o'clock last night; it has upset me. I am three hours late for my work, but what can I expect?'

Of the important calls by Ball the Guards had discovered, the one was to the shop where he had bought the stain remover. The other was to the wife of a friend. She said that Edward Ball had come to her flat on the eleventh, saying he could not pay the rent of his flat, his co-tenant having left: he had only a pound a week from his mother and one pound ten shillings a week from his father. His mother had opened and read his letters, which he could not forgive. On the fourteenth Mrs Ball had called, and she and her son had had a quarrel. Mrs Ball said Edward could not sleep in her house though he could have his meals there.

Edward Ball had left the suitcase in the woman's flat. It was taken by Sergeant Heeney on Wednesday the nineteenth in the presence of Ball. In it were bedding, towels, two shirts, a woman's black coat and underslip. All were very bloodstained. Ball admitted he had put all the things into the suitcase. The bedding was from his mother's bed, the coat was his mother's, and the shirts were his. Already Mrs Ball's house had been searched to reveal blood almost everywhere, the carpet being soaked with it. Bloodstains were seen on the mattress, bedhead and -frame, dressing table, bed lamp, hot-water bottle and other objects. They were also seen on the threshold of Ball's room, the landing, the carpets and wallpaper on the stairs, the kitchen curtains and a kitchen basin. Then Ball produced from a laundry basket hidden in the attic the pillow from his mother's bed and the missing rug, both bloodstained.

On Thursday 20 February, Ball made a further, astounding, shocking statement. It was to Superintendent O'Reilly of the Civic Guards, to whom he handed the key to his mother's bedroom, which he removed from his shoe. To the prosecution, this statement provided the essential evidence of the death of Vera Ball. For her body had not been found. Indeed, it was never found, despite the most exhaustive search by the Civic Guards on land and in the sea.

Ball said that on Monday the seventeenth, after the maid and gardener had left, he and his mother had supper together at about six-fifteen. She was depressed, saying she had failed in life and marriage, that she wished she was dead; that he must promise not to think she was a coward. She went upstairs. After he had cleared the table, he waited for her to come down. At around seven he went to her room. To his horror she was lying on her back on the bed, her neck cut on the right side, and also her cheek. A double-edged razor blade was beside her right hand. The bedclothes, which covered her to the waist, and pillow were covered in blood. There was no sign of life in his mother's body. He felt he must conceal her suicide and decided to put the body in the car. After carrying it there and putting it on the back seat, he went upstairs, changed his collar and shirt, and locked the bedroom door, keeping the key.

Downstairs, he put on a hat, opened the garage door, and drove down Corbawn Lane. Then he found his progress stopped by the barrier, the existence of which he had not expected.

A small car drew up behind his and later a second one. They had finally left around midnight. (To the Guards the driver of the second one had said he saw a man in the small car with his arm around someone whom he could not make out.)

It was raining heavily all the time, said Ball. He tried to drive the car through the opening on the right-hand side of the barrier, but it became stuck on the ground there. (Had Ball succeeded in his attempt, he could have got the car down a fourteen-foot drop into the sea, having removed the body just before. The body would have drifted out to sea, while by the time the car had been discovered every trace of blood would have been washed away. All he needed to have done then was to clean up properly at his mother's house. Then he would not have told his story to the police, and might have been safe.)

The next thing he did, said Ball in his statement, was to take his mother's body and pull it down the pathway on the side of the barrier into the sea. In addition, he dropped into the sea the parcel of newspapers into which he had wrapped the razor blade. He then walked back to the main road, where he got a lift from a motorist. At home he desperately tried to clean up. In the kitchen and garage he attempted to remove bloodstains with hot water. To try to dry the blood that had soaked through the bedroom carpet, he put on the electric fire. The bloodstained bed clothes and other items he placed into the suitcase; he put clean sheets and a pillow on the bed and, having turned off the light, locked the door. From four-thirty in the morning until six-thirty he lay on his bed, awake; then he hid the rug and pillow in the laundry basket and tried to remove the bloodstains from the stair carpet. Then he went back to his bed, staying until the maid arrived at eight-forty-five that morning.

The Guards were now watching Ball at Vera Ball's house closely. Saying he wanted to go to the lavatory, Ball went with a Guard upstairs. Hearing a suspicious noise, the Guard opened the door, to see Ball's body falling out of the window. He was found lying below, concussed. It was not a serious injury, though. There were two letters in his jacket, both dated that day. The one was to his father, saying he would never see him again, that he loved him and had loved his mother and she him. The other letter was to the coroner, saying that the events of the past few days had been unbearable and he would like to end his own life.

Later that afternoon he was arrested and charged with murdering his mother. The trial began on 18 May 1936 in the High Court before Mr Justice Henry Hanna KC and a jury. For the prosecution (nominally, the Attorney-General) appeared Martin Maguire SC (who became a judge of the Supreme Court) and Kevin Haugh (who became a member of the High Court). For the defence appeared John M Fitzgerald KC and Seán Hooper.

Ball, completely composed, pleaded 'Not guilty'.

The prosecution had been prepared to accept in general Ball's description of what had happened when he left his mother's room with her body hoisted on his back — experiments had shown that a body cast into the sea at the particular time could well never be seen again. Exploration of the ground between the barrier and the sea revealed small tufts of the deceased's hair, a hairpin with a strand of hair, fragments of red fabric similar to that of a garment she had, and blood. The ends of Ball's trousers were stained with sea water and blood, his shoes were soaked with sea water and covered with sand and mud, and the rest of his clothing was deeply stained by blood.

But the prosecution had rejected the story of the suicide. Edward Ball, it contended, had murdered his mother by violence in order to obtain the legacy bequeathed to him in her will, which would end his penury.

The method of disposal of the body could not have achieved the alleged purpose of Ball — concealment of his mother's suicide; for if the body was never found, suicide would be assumed, and if it was found the injuries as described by Ball would show she had committed suicide. The method of disposal was an attempt to hide murder. Nor could he have been fond of his mother as he claimed, Maguire SC said in his opening speech. Had he been, he would not have treated her body so callously, and he would have shed tears.

The prosecution led evidence by a previous maid of hysterical outbursts by Vera Ball against her son Edward in 1935. On one occasion she threatened him with an electric iron. On one Saturday in September 1935 she told Edward that he must leave on Monday; she would give him an allowance of a pound a week. When tempers had subsided she shook off the arm that he put around her shoulders. This maid and another witness said there were constant angry words from mother to son, never from son to mother. She would call him lazy and said he should get a job.

Mrs Ball's secretary gave similar evidence, and so too Lily Kelly. Never did Ball answer his mother back or threaten her.

Several of Vera Ball's women friends, however, testified that she was a normal cheerful person and that there were frequent signs of affection between her and her son, though she was inclined to be irritable in his company.

There was evidence that Mrs Ball had a nervous breakdown in November 1935, staying in a nursing home until December. On 13 February in the present year her son returned to stay in her house, but she told him he must leave.

Now comes an account by witnesses of the events on the crucial evening of February 1936. Mrs Ball's secretary said she had worked with her employer until around four. They and Ball had had lunch together at the house, Mrs Ball being cheerful and amicable. The two women left in the afternoon for Dublin on business. Mrs Ball returned home alone.

Lily Kelly said that her employer had returned around five-fifteen, with parcels of food for the luncheon the next day. Mother and son had been friendly all day. Lily said she had left around six, Ball still being at the house.

The gardener and odd-job man, Richard Mates, stated in court that just before six he had chopped some firewood with the hatchet that was always kept in a tea chest in the outhouse. When he had finished he put the hatchet back, said goodbye to his employer, and left.

Now only Ball and his mother were at 23 St Helen's Road. A postman testified that at about seven-ten that evening he passed the house, intending to deliver a registered letter, not uncommon at that time of night, Mrs Ball always signing for it. The house was in darkness. On returning past the house ten minutes later, he saw a light on in the garage. Now he rang the bell, and after a few minutes Ball opened the door of the hall. They spoke. Ball appeared perfectly normal and signed for the letter.

The occupier of the house adjacent to number 23 said that he saw someone very like Ball opening the garden gates. At midnight the owner of number 21 saw the lights on in Mrs Ball's room, visible through a chink in the drawn curtains.

At one in the morning of the eighteenth, according to a witness, a Mr Tanham, Ball had signalled at the top of Corbawn Lane for a lift. Tanham stopped, and Ball asked to be dropped at Ailesbury Road in Ballsbridge, a suburb closer to Dublin than Booterstown. He gave his name as Winter (? Winton) and stated that his home was in Tunbridge Wells, he being on a short visit to Ireland. Tanham gave Ball his card, which, as has been pointed out, was found in Ball's bedroom.

The next piece of evidence was that of another postman, who had delivered a batch of registered letters at seven-thirty in the morning of the eighteenth for which Ball, in his pyjamas, had signed.

At eight-thirty that morning, Lily Kelly deposed, she arrived at the house. She could not find the key of the door of the hall in its usual place under the mat, but the side door, contrary to custom, was unlocked. The kitchen floor was covered with water and there was water on the stair carpet. Mrs Ball's room was locked, but that was usual when her son was there. She then asked Ball where his mother was, to which he replied that she had spent the night with a friend but would be back for the luncheon at one.

After breakfast Ball was ready to go out. He was wearing a different suit from the previous day. She told him that she could not clean his shoes, as they were too wet. Ball left wearing his hat, which was wet, and carrying a suitcase. One of the luncheon guests had let Mrs Ball know that she was unable to come; the other guest had arrived but left on finding that her hostess was not at home.

At around six that evening, the eighteenth, Ball had returned without the suitcase. Lily then told him that his mother had not returned and detectives had arrived to whom she had mentioned the suitcase. The response of Ball was that they would come to all sorts of conclusions about the suitcase, and — surely the most significant remark — it was a terrible thing that he was the last person to see his mother alive.

Lily told the court that she could not find the hatchet that day. In searching the outhouse and garden, however, a Guard found it. He said in evidence that he had found bloodstains on the flower bed and the path to the shed where Mates had put it the previous day, but now the instrument was not in the chest but in a box below it: and there were bloodstains on it.

Evidence was given, as already pointed out, by the drivers of the other two cars that had been in Corbawn Lane on the fatal evening of the seventeenth. The driver of the last of these cars to leave said that then — it was around eleven forty-five in the evening — the baby Austin seemed to be empty.

The prosecution pinned its case mainly on the extraordinary statement by Ball just before his arrest, a statement that the defence tried, without success, to have declared inadmissible; and on the evidence of the State pathologist, Dr John McGrath, who had conducted important experiments to buttress his conclusions. The state of the carpet was a crucial piece of evidence, and its impact was enhanced by its being brought into court for the jury to look at it. Dr McGrath concluded that the deep stains on it were caused by four or five pints of blood spilling on it. The bedclothes were stained by only between a tenth to a fifth of a pint of blood. Where had Vera Ball died? Dr McGrath concluded that it was on the floor, where there had been substantial bleeding. It could hardly have been her bed unless she had been placed on it after death or she had struggled to get on to it, hardly conceivable in her dying moments. And she could not have pulled up the bedclothes, where Ball said he had seen them.

The doctor had experimented with other persons' hair, using a razor blade and then a hatchet, and concluded that the tufts of Vera Ball's hair that had been found were probably chopped off. The likelihood of her having cut her throat with a razor blade was remote. This difficult feat, which was successful only once in twenty attempts, would have required several strong cuts to a depth of half an inch on the side of the neck, through the jugular vein; the absence of spurting blood showed there had been no arterial bleeding. With a wound on the side of her neck, Mrs Ball could only have chopped or cut off bits of her hair if she had held out her hair with one hand, which was extremely unlikely.

According to Dr McGrath, death had not resulted from bleeding, for if it had, the bleeding after death would not have been so great as appeared from the blood on the towel. The hair of the deceased woman, in his view, was severed by the edge of the hatchet meeting the skull at the back of the head and neck. He had experimented with a hatchet on a corpse, and found that bleeding after death came from one of the large blood vessels, and not from the skull. The bloodstains on the hatchet were slight. The weapon had not been washed but had been wiped. An experiment had shown him that the amount of blood on the hatchet must have been small, not unexpectedly so, for lethal weapons rarely show great amounts of blood.

The defence, after an unsuccessful attempt to have the case withdrawn from the jury (it seems to me that it was a hopeless application), then outlined its case. Its main contention was that Vera Ball had committed suicide. If the jury did not accept this, then the defence was that Ball was insane, which would result in the then illogical finding of 'guilty but insane'. (I should point out that prior to 1883 it would have been 'not guilty on the ground of insanity'. In that year the British Parliament changed the finding to 'guilty but insane', it appears in order to please Queen Victoria, at whom a man had fired a bullet but had been acquitted of a crime on the ground of insanity. But today in England, under section 1 of the Criminal Procedure (Insanity) Act of 1964, the verdict once more is 'not guilty by reason of insanity'. In South Africa, in terms of s 29(1) of the Mental Disorders Act of 1916, the 'guilty but insane' verdict was introduced, but it was wisely replaced by section 78(6) of the Criminal Procedure Act of 1977 by 'not guilty by reason of mental illness or mental defect'.) Counsel for the defence of Ball decided not to call him into the witness box to give evidence. (One could imagine how he would be battered in cross-examination.) Fitzgerald KC, however, had a fine opportunity in his opening address for the defence to dwell on the depressed mental state of Vera Ball, especially on the fatal night, and on what he said were her efforts to ruin the life of her son Edward.

The first witness for the defence was a pathologist, a Dr Dockeray. His evidence was blunted in cross-examination. He knew of a case where hair cut by a razor blade had looked as if it had been cut with a blunt instrument — but agreed it was exceptional. Mrs Ball could have been the one person in twenty who succeeded in cutting her throat with a razor blade. It was possible, even if unlikely, that, though having lost half her blood, she could have got back into bed and covered herself with the bedclothes. If the hatchet had been used, there would have been more blood on it originally. He would not deny that the evidence was compatible with Vera Ball's having been struck down by violence.

Two psychiatrists gave evidence on the question of insanity. The one, a well-regarded Dublin practitioner, had seen Edward Ball in hospital and concluded then he was gravely abnormal mentally, was irrational, and had an immature and foolish outlook. Ball did not appear to understand the seriousness of being charged with murdering his mother, and seemed indifferent to her death. He was suffering from dementia praecox (nowadays called schizophrenia) in a grave monomaniacal or paranoidal form. The other psychiatrist, from London, who had seen Edward Ball in 1932 at the request of Dr Ball, confirmed this diagnosis. He was weak-minded and morally deficient, speaking cheerfully about suicide, the significance of which he did not understand. But the prison doctor, called in rebuttal, testified that he had seen no sign of insanity in the accused. The mental history of Ball showed that he suffered from adolescent instability.

At this stage Dr Ball was called to the witness box, whereupon his son began to weep. Distressed at having to give evidence, Dr Ball said he had married in 1902, and a year later, at the birth of their first child, he had noticed signs of instability in his wife. Over the years, her mental disorder had got worse. She was very neurotic, had numerous nervous breakdowns, suffered from lengthy periods of depression, insulted him in the presence of his patients, and told dreadful lies about him. Her temper was violent and she was a kleptomaniac. In 1927 he could stand the relationship no more, and parted from his wife for ever. He had assumed custody of Edward, sent him to an English public school and looked after him in the school holidays. To Edward, his mother's attitude had been the same. Dr Ball was convinced that his wife had suicidal tendencies. In her family there had been two suicides and one case of insanity.

At the age of thirteen Edward had tried to commit suicide by swallowing a large number of aspirins. To save him, Dr Ball told the court, he had used a stomach pump.

Edward had no aptitude for study, Dr Ball continued, and no ambition. When his wife complained that he had deprived her son of a mother's love, he had allowed Edward to stay with her in the school holidays. She had wanted Edward to be trained for the stage, but he refused to give his consent to so unsuitable an occupation for a boy with his mental condition. Dr Ball insisted that Edward had expressed no ill will towards his mother.

The last witness was the general practitioner whom Vera Ball used to consult. She confirmed that her patient was very excitable, nervous, apt to suffer from depression, and a kleptomaniac.

The summing-up by Mr Justice Hanna, according to Judge Deale in his fine account of the case, was not unfavourable. This, I should point out, is generally unusual; in most cases the summing-up in the type of trial found in England favours the prosecution. I also find it strange, for my reading of Judge Deale's careful analysis of what took place leads me to the conviction that Edward Ball did murder his mother by hitting her on the head with the hatchet. Had there been a knowledge of DNA in those days, I feel sure that it would have shown that the blood on the hatchet was Vera Ball's blood. Still, even if, as seems likely, the defence did not concede that it was hers, on the facts who else's could it have been?

Mr Justice Hanna expressed sympathy for the accused in his unhappy life, unwanted by his father and mother, and now homeless. I would have thought that Ball was an idle washout of a son. The judge said that Ball's description of his mother on her bed with the razor blade beside her was very convincing; if it was not true, it was the invention of a very powerful imagination. It seems to me that it was clearly the product of the brain of an accomplished liar. Why, for example, tell the lies about his name and origins to Mr Tanham? Finally, the judge said that if the mind of the deceased woman had become unbalanced, she might well have committed suicide.

The jury, after retiring for four hours, returned, asking for the recall of certain witnesses. In answer to the foreman, Lily Kelly said that she had never seen Mrs Ball use a razor blade; a police witness said razor blades had been found in Edward Ball's room; and the hairdressers of Mrs Ball said that her hair reached to her elbows. After another hour, the jury returned with the verdict of 'guilty but insane'. The judge directed, as the law required, that Ball be detained during the pleasure of the Governor-General (which meant in an asylum for the insane). (Only on the abdication of Edward VIII in December 1936 was the position of Governor-General of Ireland abolished. In July 1937 a new Constitution for Ireland was approved on a plebiscite, creating Eire, an independent republic in all but name.) What happened to Edward Ball after that we are not told, even though Judge Deale wrote about the trial twenty-three years after it had taken place.

What did Judge Deale think of the verdict? He wrote: 'Ball was, perhaps, fortunate in the verdict [I take it, not to be found guilty of murder], though the medical evidence and his family history were ample justification for the finding of insanity.'[37] On the evidence in the case, I beg to differ. And had Ball been found not guilty, to me the verdict would have been an addition to the long list of miscarriages of justice in murder trials.

Finally the author poses the intriguing possibility that Ball had planned to use the hatchet, inspired by the murder with an axe of an old pawnbroker and her sister in Dostoevsky's novel *Crime and Punishment*, a dramatic version of which had been staged in November 1935 in the theatre with which he was associated, and in which his co-tenant had played a part.

BAREND JOHANNES JACOBUS DU TOIT — *the case of the inexplicable break-in*

In the depths of the night of Thursday 11 June 1992, in her bed in the main bedroom of the mansion situated in 3 Portman Drive in the upmarket suburb of Bryanston, Johannesburg, lay the body of the slightly built Mrs Joyce Anastacia du Toit. Her head was in a pool of blood on a pillow. She had been murdered with shocking violence. A State forensic pathologist found a star-shaped wound on her forehead; a laceration below the right eye penetrating deep into the face; many communicating fractures of the skull; numerous lacerations of the left side of the brain; and five deep lacerations on the left side of the skull with brain tissue prolapsing through the wounds. No alcohol was found in the blood of the deceased.

The dead woman had been married in community of property to Barend (known as Ben) Johannes Jacobus du Toit, a strongly built man, a broker in the capital market, who was forty-four years of age and a millionaire. The couple had four children. Various witnesses close to them testified in the subsequent trial of Du Toit that they were apparently happily married.

Nothing untoward had happened to the family in the afternoon and early evening of the fatal day. As was customary with black domestic servants in Johannesburg in those days, the maid, by name Princess Ntleki, had the afternoon and evening off. She was not on the premises. Supper had been prepared by Joyce du Toit. After the children had had their meal, they watched television. Meanwhile Barend and Joyce du Toit had a drink and then discussed with interior decorators their exciting new residence which was being built. The decorators left between eight and eight-thirty, after which the couple enjoyed another drink, then apparently had intercourse, and after that ate their evening meal. When it was over they locked the house up, Joyce then retiring to the main bedroom on the extreme west side of the ground floor, in order to sleep. The children had already gone to their bedrooms, also on the ground floor, and were asleep. Barend du Toit, so he claimed, went to work in his study on the top floor on the far east side of the house. Adjoining it was a bedroom.

This picture of seeming domestic tranquillity changed radically during the night. A sliding window of the lounge on the east side of the ground floor had been broken. Shards, pieces and splinters of glass lay on the broad windowsill. The main bedroom and the adjoining dressing room were in chaos. Cupboard doors were open, and clothes and jewels lay strewn over the floor. Other jewels of the deceased were on a small cabinet. There was no sign of a murder weapon. The study was in similar chaos. Doors of cupboards had been opened and the contents pulled out and scattered over the room. Among the items found on the desk were some banknotes and coins, a round of ammunition and two Swatch watches. Two firearms lay in a cabinet. The adjoining bedroom was in similar extreme disorder.

Eventually the security firm of Eagle Watch, that had been engaged by the Du Toits, was summoned through a panic button being pressed, and its personnel arrived very soon. Shortly afterwards the police came. The story told at the time by Du Toit to Captain Tiedt of the police service and others was that he had been working for some time in his study, the television set being on, when he heard a noise. Looking up, he saw two black men at the door of the room, the one holding a pistol, the other standing watch in the ill-lit adjoining bedroom. The armed man demanded money from him. On his saying he had none, that man hit him on the face with the back of his left hand. Then, having found a length of electric cord in a cabinet, that black man tied him up with it just outside the study, his hands behind his back and his feet raised slightly towards his hands. He, Du Toit, said that he did not resist, for he had long determined, after suffering a previous robbery, to co-operate with robbers in the hope that this would result in him and his family escaping injury. He saw the robbers loading a camera, a video camera and a video machine into a black sports bag held by the second one of them.

According to Du Toit, after the robbers had searched the adjoining bedroom, they went downstairs. He did not try at that stage to escape from his bonds. Only when all was quiet in the house did he do so. It was a real struggle and took a long time. He then rushed downstairs. The light in the main bedroom was on, and he ran there. He found his wife lying on the bed with her head in a pool of blood. He felt her body. It was cold, and her hands were blue. Clearly she was dead. After pulling the duvet over the body he ran to the nearby bedrooms of the children.

They were still asleep. Having closed various doors of rooms, he pushed the panic button to summon Eagle Watch.

There was no blood on Du Toit's clothes. Nor was any blood found on any water outlet. Nor was the engine of any motor vehicle on the premises warm. There was no other eye-witness of what had taken place to cause the murder of his wife. According to the first person to arrive on the scene, one Oosthuizen of the security firm, Du Toit could give no description of the two black men. All he said he saw was the shadow of one of them. Oosthuizen wanted a description of the men to advise support groups in the area to look out for them, but Du Toit could furnish no information.

Other information furnished to the police by Barend du Toit in the view of the authorities took the matter no further. Though there were some strange aspects of Du Toit's stories, in the circumstances it was decided that no convincing case for prosecuting him for the murder of his wife could be made out.

Du Toit certainly benefited greatly financially from the death of his wife Joyce. There were enormous sums due to him as nominated beneficiary of three insurance policies on her life. With Standard General Insurance Company (Stangen) there were two policies, one of R3 million and the other of R2 million, which, together with accrued interest, yielded R5 035 576.82. With Liberty Life Association of Africa Ltd (Liberty Life) there was a policy which, with accrued interest, yielded R538 564.38. There were ten farms in the Lydenburg district. The liquidation and distribution accounts of the joint estate after the death of Mrs Du Toit showed R14.2 million available for distribution.

Then there was the apparent will of Joyce, dated 29 November 1991, which left her entire estate to her husband and appointed him as executor. There had been a previous will of 5 August 1986, leaving the estates of the spouses in trust to their children.

A further result of the tragic happenings on 11 June 1992 was that Du Toit claimed R62 833.07 from the insurance company Santam Ltd, with which he had a short-term policy covering theft, for property allegedly stolen during the break-in: photographic and camera equipment, a video machine, and jewellery. Santam replaced the equipment to the value of R17 788.07 and in addition paid Du Toit the sum of R30 045.

So matters stood for several years. All the while the mother of Joyce du Toit kept urging the State authorities to charge Du Toit with the murder of her daughter and the forgery of her will. Eventually Captain Luke Enslin of the Brixton Murder and Robbery Squad (since disbanded) investigated again all the circumstances of the case. He became worried over several aspects. If there had been a break-in in the lounge by the robbers, why was there glass from the shattered window outside the house? It surely must have come from a blow from inside. Why hadn't the dog barked? According to the domestic servant, the dog barked so much at night that the neighbours used to complain. The reason why it was quiet that night was that it was found locked in a cupboard in the garage. (It was not for the reason that the dog kept in the stables had not barked in the account of Sherlock Holmes's investigation of the missing racehorse Silver Blaze: that it knew the intruder well. Du Toit's dog could not have known the intruder or intruders at all. Was it not a planned intrusion?) Captain Enslin concluded that Du Toit had been involved in the murder of his wife and other crimes.

The police now as a whole agreed with him. There were further suspicious circumstances. If the sliding window in the lounge gave access to the house for the intruders, why on earth did they close it neatly, so blocking a quick escape route should they encounter resistance? It was not as though the broken window could be seen from inside, owing to the shut curtain, or from outside, owing to the high wall surrounding the property.

No footprints were found either in the flowerbed before the broken window or inside the property. So there was apparently no indication where and how the intruders had entered the premises or indeed if they had entered through the sliding window.

There were no fingerprints on the movable window, which was explicable only if the intruders had worn gloves.

The many valuable items scattered in the rooms that had been found in chaos would not have been left by the ordinary run of housebreakers.

Why was the wife of Du Toit murdered and not he?

The upshot was the trial of Du Toit that began on 30 July 1997 on twelve charges. Charge one was for the murder of his wife; charges two, three and four were for defrauding the insurance companies Liberty Life and Stangen in contending that he was entitled to the proceeds of three insurance policies on the life of his wife and failing to disclose that he was responsible for her death, which disentitled him to the proceeds; charge five was for forging his wife's will; charge six was for defrauding the insurance company Santam by falsely making out that there was a break-in at his residence that led to the loss of certain items. To all these charges Du Toit pleaded not guilty. Charge seven was that of fraud arising out of a claim against the insurance company Santam that was made two years after the death of Joyce du Toit. To this charge, the circumstances of which will be outlined later, Du Toit pleaded guilty. Charges eight and nine were that Du Toit had stolen the two guns and the rounds of ammunition that had been found in his possession on 22 July 1996; and charges ten and eleven were that he had been in unlawful possession of them. Finally, charge twelve was that he had been in unlawful possession of a pistol that had belonged to his deceased wife. On each of these charges Du Toit was given the benefit of the doubt and found not guilty. There is no need to refer to them again.

The trial was held in the Witwatersrand High Court before the Hon Miss Justice Suretta Snyders* and two assessors, Professor George Barrie,† a professor of law in the Rand Afrikaans University, and Mr P H S van Zyl, a retired regional court magistrate. In terms of sections 145 and 146 of the Criminal Procedure Act of 1977,[38] a presiding judge in a criminal trial in a High Court may summon one assessor or two assessors to assist him or her at the trial. An assessor is a person who, in the opinion of the judge, has experience in the administration of justice or skill in any matter that may be considered at the trial. If only one assessor is summoned, all decisions of fact and law are those of the judge. If two assessors are summoned, which is almost always the case where the judge decides not to sit alone, the decision of the majority of the members of the court on any question of fact becomes the decision of the court; but questions of law are decided by the judge alone. The reasons for a decision of law are given by the judge; when the judge sits alone he or she gives the reasons for a decision of fact, but if the judge sits with an assessor or assessors and there is a difference of opinion on a question of fact, where there are two assessors the judge must give the reasons for the decision of a member of the court who is in the minority; and, if there is only one assessor, the reasons for any different opinion of the assessor even though here the opinion of the judge prevails. The judge determines the sentence but may consult with the assessor or assessors before finally deciding on it.[39] While judges vary in their attitude to the summoning of assessors, there is a general tendency to summon them if a sentence of imprisonment for life or a very lengthy period is possible.

---

* She had been a judge since 1 February that year. Miss Justice Snyders was born in 1959 in Prieska, had obtained the degree of BCom in 1980 and LLB in 1982 at the University of Stellenbosch, and had worked for the Department of Transport after 1982 until 1984, when she joined the Johannesburg Bar. On 21 November 1996 she took silk. She had been married to Colonel Robert Blake, who died in 2001, and has a son. See *Consultus* (SA Bar Journal) vol 10 no 1 May 1997 p 21.

† George Barrie had early in his career for six years been a State advocate, a person who conducts prosecutions in the superior courts. He holds the degrees of BA LLB (Pret) and LLD (Unisa). I am indebted to him for drawing my attention to the case, for arranging for copies of the judgments (by courtesy of Miss Justice Snyders) to be furnished to me, and for elaborating on certain details that do not emerge from the judgments in the case.

The State advocates (counsel for the prosecution) were Mr J Henning SC and Mr K Nienaber. Counsel for the defence were Mr W L Wepener SC and Mr J I du Toit.

The case ran for eighteen court days, within the period 30 July to 1 September 1997. Judgment was delivered on 8 September that year. It occupied eighty-five typed pages in Afrikaans. The findings of the court were unanimous. The judgment is closely reasoned.

Du Toit elected to go into the witness box. In his examination in chief and particularly in cross-examination he fared badly. In her judgment Miss Justice Snyders found him to be an arrogant witness who was far from impressive and who uttered glaring lies on many occasions.

The court rightly warned itself, though, not to find the accused's falsehoods in certain respects to cause it to conclude that he had lied in all respects. The accepted test, it pointed out, was whether the accused's account was reasonably possibly true, even though in some aspects it was false.[40]

One of the blatant lies told by Du Toit was in his account of threats by certain Chinese who, according to him, had lost considerably by not following his advice on making investments in the capital market. They had threatened, so he said in examination in chief, to spend R100 000 to injure him. In cross-examination he revised the threat to be to injure him and his family.

What Du Toit related in evidence about being assaulted by one intruder was found to be unacceptable, to be a result of much improvisation in cross-examination. Initially he said that he did not know how many times he was hit by the intruders, but later spoke of a second blow. First of all he demonstrated how the intruder had hit him with the back of a flat hand and later changed his story to a blow with the knuckles of a closed hand.

Du Toit could not explain in his evidence at the trial why, immediately Oosthuizen of the security firm arrived, he showed him the broken window in the lounge where he said the intruders must have entered, and not the bedroom where there was also a window without bars which could have served as a potential point of entry. When asked in cross-examination how he knew to look in the lounge for the entry of the robbers, Du Toit suddenly remembered that he had also looked in the small lounge for signs of a break-in.

The story Du Toit told of the robbers and money was held to be totally unacceptable. He said that one of them had demanded money, threatening him with a firearm; that if he had had money he would have handed it over, as he had made up his mind to co-operate with the robbers to save the lives of himself and his family. But according to his own account, he had between R50 and R100 stored in the drawer of his desk, and this was confirmed by the domestic servant, Ms Ntleki. Yet he did not tell the robbers that possibly there was money in the drawer. And when one of the robbers searched the drawer of the desk and found small sums of money, they left them. Du Toit gave the lame reason that the R2 notes were out of circulation and valueless. He could not give any explanation why a R5 note was not taken.

Du Toit stated in his evidence that the robbers had searched his study and the adjoining bedroom for valuables, yet he could not explain why they had not taken any of the visible watches, jewels, leather jacket, video and television machines or additional items.

A number of other unacceptable accounts by the accused were set out by the judge. Among these accounts were the following: Despite the robbers finding a round of live ammunition, they did not ask Du Toit if there was a weapon that they could steal. From his previous experience Du Toit must have known of the need to look carefully at the robber with whom he had a confrontation so as to be able to give a description of him; Du Toit saw him in a clear light and while he was being bound he had a good chance to see the robber's trousers and shoes; yet all he could describe to the police was the facial appearance of the robber. Du Toit said that he did not call to his family even when all was quiet, as he was not certain if the robbers had left, but nevertheless he hastened downstairs after he had freed himself from his bonds without taking one of the two firearms which lay on a chest. Du Toit said that the cord with which he was bound left red marks on his wrists through his struggling to release himself, marks that were still visible by the following morning, but they were not seen by any State witness, nor did he show the marks to anyone. And his account of the Chinese clients was full of inconsistencies; moreover, he did not give the name of any one of them.

The court concluded that there had not been a break-in on the evening of 11 June 1992 by a person or persons with the intention to steal. Some person or persons had entered the house, with the co-operation of the accused, with the intention of killing Joyce du Toit and to make the scene appear to be an ordinary case of housebreaking. Clearly he or they had wielded the blows that had killed Joyce du Toit. Barend du Toit himself had not done so, for there was no bloodstain or other evidence pointing to his being the actual hand. But had he caused the death of his wife by using some person or those persons to administer the fatal blows? (That person or those persons were never apprehended.) Before the court decided this awful question it analysed the evidence relating to the jewellery and the accused's financial means.

After a detailed and careful analysis of all the relevant evidence, the court concluded that the accused took jewellery of his wife's after her death and nevertheless claimed compensation for its value from the insurer on the ground of its having been stolen.

Then the financial means of Du Toit were considered. The State had led evidence showing that for a period prior to the death of Joyce du Toit her husband had had serious financial problems, and argued that this was a motive for his killing her.

The joint estate of the spouses was of considerable value. There were a farm in the Lydenburg district and other immovable property, including the family residence at 3 Portman Drive, Bryanston, and an adjacent three acres on which a new residence costing R3.5 million was being built. The accused had shares in a company that owned real estate, and also local and Eskom shares of a total value of about R3 million.

The evidence of Allan Greyling, an auditor and a director of the leading firm KPMG, in essence was that while Du Toit at all relevant times was solvent, he had had serious cash-flow problems from 1991, which had reached a climax in 1992. The accused did not effectually challenge this contention. Evidence led on his behalf that the balance sheet of the farm in reality reflected an underestimate of R700 000 was accepted by the trial court. But the court pointed out that this was of little significance, as the assets of Du Toit anyway exceeded his liabilities by millions of rand. The court went carefully into the bank accounts of the accused. Greyling testified that the interest Du Toit had to pay on his debts to Trust Bank, Saambou and Prima Bank amounted to around R90 000 a month. Then there was a monthly charge of R8 000 on the insurance policies. The accused did not challenge the accuracy of these figures. On top of all this were the obligations of the Du Toits arising out of their grandiose new residential project, the fulfilment of a dream. Thus the accused did not have the income to meet his liabilities.

Furthermore, his broker's business had been doing poorly for some time. While for the financial year ending 28 February 1991 there had been a profit of R307 225, for the next financial year there had been a loss of R1 868 194, and for the following one a loss of R664 073. With the farming operations things were no better: for the financial year ending 28 February 1991 there had been a loss of R177 243, for the next financial year a profit of R9 148, and for the following one a loss of R228 659. The only answer of the accused when he was asked how he was to meet his debts was that he had in progress various projects that would enable him to meet them. A look at the projects may be of interest.

Du Toit in his evidence, the court found, had spun an unbelievable story that he had hoped to earn about R220 000 a month from a contract with the Defence Force to supply it with meat, but that the death of his wife gave him so great a shock that he became a 'zombie' and abandoned the project.

The second project of Du Toit's, according to his testimony, had been to be the broker of a transaction between the South African Reserve Bank and a foreign supplier of maize. But the evidence of Dr Jacobs of the Reserve Bank was to the effect that the maize was imported through the employment of the Mealie Industry Control Board as agent; there was no room for involvement of a private person.

The third alleged project was to act as the broker of a transaction of purchase of cobalt from abroad that should yield an income of between R2 and R3 million. Du Toit gave the same unacceptable explanation of its failure through his becoming a zombie.

A fourth proposed project, that of a coal transaction with certain Japanese, again had come to naught.

The court rejected Du Toit's explanation of the failure of every transaction being attributable to his shock at the death of his wife. He had immediately acted in many respects with resolution, even supposing he had had a shock and had become emotional.

Du Toit's account of the income he hoped to get was found not to be reasonably possibly true. Furthermore, in cross-examination he conceded that there was pressure on him to pay his debts.

In her judgment Miss Justice Snyders pointed out that Du Toit in the first half of 1992 (the murder of his wife, you will remember, took place on 11 June) found it necessary to tell lies about his income. One of the lies was in his declaration in an application form for life insurance of R3 million that R1.5 million a year came his way from dividends.

The conclusion reached by the court after a painstaking analysis was that while Du Toit could have solved his financial problems finally by realizing his fixed assets, it was understandable that he had not been keen to do this. Still, he was under such financial pressure that he had had to sell his shares, and had placed the family residence and a property in Randburg on the market. But his problem was if these assets had realized respectively R1.5 and R1 million rand, this would not eliminate even his debt to Prima Bank. To make matters worse, he did not have an income to cover his expenditure. It was unthinkable that he, a sharp businessman in others' and his own description, did not fully appreciate his dilemma.

The accused's account of his financial position, the court held, was altogether improbable. That he had any hope of drawing an income from such negotiations there might have been before the death of the deceased was not reasonably possible.

The judgment of Miss Justice Snyders then proceeded to an analysis of the facts in the case. She pointed out that it had been laid down by the courts that it was not necessary for the State to prove every piece of evidence in isolation as beyond reasonable doubt; it had to satisfy the trial court, not that each separate fact was inconsistent with the innocence of the accused, but only that the evidence as a whole was beyond reasonable doubt inconsistent with such innocence.[41] Bearing this rule in mind, the court found that while the accused's assets far exceeded his debts, he had serious problems of cash flow. As pointed out above, it was held that the accused could not himself have inflicted the blows that killed his wife. After her death he took possession of her jewels but nevertheless made a claim for them on the insurance policies.

The case against Du Toit rested on circumstantial evidence. The prosecution rightly relied on certain rules expounded by our highest court.[42] The State need not close every avenue of escape for the accused, but only establish such a high degree of probability of guilt that an ordinary, reasonable person would conclude that there was no reasonable doubt that the accused committed the crime charged — would be morally certain of his guilt. Where reliance is placed on circumstantial evidence, there are two cardinal rules of logic: (1) The inference sought to be drawn must be consistent with all the proved facts; and (2) the proved facts must exclude every reasonable inference from them other than the one sought to be drawn.

Applying these rules to the circumstances of the case, the court held that the inevitable conclusion was that the accused had caused the death of his wife by using some person or persons to physically inflict the fatal blows.

It followed from this finding, the judgment continued, that the accused was also guilty on charges two, three and four: defrauding Liberty Life and Stangen in contending that he was entitled to the proceeds of the insurance policies, which were then paid to him, whereas, through murdering his wife, he was not so entitled. It was to lead to a finding of guilty on charge six, that of defrauding Santam in falsely claiming that certain goods were stolen by the fictitious robbers.

The court then proceeded to consider charge five, the one peculiarly relevant to this book: that Du Toit had forged the document bearing the date 29 November 1991 and purporting to be the last will of his wife. As has been shown, it disinherited the children and instituted Du Toit as heir to the whole of her estate.

The document bore two apparent signatures of 'J du Toit'. There were two witnesses with the legible signatures of Labuschagne and Bosman. This very simple document, extending over only two typed pages, contained the usual provision of repeal of all previous wills and codicils, and appointed the husband of the testatrix as executor, with exemption from the obligation to provide security. (Actually, in law there is no need for a surviving spouse to give security.) The only bequest read in this simple form: 'Indien ek te sterwe kom, bemaak ek my boedel aan my eggenoot.' (If I come to die, I bequeath my estate to my husband.) There followed the usual provision of exclusion of any community of property of the beneficiary and exclusion of the retention of any marital power.

The document was drawn up by one Christiaan Nel, of the firm of chartered auditors and accountants, Van Niekerk, Wessels & Weber of Randburg. The accused was a regular client of the firm, and particularly of Nel. The two witnesses to the 'will' were Mrs Bosman and Mrs Labuschagne, both of whom were in the employ of the firm when the document was signed. Neither had independent recollection of signing as a witness, but each from the presence of her signature believed that the testatrix must have signed in her presence, as the custom (necessarily so, it should be said) in the office was for witnesses to sign in the presence of a testator or testatrix. Both remembered that the accused, whom they knew as a client, was also present at the time, and on the same day had signed his own will with them as witnesses. These two ladies who were witnesses to the 'will' of Joyce du Toit identified their signatures. They did not know the deceased. The accused was accompanied by a woman whom he introduced as his wife, and they then had no reason to believe that she was not. The woman signed the will as testatrix. When Mrs Bosman and Mrs Labuschagne saw the photographs of the deceased Joyce du Toit in the newspapers that reported her murder, they did not recognize them as being of the testatrix. The photographs rang no bell.

The State argued that the signatures were not those of Joyce du Toit. It adduced the evidence of two handwriting experts to this effect: that of a Mr Landman, with twenty-five years' experience in his profession, and of Senior Superintendent Quinton of the South African Police Service.

The accused adduced the evidence of two overseas handwriting experts who considered that the signatures were that of the deceased: a Mr Gregory and a Mr Blanco. The court pointed out that there were substantial differences between the contested signatures and previous signatures of Joyce du Toit, the agreements between them being mainly only of a general character. That external factors could have caused the differences had never been put to the witnesses for the prosecution. Mesdames Bosman and Labuschagne had no recollection of the woman who had signed as testatrix having a child with her. They had not been asked whether she smelt of drink or appeared to be physically uncomfortable when affixing her signatures.

After a very careful and impressive analysis of the testimony of the four experts, of the approach laid down by the courts and the leading textbooks to the evaluation of this type of evidence, and of what the accused had stated in the witness box, Miss Justice Snyders in delivering the judgment of the court concluded that the prosecution had beyond reasonable doubt proved that the disputed signatures were not those of the deceased. Thus charge six had been proved.

This left only one disputed charge against Du Toit for the court to deal with, that of defrauding the insurance company Santam by falsely making out that there had been a robbery, some two years after the murder of his wife, at the family farm Goedevooruitzicht (nomen est omen!) in the Lydenburg district. Du Toit pleaded guilty to this charge, but the State wished to lead evidence on it.

The accused had given the farm foreman instructions to help him remove household goods, clothing and groceries from the house on the farm and then, during the night, break windows in the house and cause such disorder inside as to give the false impression that there had been a break-in and consequent loss. After this sham break-in and theft Du Toit made a claim under a short-term insurance policy with Santam, with a full list of the alleged stolen property, in the amount of R137 322. On the charge both Du Toit, in defence, and the foreman, for the prosecution, gave evidence.

The essence of the evidence of Du Toit was that he had suffered previous losses through break-ins on which he had not claimed and for which he now wanted to get compensation. The only explanation he could offer for not putting in a genuine claim was that his employees on the farm had not been careful enough. He had to concede that there had been no need for him to commit fraud if there had actually been a

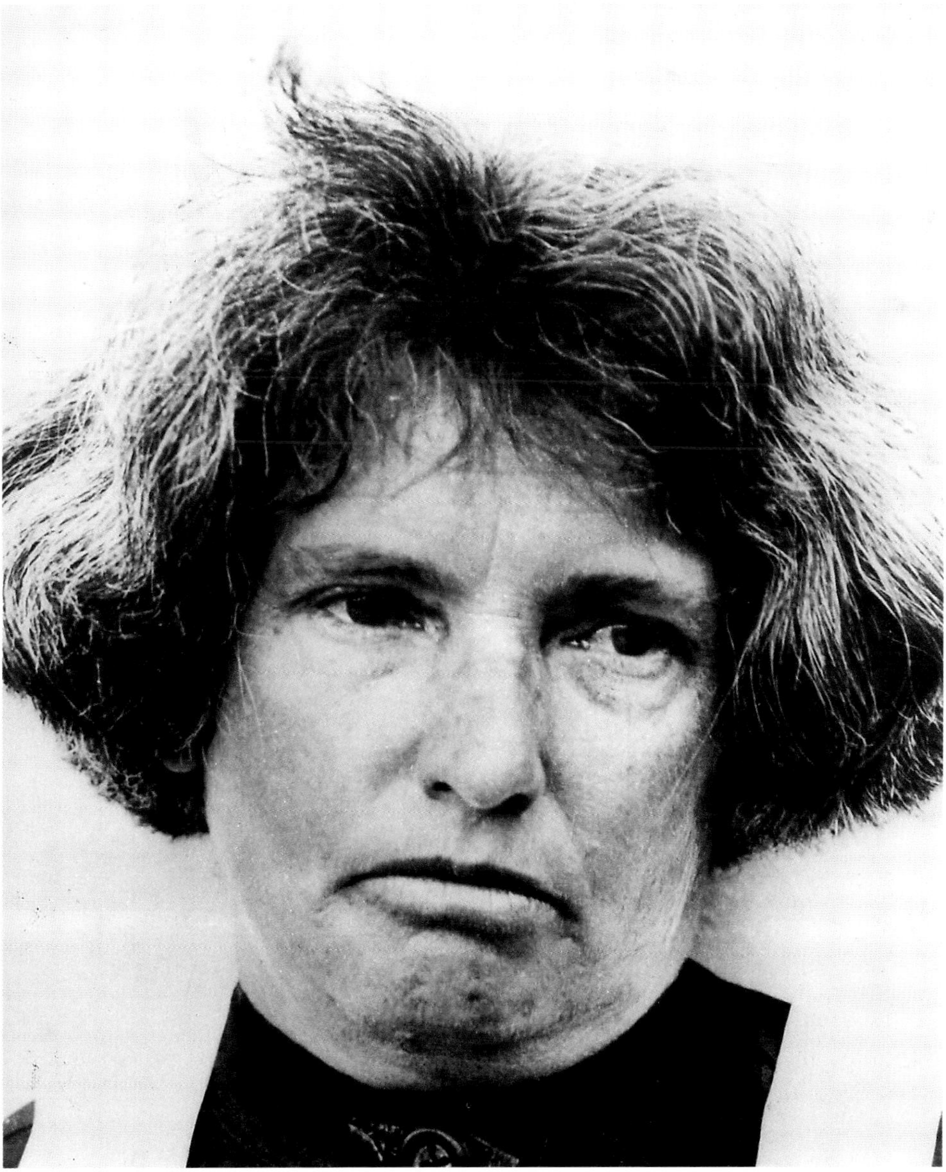

1 Daisy de Melker, South Africa's most infamous poison killer
(Picture: PictureNET Africa)

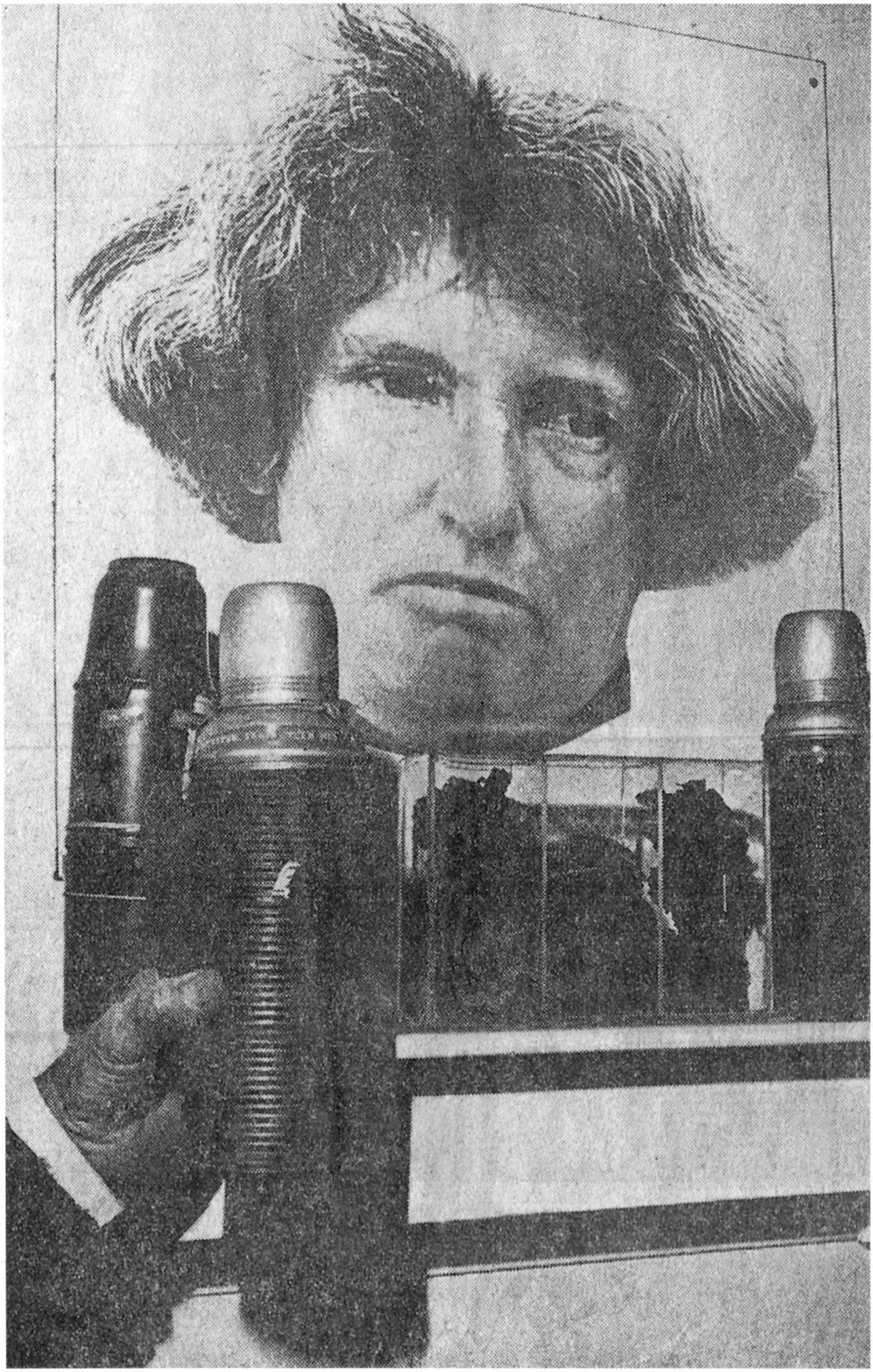

2 Daisy de Melker: in the foreground are the tea flasks she used for her killings

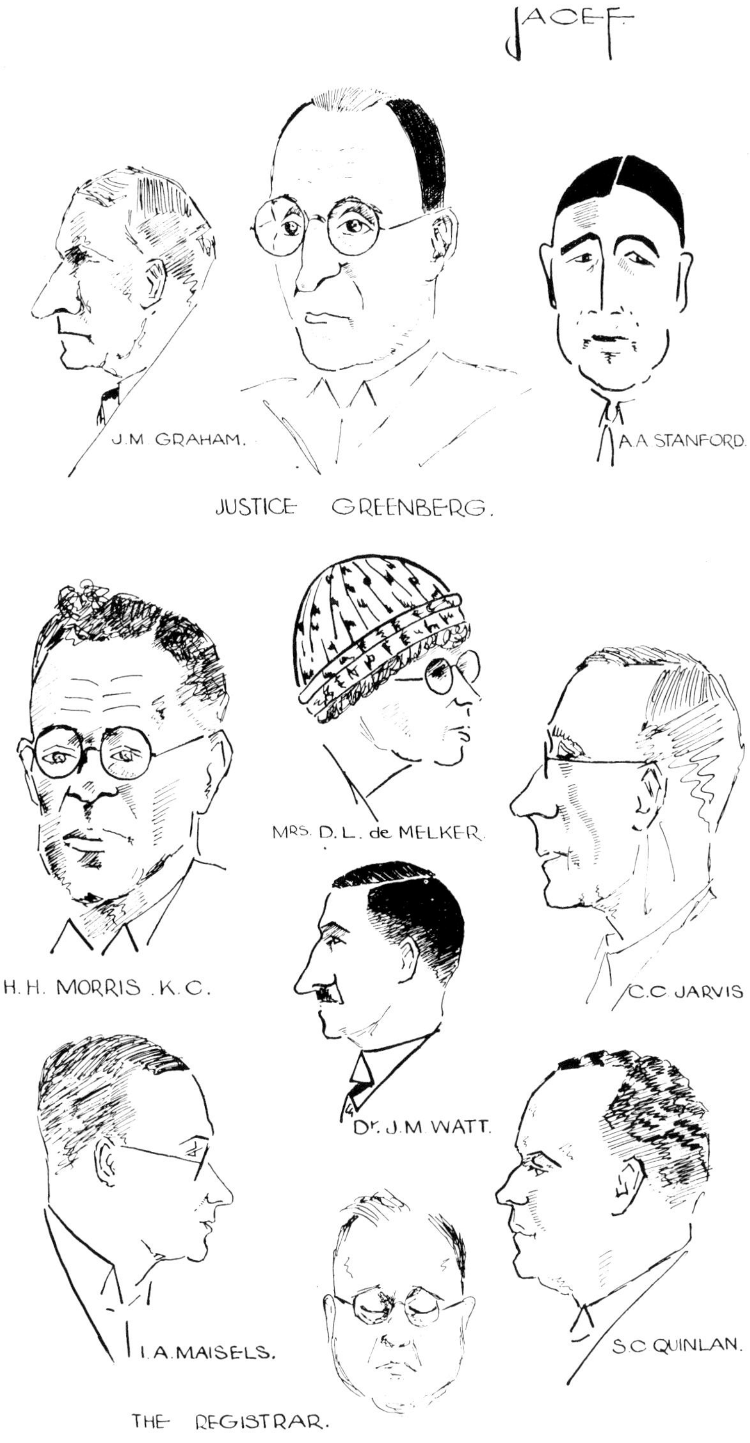

3 Figures in the De Melker murder trial

Sketch by 'Jacef' (Jack Franklin 1902-65)

4 Rhodes, Daisy de Melker's son (and one of her victims)

5 H H Morris KC

6 Mr Justice Leopold Greenberg

7 Professor J M Watt

8 George Joseph Smith
(From an official photograph taken in Brixton Prison)

9 George Joseph Smith
(From an official photograph taken in Brixton Prison)

10 Beatrice Constance Annie Mundy

11 Margaret Elizabeth Lofty

12 Alice Burnham

13 Mr Justice Scrutton

14 E Marshall Hall KC

15 Archibald Bodkin: helped convict several notorious murderers, including George Joseph Smith

16 Sir Bernard Henry Spilsbury

17 Lord Darling

18 Lord Darling

19 Armstrong's wife

20 Herbert Rowse Armstrong, a killer who was determined to have his way

21 Sir Henry Curtis Bennett KC

22 Sir Earnest M Pollock KC, the Attorney-General

23 William Palmer: "It was the riding that did it"

(From a drawing by Joseph Simpson)

Ὁ ἐναγὴς ἰατρὸς ἐξηγνίσθη ἐπὶ τῆς ἀγχόνης
τὴν 14 Ἰουνίου 1856 ἐν Σταφφώρδ.

24 "The Accurst Surgeon", executed by the halter on 14 June 1856 in Stafford

break-in. Owing apparently to the reservations that Du Toit's short-term insurance agent had, the claim was not met by the insurers. Du Toit was naturally found guilty on this charge.

In the event, the accused was found guilty of murdering his wife, of forging her will, and of defrauding insurance companies on five occasions. On all except charge seven, the sentences of imprisonment imposed were specified to run concurrently, so that the effective sentence was that of twenty-five years.* On charge seven a separate sentence of seven years was imposed, resulting in a total sentence of thirty-two years.

Du Toit applied in terms of section 316 of the Criminal Procedure Act for leave to appeal against his convictions on charges one to six and against the sentence imposed on charge seven. Leave to appeal against the convictions was granted by the trial court and against the sentence by the Supreme Court of Appeal. The appeal went to a bench of three judges of the Witwatersrand High Court, Mr Justice H C J Flemming (the Deputy Judge President), Mr Justice C J Claassen and Miss Justice Kathleen Satchwell.† The judgment of this appeal court was delivered in February 1999 by Mr Justice Claassen in an admirable judgment in Afrikaans extending over thirty-nine typed pages, which was concurred in by the other members of the court. An attempt by Du Toit to appeal further to the Supreme Court of Appeal failed. The judgment of the Witwatersrand appeal court expands on certain aspects of law of the trial court, and merits careful consideration.

---

* The perceptive reader who is not a lawyer may well ask why lifelong imprisonment was not imposed. The answer is that at the time Du Toit was sentenced by the trial court section 51 of the Criminal Law Amendment Act 105 of 1997 had still to come into operation (that happened on 1 May 1998). It would then have required in the circumstances (a planned or premeditated murder) a sentence of life imprisonment for the murder unless the court was satisfied that substantial and compelling circumstances existed that justified a lesser sentence. It is most doubtful whether they existed. At the time of the trial, however, the general practice was that of not imposing a sentence over twenty-five years.

† The lay reader will understandably be puzzled about the structure of the courts and their judges. The Republic of South Africa Constitution of 1996 left several mysteries that still await solution by Parliament. The Constitution apparently created thirteen separate High Courts, replacing the previous six provincial and three local divisions of the Supreme Court (no longer existent) and the four surviving courts of the one-time Transkei, Bophuthatswana, Venda and Ciskei. The Supreme Court of Appeal took the place of the Appellate Division of the Supreme Court. But the previous structure of the judiciary was not changed in all respects. The Witwatersrand High Court still shared the judges of the Transvaal High Court, as was the case with their predecessors. The Transvaal High Court still in a way remained superior to the Witwatersrand High Court. At the head of both courts was the Judge President of the Transvaal High Court.

Mr Justice Flemming had been on the Bench since 1978 (initially in the Orange Free State Provincial Division) and had become Deputy Judge President of the Witwatersrand Court in 1990. Mr Justice Claassen had been appointed a judge in 1995 and Miss Justice Satchwell in 1997.

Mr Justice Claassen rejected the criticism of counsel for Du Toit that Miss Justice Snyders did not set out the grounds for saying that Du Toit was an arrogant witness when she rejected his contention that two or more intruders had murdered his wife. It was a finding based on his demeanour and was supported by the two assessors in the unanimous judgment. The appeal court did not have the benefit of seeing and hearing the accused person. And the rejection of Du Toit's contention had not been based only on his arrogance but also on his many blatant lies.

In his judgment Mr Justice Claassen said that the trial court could also have alluded to further lies by the accused (strictly in the appeal, the appellant; but for the sake of consistency the word 'accused' will continue to be used). He had been quick to show the police the place he said was that of the break-in, and one would therefore have expected him as rapidly to have drawn the attention of the police to the red marks on his wrists if he had in fact had them as a result of his lengthy attempts to escape from his alleged bonds. According to his testimony, the marks must have been clearly visible, since they could be seen also the following morning. Yet Tiedt and other relevant witnesses were unanimous that Du Toit showed no visible signs of his trauma. When asked why he did not display the red marks on his wrists to the police, he answered that they had not asked him about them. In contradiction to this he said later in his evidence that he could not remember if he had told the police about the red marks. These patent lies affected a substantial part of his account of the happenings on the fatal night.

Then Du Toit's evidence was also manifestly false on the question why he did not fetch the firearms from the study before he descended the stairs to inspect the ground floor. It would have been logical from the viewpoint of the accused to have done this, particularly as he had suffered a previous break-in, had there really been a break-in that night. Du Toit testified that he did not want to call for help while he was still bound, as he was uncertain if the intruders were still in the house: all the more reason for him to have armed himself to protect himself and his family before descending the stairs.

In his statement to the police immediately after the happenings of the night, Du Toit specifically said that he did not know of anyone who had a grudge against him; yet, in contradiction to this, in his evidence in court he made great play of Chinese businessmen who allegedly had threatened him.

Du Toit in his evidence five years after the happenings recollected that when he rapidly descended the stairs to go to the main bedroom, he saw that the front door was open. This was of importance as indicating that the robbers had left the house through the front door and not the window. But he had said nothing to the police on the day of the happening about the open front door. And in answer to a question by the trial court, he said that he could find no place of exit other than the window.

Mr Justice Claassen pointed out that it is an established rule that a court of appeal will not readily reject the finding of a trial court on the credibility of a witness.[43] The trial court had had the advantage of over three days listening to the accused and seeing him give evidence in chief and on cross-examination. The three members of the trial court had rightly unanimously rejected his evidence as false in essential aspects beyond reasonable doubt.

The conclusions reached by the trial court on the improbabilities in the account given by Du Toit on what happened on the fateful night were accepted by the appeal court, which added several improbabilities: First, even a defence witness had expected the window of alleged entry to show fingerprints unless the intruders had worn gloves, but the accused never suggested they had, and had contended that one had attacked him with bare hands.

Secondly, the breaking of the window pane must have caused a noise at a time when the intruders could not have been sure that it would not awaken someone; indeed, the light in the study showed anyway that people were awake. In these circumstances it was highly unlikely that intruders gained access in this way.

Thirdly, if the intruders intended to get rapid entry to the house and avoid any opposition, they would more likely have gone immediately to the one room where a light was on, the study, to eliminate any opposition from there; but the accused said they had at once gone to the dark bedrooms.

Fourthly, the violent attack on Joyce du Toit must have caused considerable noise; so too the pulling out of the drawers and the throwing of their contents on the floor. Moreover, the robbers didn't try to speak softly, for Du Toit said he heard them from his study on the top floor even though the television set was on. According to him, the doors of the children's bedrooms were then open, for he closed them only when he discovered that his wife was dead. Yet the children did not wake up, which was inconsistent with a break-in on the scale described.

Fifthly, if the intruders had intended to steal and gone off with a video machine and two cameras secreted in a black bag, it was very likely that they had left the murder weapon behind. The fact that one was not found was inconsistent with a real break-in.

Sixthly, the deceased had been murdered where she lay, as the police photographs showed no signs of a struggle or of bloody marks of dragging. Why did the intruders go directly to the main bedroom and kill Mrs Du Toit with violence before proceeding with the robbery? It could only be because there had been a plan to murder her and then to arrange the cupboards and drawers to give the appearance of a break-in.

Seventhly, if in fact the deceased had woken up and begun to resist, causing the miscreants to kill her so that she could not give evidence against them, why didn't they eliminate the accused, who had seen them, for the same reason? Only because there was a feigned break-in, following a plan to murder the deceased and not the accused.

Eighthly, if there had been a genuine break-in, it was highly unlikely that the intruders had closed the movable window.

Ninthly, anyone intending to break in would have noticed the signs on the walls showing that the house was protected by Eagle Watch. The accused had conceded that there was no way in which would-be intruders would know whether the alarm system was on or off. It was thus highly unlikely that anyone not acquainted with the condition of the system would have tried to gain access to the house, when some lights were still on, by breaking a window pane, which in all probability would have set off the burglar alarm.

The appeal court decided that the trial court had been justified in its finding that the accused's account of the occurrences on the evening that his wife had met her death was not reasonably possibly true; that there had not been a break-in by a person or persons with the intention to steal; that what actually happened was that some person or persons had entered the house, with the co-operation of the accused, with the intention of killing his wife and of making the scene appear to be an ordinary case of housebreaking.

Mr Justice Claassen then said that this conclusion was clearly sufficient for a finding that Du Toit was guilty of murder. But, as it were involuntarily, so he went on to say, the question arose why Du Toit would want to murder his wife. What was his motive? In law, stressed the judge, it was not necessary to show a motive. Still, the prosecution had adduced evidence to show that Du Toit was under such financial pressure that he murdered his wife for monetary gain. (It will be recollected that the trial court had gone into this matter in detail.) Mr Justice Claassen stated that the prosecution had done this apparently because of what Mr Justice Malan had said in 1957 in the case of *Rex v Mlambo*,[44] that 'proof of motive for committing a crime is always highly desirable, more especially so where the question of intention is in issue'.

The appeal court held that Miss Justice Snyders had dealt with the financial situation in a great measure of detail. No criticism had been made by counsel for Du Toit in the appeal of her handling of the evidence and the documentation. It was common cause (that is, accepted by both sides) that in June 1992 Du Toit experienced problems with cash flow. It was also common cause that none of the projects he said he was busy with yielded any income. Even the accountant testifying for the defence could not say if any would yield income. The explanation for the failure of the projects to yield income which the accused gave, that after the death of his wife he was like a 'zombie', did not hold: in various respects he acted perfectly rationally, among them the following: the day after the murder he opened a new banking account, took the rational decision to remain in the house so as to avoid building up a fear of it, and asked his sister-in-law and brother-in-law to exchange the bloodstained mattress for a new one. Thereafter he assisted rapidly with the winding-up of the estate, which took place in a very short period. He installed an au pair to look after his children; met weekly with his brother-in-law, who acted as a manger of his farm; negotiated with the banks to get further time to pay off his debts on the life policies; claimed under an insurance policy the sum of R62 833.07 to cover jewellery he claimed was stolen on the night of the murder.

The appeal court agreed with the trial court's conclusion that Du Toit's account of his financial position was totally improbable. Mr Justice Claassen found that on 11 June 1992 Du Toit was confronted with the following situation: He knew that he was solvent but that the bulk of his assets consisted of immovables which would take a long time to realize. His easily realizable shares had been sold in 1991 to reduce his debt of R6.1 million to Prima Bank. At that stage his total debt to Prima Bank, Saambou Bank and Trust Bank was around R5.3 million, carrying interest of about R90 000 a month. He was also burdened with monthly premiums on his life policies of R8 000. And all this before meeting his living expenses. Nor for the six months prior to his wife's death had he earned any actual income. For the year ending 29 February 1992 his broker's business had a net loss of R1.8 million, and his farming activities had yielded a profit of only R9 148. On 31 May 1992 the outstanding balance on his debts to Prima Bank was some R2.7 million, and since October 1991 he had not been able to reduce this sum. By then he had exhausted all his overdraft facilities. On 16 June 1992 he had to pay R186 290.29 on the architect's certificate as an instalment of the contract price to the builder of the new residence. Even if Trust Bank did grant a bond of R3 million for the new residence, the existing bond of R1.2 million would first have to be paid off. Furthermore, the monthly payment to cover interest and repayment of the capital was R50 000, for which Du Toit did not have the funds. To try to secure the bond, he made false statements as to his financial position, such as his estate amounting to R30 million, while it was only R19.6 million. His income had dried up; financially, he had reached a dead end.

Du Toit's wife had been suffering from depression for a year, and was on the antidepressant drug Prozac. According to the evidence, she liked to live on a lavish scale, which must have been a heavy financial burden on Du Toit. It was she who was the driving force behind the building of the very expensive new residence.

It was common cause that Du Toit was the sole beneficiary in the joint estate from insurance policies on the life of his wife, which were to the value of R5.5 million. Were she suddenly to die, he could discharge his short-term debts of R5.2 million.

Mr Justice Claassen then arrived at the memorable deduction that 'die versoeking om sy vrou in te ruil vir die opbrengste van die lewenspolisse moes enorm gewees het'.[45]

The appeal court endorsed the approach of the trial court as to the cumulative effect of the facts, circumstances and probabilities in the case, and its judgment that Du Toit was guilty of the murder of his wife and the defrauding of the insurance companies. It then turned to charge five, that of forging Joyce du Toit's will.

The appeal court held that the approach of the trial court had been correct. It also stressed the fact that the two signatures of the purported testatrix, 'J du Toit', did not appear to be in her ordinary handwriting. It was argued on behalf of Du Toit, however, that the differences were due to Joyce du Toit's having drunk intoxicating liquor at the previous luncheon and was taking Prozac, both of which could have affected her handwriting, as did her having a child on her hip when she signed. Furthermore, Du Toit would have taken a tremendous risk in bringing a strange woman to sign as his wife in the office of Nel, who knew his wife well. These arguments were rejected by the appeal court. It pointed out what the trial court had said of the allegations, and added that it was most unlikely that a person would sign so important a document as a will with a child on her hip and that the accused had lied in relating what had happened. Alcohol could not have influenced the signature; Du Toit in his own account of what took place said that she had not been affected by it; she was in any event used to moderate imbibing of liquor; and the defence witness Blanco could find no indications of its having had an effect on her. Prozac, too, could not have played a role, as

Mrs Du Toit had been on it for a year, it had not affected her signatures on the examples that had been analysed, and the medical expert Dr Hart had testified that it did not affect motor co-ordination and so could not influence writing. As for the alleged great risk of signing in the office of Nel, the accused himself had testified that he did not know if Nel was then present in his office, and had admitted that they did the signing rapidly.

The falsification of the will would indeed at that stage be a considerable advantage to Du Toit were his wife to die.

The appeal court expressed its complete agreement with the finding of the trial court that the disputed signatures on the 'will' were not those of Joyce du Toit. It also held that the accused had rightly been found guilty on charge six, that of defrauding Santam.

That left charge seven, the one on which Du Toit had actually pleaded guilty, that of defrauding the insurer Santam by falsely claiming there had been a robbery on his farm in 1994, some two years after the murder of Joyce du Toit. Here the accused met with some success in appealing against the sentence of seven years' imprisonment. Mr Justice Claassen held that the trial court had not paid sufficient attention to the fact that when he had committed this crime, Du Toit was still a first offender, not having been convicted of the crimes he had committed before 1994, and so he was without the disciplinary effect of an imposed sentence that would yield the opportunity of pulling himself together. In the circumstances a sentence of seven years' imprisonment was unjustifiable, and should be replaced by one of three years. So Ben du Toit went to gaol for twenty-eight years.

A clutch of murderous or possibly murderous medicos[46]

When the murderer who aims at benefiting from the death of a recipient of his or her attention is a medical practitioner, public interest tends to be heightened. After all, a doctor is meant to save life, not take it. And, moreover, it should be so easy for him or her to get away with murder.[47] In his autobiography[48] the distinguished forensic pathologist Professor Keith Simpson, who had conducted over a hundred thousand autopsies, conceded this, and concluded that the medical murderers who were caught out had been either foolish or unlucky. Still, looking at the mere handful who were convicted over the years, Simpson felt that the number spoke 'very highly of the moral fibre' of medical doctors 'or the ease with which they can conceal crime'.

What follows is a description of a few of the relevant classic crimes of murder, or alleged murder, to obtain a benefit from a will, which involve a medical practitioner. What crimes are 'classic'? They are the crimes that — sometimes for doubtful justification — engage great public interest and become the subject of many books and articles. From a merely legal point of view, very few add anything to the elucidation or development of the law. Nor do many raise the 'who did it?' problem of so much of detective fiction. Our fascination with them may lie in our having something in common with the aims of the criminal — such as greed, jealousy, sexual satisfaction — though we do not do what they do; indeed, part of the fascination, then, may also lie in the *actions* of murderers being so different from those of us normal people. We who are concerned with life are both horrified and intrigued by the takers of life.

Bear in mind that this essay is concerned only with wills and crime. That is why a number of the most malign of medical practitioners executed for murder rate no appearance. You must not ask: where is Thomas Neill Cream, a sadist whose very name for long in the eighteen-nineties caused even respectable women to get the shivers, let alone young prostitutes, several of whom he murdered in London by the administration of strychnine; where is Marcel Pétiot, a sadistic and avaricious murderer of at least twenty-seven, who in Paris during the war lured people, mostly Jews, seeking to escape the Germans, into his surgery by making out he belonged to the French Resistance, there watched them die in agony from an injection he had given them, and then took their possessions; where is Professor John White Webster MD, a professor at the Harvard Medical College, who killed his colleague George Parkman, another Harvard MD, to whom he was owing money, and tried to dispose of the body by burning it in a furnace in the medical school; where is Hawley Harvey Crippen, who in London murdered his wife Cora by the administration of hyoscine to be free of her and her demands so he could marry his young mistress Ethel de Neve, and who in 1910 fled with her on a ship en route to Canada, both being caught through the earliest use of wireless; and where is 'Buck' Ruxton, who in Lancaster murdered Isabella Kerr, who passed as his wife, and Mary Jane Rogerson, nursemaid of their three children, probably after a terrible quarrel, dismembered their bodies and deposited the remains in a river, the remains being identified by the consummate skill of medical and dental experts?

WILLIAM PALMER — *'it was the riding that did it'*

I start with the trial of Dr William Palmer, the mass poisoner of Rugeley, England, in the mid-nineteenth century. Palmer had the honour of having his life story recounted in the *Dictionary of National Biography*. Sir James Fitzjames Stephen, the eminent English jurist and judge, in his *History of the Criminal Law* recounts how he was present at the trial, which he regarded as one of the greatest in English history.

There is no doubt that Palmer was wickedness personified: the very embodiment of Evil. Sir James Stephen — to be sure, a person who believed in criminal punishment being essentially retribution — said that Palmer was perfectly sane (today one may question this: some might say he was a psychopath) but he was as cruel, treacherous, greedy of money, sensual and brutally hard-hearted as was possible to imagine. Of common or garden criminals — I leave out of account recent war criminals — he reaches the apogee of sinfulness among men: just as, in my view, our own Daisy de Melker reaches it among women.

Yet the strange thing about his trial is that the prosecution was unable to establish that the body of Palmer's last victim, John Cook, of whose murder he was charged, did contain strychnine, though the whole case of the prosecution rested on Palmer's having administered it to him.

But let me rapidly survey Palmer's short, shocking life.[49] Born in 1824 of a respectable family, at an early age he started his career of crime with thefts. At the age of eighteen he began studying medicine, qualifying after five years. During that time, so some writers claim, he ran an abortion practice and had fourteen illegitimate children. Shortly after qualifying — again, this is a conclusion certain writers have arrived at — he poisoned a man named Abbey with strychnine in a glass of brandy just to see what happened. No one suspected that the man had been poisoned. Very little was known in those days about strychnine (strychnia), and scientific tests were in their infancy. He then appears to have poisoned one of his illegitimate children; a creditor named Bladon (a doctor, well in his eighties, Dr Bamford, was called in and had no suspicions); another creditor named Bly; probably several more of his illegitimate children; very likely four of his five legitimate children; and his uncle, 'Beau' Bentley, and his mother-in-law, from both of whom he inherited. Then, in 1853, came the end of his wife, whose life he had insured for £13 000, a very large sum in those days. Dr Bamford certified death from 'English cholera'. By now Palmer had given up the practice of medicine; his life was devoted to horse-racing, but he kept on losing bets. Insurance had paid off, so he tried it again, taking out a life policy on his brother Walter for another £13 000. Walter went the way of so many others, but the boots at the hotel where he met his agonizing end had seen Palmer slip something into Walter's drink, and the insurance company refused to pay. Still the police were not on Palmer's track. But then Palmer performed his last murder, that of Cook, whose signature he had forged to various documents. On the morning of Cook's death Palmer bought six grains of strychnine. Cook, who had been taking pills given him by Palmer, now became so convulsed that his head touched his heels. His father demanded a postmortem examination.

The postmortem examination was Gilbertian. Palmer was allowed to be present and he almost escaped with a jar containing the contents of the stomach and intestines. This was telling circumstantial evidence against him. It was decided to charge Palmer with murdering Cook. As I have pointed out, in those days only one charge of murder could be tried at a trial.

One main expert witness for the Crown was the esteemed Professor Alfred Swaine Taylor, Professor of Medical Jurisprudence at Guy's Hospital, author of famous works on medical jurisprudence and of a book on poisons. He could find no trace of strychnine in the remains. Taylor was later to disgrace himself in the trial of Dr Smethurst, as I shall show, but on this occasion he did well. For the defence appeared his notorious opponent, Professor William Herepath of Bristol Medical School. Of Herepath you will also hear. The medical evidence was very confusing. There was a tendency to relate strychnine to tetanus, because they produced similar seizures. Remember that it was only in 1889 that the bacillus tetanus was isolated by Kitasato of Japan.

The prosecution was conducted with great ability and scrupulous fairness by Sir Alexander Cockburn, the Attorney-General, who later became Lord Chief Justice. You will remember the convention that a charge of murder by poisoning had to be prosecuted by this senior law officer of the Crown. Cockburn's cross-examination of certain defence witnesses was devastating. Palmer wrote on a slip of paper the immortal words — they are in racing parlance — 'It was the riding that did it'. The circumstantial evidence was very powerful, and the members of the jury took just over an hour to reach the unanimous verdict of guilty. Had they acquitted Palmer, he would have been arrested on a further charge, as there were indictments against him for the murder of his wife and brother; just as Daisy de Melker would have been arrested had she been acquitted of the murder of her son as well as that of her two husbands, for police were waiting for her on charges of murder in Southern Rhodesia.

Two interesting points remain to be made. Palmer said before he was hanged at Stafford in public before a crowd of 50 000 on 14 June 1856, 'I am innocent of poisoning Cook by strychnia'. It has been suggested that perhaps he chose a poison allied to strychnine, such as brucin, and the experts of the day did not know strychnoid poisons well enough to see the difference. Secondly, Prince Albert, consort of Queen Victoria, bought Palmer's blood mare 'Trickstress', rather an appropriate name.

THOMAS SMETHURST — *impure copper in an arsenic test*

In the same decade that Palmer met his end another trial of a doctor aroused equal public interest. It was the trial of Dr Thomas Smethurst in 1859, which had a fascinating sequel. In his foreword to the account published in the Notable British Trials Series published in 1931,[50] John Flowers KC, reflecting on the conviction of Smethurst for murder, said: 'I venture to say definitely that, if this case had been tried in the twentieth century, not only would the accused have been acquitted, but in my opinion he would have been acquitted when the prosecution closed, on the ground that no case had been made out for the accused to answer.' But, as Sir James Comyn, a retired judge of the High Court of England and Wales, points out,[51] 'Sentence of death was duly passed and in those days there was no appeal. If there had been a Court of Criminal Appeal, it is reasonably certain that an appeal would have been allowed if only because the evidence was unsafe and unsatisfactory.'

Lest you now believe that an innocent man was hanged, let me put an end to your concern. Smethurst was given a free pardon. But I must add: he was almost surely guilty; only his guilt was not proved. A leading medical journal of the day, *Medical Times and Gazette*, put the matter very well:

'Is the prisoner guilty? — We believe he is.

'Was he *proved* guilty? — Certainly not.

'The balance of probabilities was against him, but there is a *possibility* that he may be innocent. Innocent men have been hanged upon circumstantial evidence as strong as that which led to Smethurst's sentence.'

It stated that, '[w]hile retaining the conviction of the guilt of the prisoner . . . and without a particle of sympathy for him personally', it believed Smethurst should not be hanged.

The same attitude was adopted by the *British Medical Journal*, though it dwelt on Smethurst's defects of character — he was a liar, a cheat, and a scoundrel in all walks of life.

Who was this man? Thomas Smethurst, who is said to have been a small insignificant-looking person, with a reddish-brown moustache (I have seen no portrait of him), was born in 1805. At the age of twenty-four, while still studying for his medical qualification at the Society of Apothecaries, he married Mary Denham, twenty years his senior. In 1830 he obtained his licentiate in medicine and surgery from the Society, so becoming properly qualified, so far as this was then possible. Later he obtained the degree of Doctor of Medicine in Germany from the University of Erlangen. For nine years he practised medicine in London, and thereafter for three years in Ramsgate. Then he studied hydropathy — 'water cure' — the pseudo-scientific method of treating disease through the use of large quantities of water internally and externally, and set up a water-cure establishment. It was so successful among the wealthy of Surrey that he sold it and more or less retired at the age of forty-nine.

In 1848, when he and his wife were living in a boarding house in Bayswater, he began an affair with another lodger, Miss Isabella Bankes, an attractive spinster of forty-two, possessed of a capital sum of some £1 800, bringing in £80 a year, and an income of £150 a year from an estate of £5 000, which would end on her death. To get the present-day equivalent, one would have to multiply the sum by about fifty. She was well away financially.

Isabella was ordered by the prim and proper landlady to leave the house, which she did. Smethurst followed her, and on 12 December 1858 the two entered into a bigamous marriage, settling down in Richmond.

Isabella had hitherto been quite healthy, though subject to bilious attacks. On 27 March 1859 she took ill, suffering from violent diarrhoea and vomiting. As she did not recover on the ministrations of Smethurst, on 3 April he called in a Dr Julius, a well-known medical practitioner. (I cannot refrain from mentioning a qualification Dr Julius claimed when cross-examined at the trial. He was asked whether he was a Doctor of Medicine. 'Yes.' 'Is yours a London degree?' 'Yes.' 'What degree is it?' 'It is the Archbishop of Canterbury's degree.' 'What! Can he make a Doctor of Medicine?' the judge interposed: 'Yes; and he can also make a Master of Arts.' In fact the Archbishop did have that power, a remnant of papal authority; but if the degree was awarded after 1857 it did not give the right to practise medicine. Fortunately, Dr Julius was also a Member of the Royal College of Surgeons and a Licentiate of the Society of Apothecaries, both proper medical qualifications.) Julius's drugs proved useless, and Isabella complained of a sore mouth and a burning sensation in the throat and intestines. Julius and his partner began to suspect that an irritant poison was being administered to her. On 30 April Smethurst brought a solicitor, a stranger to both of them, to the house to execute Isabella's will, in which she, described as a spinster, left her entire estate (apart from a brooch, left to a Miss Jenkins) to 'my sincere and beloved friend, Thomas Smethurst, doctor of medicine'.

Isabella got no better. Dr Todd, a well-known consultant, was now called in. A stool was sent to Professor Alfred Swaine Taylor, who had given evidence in the trial of Palmer. He reported that he had found arsenic in it. On 2 May Smethurst was arrested on a charge of administering poison to Isabella, but was released on his own recognizances. Lord Chief Baron Pollock, the presiding judge at the trial, in his summing up to the jury made this strange remark: '. . . [H]e pleaded that he was torn from the bedside of his dying wife . . ., he implored that he might be sent back to her assistance, and undoubtedly it was a scene that might well have affected a magistrate . . . and he might have said, "Well there is nothing but a charge of administering poison".' The next day Isabella died, and Smethurst was arrested on a charge of murder. His trial began on 15 August, and so, too, began an extraordinary story that brought much discredit to the medical profession and some discredit to the processes of the law.

The prosecution had to rely on circumstantial evidence — on motive, on opportunity, and on any clinical, pathological and toxological evidence. The motive alleged was the obtaining of Isabella's money; the defence pointed out, however, that Smethurst would cease to get the income from the £5 000 on Isabella's death. To which the presiding judge made the comment that the capital sum of £1 800 was equivalent to twelve years' return on the £5 000, which was a doubtful prospect. The opportunity was obvious: Smethurst had for most of the time been the sole provider of medicine, food and drink to the deceased. He had knowledge of poisons. Did he possess them? Here there was an amazing retraction by the eminent Professor Taylor. He had sworn in the preliminary hearings before the coroner and the magistrates that in one of the forty bottles found in Smethurst's possession — bottle no 21 — arsenic was present. Subsequently, and before the trial, he notified the prosecution and the defence that he had made a mistake: the presence of the arsenic had been due to an impurity in the copper gauze he had used in his tests. It was a grave mistake, and if it had not been discovered Smethurst *would* have gone to the gallows. Dr Leonard Parry, who edited the account of the case in the Notable British Trials Series in 1931, states that this preliminary error by Taylor — who still persisted in his conclusion that Isabella had died of irritant poisoning — prejudiced the position of the accused: the atmosphere of the trial was of hostility to him from the start.

The conflicting medical evidence as a whole was bizarre. The autopsy showed no trace of arsenic in the body. Professor Taylor found up to half a grain of antimony in the small intestines, the caecum (the blind end of the first part of the large intestine) and one of the kidneys (the other had not been examined): but no antimony was found in the possession of the accused, nor was there any evidence of his having bought arsenic or antimony. Ten medical men gave evidence for the prosecution, concluding that Isabella had been poisoned: her death could not be attributed to any natural cause. Seven medical men for the defence contended that she had died from natural causes: from dysentery and the effects of pregnancy, a condition that was discovered only at the autopsy.

The presiding judge at the trial at the Old Bailey, Lord Chief Baron Pollock, was then seventy-six years old. Sir Jonathan Pollock was to continue sitting as a judge until he was eighty-three, dying four years later. He had an enormous family: eleven children by his first marriage, which ended after fourteen years by the death of his wife, and ten by his second. All but one of his children survived him. The Pollock family, like many legal families, was a long-lived one. The Lord Chief Baron was a true Victorian, and in his summing up to the jury, which was strongly against the accused, he expressed disapproval of his bigamy — 'the iniquity, the sin, the crime of that act'. But according to a letter written to *The Times* by one of the jurors, eleven of the twelve had already decided to convict. It took only forty minutes before they returned with their verdict. The judge, saying that it would have been difficult for them to reach any other conclusion, then passed sentence of death.

That was the position on 19 August 1859. There was an immediate and unprecedented reaction, medical, legal and public. Petitions flooded in to the Home Secretary, Sir George Cornewall Lewis. Thirty medical practitioners signed a memorial asking for a reprieve, on the ground that the evidence was insufficient. There was a similar memorial from twenty-nine barristers. The true Mrs Smethurst added her plea in a warm testimonial. The documents were forwarded for consideration to Lord Chief Baron Pollock, who answered that he still felt that the conviction was warranted. The next month, however, a reprieve was granted. Then the Home Secretary took an unprecedented step: he asked the eminent Sir Benjamin Collins Brodie, Serjeant Surgeon to the Queen, to consider all the papers. Brodie reported on 28 October that while there were grave suspicions, 'there is not absolute and complete evidence of Smethurst's guilt'. On 15 November Lewis wrote to Pollock that 'there is sufficient doubt of the prisoner's guilt to render it my duty to grant him a free pardon', but that 'it is my intention to institute a prosecution against him for bigamy'. The letter, which was published in *The Times*, ended by saying that the pardon did not arise from any defect in criminal procedure or tribunals, but 'from the imperfection of medical science'. This conclusion gave umbrage to certain of the medical fraternity, but Dr Parry was generous enough to write in 1931 that 'it is hardly to be wondered at that a layman should have doubts as to the value of scientific testimony, if that were a sample'.

I should not give the impression that in 1859 the whole of the medical profession was happy with the medical evidence.

The *Dublin Medical Press* poured vials of scorn on the head of the hapless Professor Taylor. This 'pillar of medical jurisprudence', it said, 'is the same who has now admitted the use of impure copper in an arsenic test where a life hung upon his evidence. . . . He has brought an amount of disrepute upon his branch of the profession that years will not remove. . . . We must now look upon Professor Taylor as having ended his career, and hope he will immediately withdraw into the obscurity of private life, not forgetting to carry with him his favourite arsenical copper. . . .' The *British Medical Journal* was scathing in its condemnation of the public sneering at one another by the three eminent toxicologists, Taylor, Herepath and Letheby. 'The public at large are scandalised, and ask in amazement, whether there can be anything in poison-hunting which breeds these unnatural storms. . . . The public should no longer have exhibited to them the spectacle of professional men stabbing each other's reputation over the bodies of malefactors. . . .'

Dr Parry in his introduction to his book on the trial, published in 1931, stated that he was much inclined to the view that on the clinical evidence it was a case of irritant poisoning, not of severe vomiting or pregnancy complicated by dysentery, but that he could not deny the possibility of the latter. On the pathological evidence, he could draw no conclusion. 'The chemical evidence', he found, 'was very definitely against arsenical poisoning'; if arsenic had actually been present in the motion examined by Taylor, it could possibly have been accounted for by impurities in the many metallic drugs that had been administered. It was 'not at all conclusive of antimonial poisoning. No modern toxicologist would dream of considering the facts proved on this point as conclusive of this condition.' His opinion of what the Lord Chief Baron said was one of the most remarkable prosecutions he had ever met with, was that 'the evidence, both circumstantial and scientific, completely failed to prove the guilt of Smethurst'.

The accused was thereafter duly convicted of bigamy and sentenced to a year's imprisonment with hard labour. Two years after his release he had the cheek to prove the will of Isabella. Those opposing, who included two sisters of Isabella, who would have been one of the four heirs on intestacy, contended that she had signed through Smethurst's undue influence or fraud. The jury found in favour of Smethurst, but he had to pay his own costs. He also petitioned the Crown for compensation, but in vain.

Apparently Smethurst returned to the bosom of his elderly and forgiving true wife. What happened thereafter no one seems to know. What conclusion does one draw from this strange case? At least that things medical and legal have improved.

GEORGE HENRY LAMSON — *a fatal risk*

Mr Justice Hawkins, who presided at the trial of Dr George Henry Lamson for the murder of his brother-in-law Percy Malcolm John, in his reminiscences called it 'one of the most diabolical cases which came before me while a judge'.[52] Born in 1850, Lamson qualified in medicine in 1871. He then served in the siege of Paris; subsequently, in 1876–7, he served with distinction as a volunteer surgeon in the army in Serbia and Romania. But in everyday life, as a medical practitioner he was a failure, partly because he was addicted to drugs, and he looked to fraud and murder to obtain finance.

In 1876 he married a Miss John, who was a ward in chancery, as were her two sisters and two brothers, their mother, the surviving parent, having died in 1868. One child of hers died in 1873, before reaching the age of twenty-one. According to the mother's will, each child on attaining majority or marrying became entitled to an eighth share of certain property. The share of one who died before majority passed to the survivors.

On her marriage, Mrs Lamson made a settlement on her husband, so her share became his property. In 1879 one of her brothers, Herbert John, died unexpectedly and mysteriously before attaining majority, so his share went to his surviving sisters, a Mrs Chapman and Mrs Lamson, and to his brother Percy Malcolm John, who each received £479 in India stock and £269 in Consuls. It is very likely that Lamson murdered Herbert.

The inheritance that came through the death of Herbert was soon spent by Lamson. He was in such financial straits that he pawned his watch and his surgical instruments. Despite his attractive appearance and outward personality, he had failed to make a go of a medical practice he had bought in Bournemouth and had started writing cheques that his bank would not meet. Lamson's mind now turned to his remaining brother-in-law Percy. He was only eighteen years old. Should Percy die before turning twenty-one, half of his inheritance of £3 000 would go to Lamson through his wife. It was an enticing prospect.

Percy went to a private school, Blenheim House, at Wimbledon. He was paralysed in both legs, and suffered from curvature of the spine, but was otherwise in reasonably good health. During the school holidays he stayed with the Lamsons.

Lamson decided to poison Percy with aconitine, a deadly poisonous vegetable alkaloid, containing the active properties of aconite, distilled from the root of monk's-hood. At the time — 1881–2 — very little was known of the poison, and there was no chemical means of detecting it.

On 28 August 1881 Lamson bought from a pharmacist, Albert Smith, three grains of sulphate of atropine and two grains of aconitine. Smith knew that Lamson was a medical practitioner and supplied the drugs without any inquiry. On 24 November 1881 Lamson bought two grains of aconitine from the well-known firm of pharmacists, Allen and Hanbury, of Lombard Street. Having checked in the medical register that Lamson was a qualified doctor, the assistant supplied the drug.

Lamson tried to poison Percy when he was staying with him, by putting the drug in a capsule, which he said contained quinine. Percy was violently ill, but survived. The next attempt by Lamson was successful.

He wrote an affectionate letter to Percy on 1 December 1881, saying he would like to see him shortly before leaving for Paris and Florence on the third. Lamson arrived at the school at seven in the evening of 3 December. He met Percy with the headmaster, Mr Bedbrook, and produced a parcel containing capsules and a Dundee cake. One of the capsules he filled with sugar from a bowl on the table, saying it would disguise the nauseous taste. He also cut a slice of the cake for Percy, a slice for Bedbrook and a slice for himself. Then Lamson left to catch the train for Paris.

Some twenty minutes later Percy complained of feeling very ill, just as he had felt when Lamson gave him a capsule during the holidays. A Dr Berry happened to be calling at the school. A Dr Little was also summoned. The two medical practitioners suspected a vegetable poison. They did what they could for Percy, who was suffering from great pain and vomiting violently, but he died at eleven. The doctors took some of the vomit and urine.

In a pill box of Percy's were found certain pills, with a label 'George Henry Lamson, M.D.' and described as quinine. On analysis they were found to contain aconitine, each containing a lethal dose of eight-tenths of a grain of the poison.

There was then an autopsy. A chemical analysis of the viscera, vomit and urine showed that death had resulted from a vegetable poison. There was damning evidence from medical forensic experts. An extract from the fluid in the stomach produced 'a biting and numbing effect' precisely like that of the taste of aconitine. A subcutaneous injection of the vomit into mice had caused them to die.

Did Lamson insert poison into the capsule that Percy swallowed? The Crown believed he had, but it was most unlikely, for then the poison would have taken effect much sooner than it had. The judge believed that the administration of the capsule had been to hoodwink the doctors and professional authorities. Almost certainly the poison had been inserted in a raisin in the slice of cake that Lamson had carefully cut for Percy. This would cause the poison to react in the body at a considerably later time.

Suspicions were aroused against Lamson. On his return from abroad on 8 December he went straight to Scotland Yard to clear his name. But he was taken into custody and charged with the murder of Percy. In a box of his lodged at Euston Station were found pages in his hand describing the effects of acrid vegetable poisons.

The powerful prosecution team was headed by the Solicitor-General, Sir Farrar Herschell QC, who later became Lord Herschell, Lord Chancellor. The defence team was led by Montagu Williams, an experienced and able counsel. The circumstantial evidence of guilt was overwhelming, and the jury was not persuaded by the argument of Williams that the accused, had he intended to kill Percy, would have waited another three weeks, when the youth would be staying with the Lamsons on holiday, and would then have been at the mercy of his brother-in-law. It would seem that Lamson was so desperate to get the inheritance as soon as possible that he took a fatal risk.

The jury found Lamson guilty. Shortly before his execution he confessed to the crime, but he strenuously denied having murdered Herbert John. Montagu Williams believed he did.[53]

EDMÉ CASTAING — *at the Blackamoor's Head at St Cloud*

Dr Edmé Castaing of Paris was another young doctor who murdered to acquire wealth through an inheritance.[54] In 1823 at the age of twenty-seven he decided there was a quicker way than the practice of family medicine of attaining the large sum he needed to cater for his liking for luxuries. The way was through the dispatch of two patients of his, the brothers Hippolyte and Auguste Ballet. Hippolyte, slowly dying of tuberculosis, had made a will disinheriting his young brother Auguste. Were the will to be destroyed and Hyppolyte to die, Auguste would inherit his large estate on intestacy. Castaing administered to Hippolyte morphine, an alkaloid, a narcotic analgesic extracted from the head of the opium poppy, used as an anaesthetic or a sedative, in sufficient a quantity to cause the death of his patient. This was the first known use of this recently discovered drug with the intention to cause death. Auguste got hold of his late brother's will and destroyed it. Though he was well paid for his services, Castaing was not satisfied. Somehow he got Auguste to make a will appointing him his heir, having been assured by a lawyer that it was quite in order for a person to make his medical adviser his beneficiary. Then Castaing went with Auguste for a drive in the country to inspect some property. At the Blackamoor's Head Inn at St Cloud, Castaing called for mulled wine. Into Auguste's glass Castaing put sugar from a supply he had brought. A sip was so bitter that Auguste refused to drink more, saying he felt ill. Castaing then booked a room for the night. From a local pharmacist he bought more morphine, which he put in a glass of milk, which Auguste drank, causing him to vomit and be violently ill. In agony, Auguste asked for another doctor. Dr Pigache, the local physician, was summoned, who immediately sent for Professor Pellatan of the School of Medicine in Paris. Both these medical practitioners observed the 'pinpoint' condition of Auguste's eyes, one of the already recognized symptoms of morphine poisoning. Auguste died while the two doctors were still at the inn.

Pellatan ordered a postmortem examination. It revealed all the signs then known of poisoning by morphine. Castaing was obviously suspected of murdering Auguste: he had a strong motive, knowledge, possession of morphine, and an opportunity to administer it. He was charged not only with the death of Auguste but also that of Hippolyte.

The medical evidence on the death of Hippolyte was conflicting, for little was known then of the effects of morphine, and Castaing was found not guilty of murdering him. But the evidence in support of the charge relating to Auguste was so strong that it was inevitably sustained. Castaigne paid the penalty under the guillotine.

JOHN BODKIN ADAMS — *the classic enigma*

Many years have passed since 9 April 1957, when the famous trial of John Bodkin Adams came to an end. Adams (21 January 1899–5 July 1983) had been charged with murdering his patient Mrs Edith Alice Morrell on 13 November 1950. Yet the trial is of abiding interest. There is its extraordinary complexity — in the words of the presiding judge, Mr Justice Devlin, 'quite outside the usual pattern and fascinating in its twists and turns'.[55] There is the continuing great difference of opinion among lawyers and members of the public on whether or no Adams was a mass killer of patients for gain. There was the continued belief of the prosecuting authorities and the police that he was. And there is the unique detailed analysis by the presiding judge (who had become Lord Devlin) of his conducting of the trial, set out in a book published in 1985. 'For the most part', he wrote, 'it was what was passing through my mind.' And the book also shows what caused him to make the decisions he did. It was written with panache, shot with irony and wit; it was scholarly, detailed, self-revelatory and most informative on the content of criminal procedure and how it had changed (such as the 1898 legislation that permitted an accused to give evidence and the desirability or not of putting him or her in the witness box).

The trial began in London at the Old Bailey (the Central Criminal Court) on 18 May 1957. For eight months certain newspapers had published accounts of Adams and his many supposed victims. One hundred and thirty deceased patients of his had left legacies to him, and the great majority of the patients had been cremated. Not that many legacies were large. Between 1944 and 1955 they amounted to £21 000 in cash, an elderly Rolls-Royce, and a chest of silver. On the other hand, Adams pestered many patients for a legacy, which a sensible person would not have done — but then, as Devlin wrote,[56] Adams was 'a stupid, obstinate and self-righteous man' who was prone to prescribe large doses of heroin and morphia to elderly ill patients. It was not that the doctor accepted a lower fee in return for a promise of a bequest: 'He seems to have thought of it more as a golden handshake from beyond the grave.'[57] Lord Devlin went on to say that such handshakes do not become a person whose business it is to keep death at bay.

Who was this Eastbourne general medical practitioner whose actions gave rise to this enormous public interest and protracted trial? On the face of it he was well qualified: he had obtained a bachelor's degree in medicine and surgery from Queen's University, Belfast in 1921, a doctorate in medicine from there in 1926, and a diploma in anaesthetics in 1941. Despite his unattractive appearance — he was small, fat and ugly — he built up a substantial practice in Eastbourne from 1922; later he had several partners; to the end he had patients, both private and National Health ones, who were attached to him; and he devoted care and sympathy to all his patients.

Mrs Morrell was a wealthy widow. On 25 June 1948, when she was visiting her son in Cheshire, she had a stroke that left her paralysed on the left side. She then moved to Eastbourne, where she became a patient of Adams, who started prescribing doses of morphia and heroin for her. On 9 June 1949 Mrs Morrell made a new will in which she left Adams a canteen of silver of the value of £276. Adams was not satisfied and on 6 March 1950 called on his patient's solicitor to inform him that she had promised him to bequeath to him a case containing jewellery and her Rolls-Royce motor car. The last will executed by Mrs Morell was on 24 August 1950. In it she left Adams legacies of an oak chest containing the silver and, if her son Claude predeceased her, the Rolls-Royce and an Elizabethan court cupboard. But when Adams went on holiday on 12 September 1950, Mrs Morell was furious and made a codicil disinheriting him. She forgave him when he returned from holiday for a day to attend to her, and she tore up the codicil. She died on 13 November 1950. Claude survived her, but he quietly told the family chauffeur to take the car to Adams, who believed that it came to him through the will.[58]

Adams filled in the cremation form, saying that as far as he was aware he had no pecuniary interest in the death of his patient, Mrs Edith Morell. So she was cremated. In the trial, years later, of Adams for her murder, the Crown was to contend that had he told the truth there might have been a postmortem examination, leading to the discovery of the amount of drugs in her body; and this would have helped establish the prosecution's case that her death was caused by increasing amounts of morphia and heroin given to her in the previous ten and a half months, which were not necessary, as she was not in acute pain, but deliberately given to prevent her cutting Adams out of her will again. When, six years later, Detective-Superintendent Herbert (Bert) Hannam of Scotland Yard interviewed Adams and asked him why he had given that answer on the cremation form, Adams replied that it was not done wickedly: 'We always want cremations to go off smoothly.'

The passing and cremation of Edith Morrell led to no comment in the press. The interest of the police was aroused only five years later when Adams's patient Mrs C J Hullett died and was cremated. Her husband, M J (Jack) Hullett, also a patient, had died in his sleep on 14 March 1956, some hours after Adams had given him an injection. He had been seriously ill. The will of Hullett (he left £94 644) had given all to his wife except for a few small legacies, among which was one of £500 to Adams, who, as before, wrongly made no mention of it in the cremation form.

The death of her husband caused Mrs Hullett to become desperately depressed. She spoke of committing suicide. On 14 July 1956 Mrs Hullett signed a cheque of £1 000 in favour of Adams, to make good her deceased husband's unfulfilled promise to him to buy him a motor car. Adams presented the cheque to the bank on the eighteenth, asking for a special clearance. On the nineteenth it was cleared, two days earlier than it would usually have been; but if Mrs Hullett had died before then, it would not have been cleared at all. Plainly, Adams was taking no chances.

On the evening of the nineteenth Mrs Hullett took a massive dose of barbiturates and fell into a coma which continued until her death on the twenty-third.

Dr R V Harris, one of Adams's partners, had been called in on the twentieth, as Adams was out of town. Shortly after Harris arrived, Adams turned up. He arranged with a consultant pathologist to analyse his patient's urine to see if it revealed poisoning by barbiturates. But she died before the analysis was ready. In the meantime Adams decided, in case she had taken too much of barbiturates, to try megimide, which he had heard was an antidote. At the hospital he was given a new box of megimide. Instead of reading the instructions on it, he took the word of the house surgeon as to the dosage. It was quite wrong. This negligent procedure was later criticized by the coroner.

Harris had told Adams that if the patient died, a postmortem examination would have to be held. Later on the morning of the death of Mrs Hullett, Adams wrote a report saying that he had strictly doled out her sodium barbiturate and she could not have secreted any of it. On that day the coroner ordered a postmortem examination. The popular press now picked up a possibly titillating story. On 21 August the inquest resumed. By then the Chief Constable of Eastbourne had summoned Scotland Yard for help, but Detective-Superintendent Hannam made no application for the adjournment of the inquest. The evidence at the inquest was hardly to the credit of Adams. Mrs Hullett had clearly died of an overdose of barbiturate tablets. The jury found she had taken them of her own free will. But the examination of Adams by the coroner showed that Adams had exercised very poor judgement in not ensuring that a patient who had threatened suicide could not get her hands on a large quantity of the drug he had prescribed.

The following day the *Daily Mail* published, together with a report of the inquest, an article stating that Scotland Yard was investigating the poisoning of four hundred wealthy women in Eastbourne during the past twenty years. Other national newspapers soon followed with similar, though not quite so sensational, allegations. Their proprietors and editors were to regret what had been done.

The chief crime reporter of the *Daily Express*, Percy Hoskins, the only journalist who expressed conviction of the innocence of Adams, happened to meet the doctor the day after the inquest finding. Any ordinary doctor would have been crushed by the adverse publicity; but Adams was unperturbed, and did not heed Hoskins's plea to take care what he said.

Bert Hannam had with him, in the police inquiries into the activities of Adams, Detective-Sergeant Charles Hewitt, also of Scotland Yard. Assisting them was Detective-Inspector B Pugh of the Eastbourne Borough Constabulary. They and all others active in the prosecution of Adams believed (and many continued to believe) that he was a mass murderer of the worst type. Inquiries at Somerset House revealed 132 wills in which Adams had been left a legacy. The police believed that Adams had murdered twenty-five patients and 'eased' others from life by making them dependent on morphine and heroin. His death certificates showed the cause of death in 68 per cent of cases as being due to cerebral haemorrhage or cerebral thrombosis, a suspiciously high number. The police investigated over four hundred deaths of patients and prepared cases of murder in nine of them. It was decided to concentrate on the Morrell and Hullett deaths, and that Hannam was to question Adams to see if he would crack. He did, in the sense of talking incessantly and saying things that could be understood in two ways.

A preliminary inquiry before examining magistrates followed. The procedure was very similar to that of the one-time South African preparatory examination. The inquiry in England was open to the public and the press until 1967, when it became a closed one as a result of the Adams trial, which had shown the harm that an open hearing could do to an accused where no case is found or there is a jury trial. Later the United Kingdom Parliament limited the reporting of committal proceedings, leading in fact to the defence accepting the statements of witnesses the police regard as informing the defence what it wants to know. The defence today in England has the case of the prosecution before it, but the prosecution will not have knowledge of the defence case if the defence chooses to be silent, which almost always it does. The history of the criminal trial in South Africa is similar.

The Attorney-General at the time was Sir Reginald Manningham-Buller QC MP. He decided on a prosecution of Adams for the murder of Mrs Morrell. The Crown also alleged that he had murdered the Hulletts, but you will remember that in 1957 there were two rules of practice in a murder trial: only one charge could be entertained, and if it was murder by poisoning, as it was contended with Mrs Morrell, the prosecution normally had to be led by the Attorney-General. So while at the preliminary hearing the head of the Crown team was Melford Stevenson QC (it was unheard of for the Attorney-General to appear at that stage), at the actual trial Stevenson, this 'last of the grand eccentrics',[59] was only second in command and actually did little. At the end of 1957 Stevenson was elevated to the Bench, where he was known to favour stiff sentences.

It is now time to devote some attention to the principal figures in the trial, other than Adams: Manningham-Buller QC MP, the Attorney-General; Mr Justice Devlin, the trial judge; and Geoffrey Lawrence QC, leader of the defence team. The life stories of Manningham-Buller and Devlin after the trial I shall recount only when all aspects of the trial and its protagonist have been told.

Reginald Manningham-Buller (1 August 1905–7 September 1980), the son of Lieutenant-Colonel Sir Mervyn Manningham-Buller, 3rd Bart, whom he succeeded in 1956, was the only one involved in the trial to have aristocratic antecedents.[60] His educational background was typical: Eton and Magdalen College, University of Oxford. In 1943 he was elected an MP. In 1946 he became a KC, what Devlin called a 'career silk'. An MP was entitled to take silk if he wished, whereas others had to be appointed by the Lord Chancellor, and the competition among applicants for choice by him was severe. Manningham-Buller never had a large private practice, and his experience in running trials was limited.

Still, he always mastered his brief and was normally admirably capable. On 1 November 1951, at a time of shortage of Conservative political counsel, he was appointed Solicitor-General, who is the junior Law Officer of the Crown; he became Attorney-General, the holder of the senior post, on 18 October 1954. That post he occupied until 13 July 1962. In his lengthy period in it he was greatly appreciated by the Conservative politicians for his dedicated work, his talent as a debater, and his clear, confident advice. He did not have outstanding intellectual qualities, but he was competent. While as a person he was respected and while his sense of humour was valued, he did not arouse affection by those subordinate to him; indeed, many feared him. According to Devlin, he and his career were almost unique in 'that what the ordinary careerist achieves by making himself, falsely or otherwise, agreeable, Reggie achieved by making himself disagreeable'.[61] Some parts of the press he had antagonized called him Sir Bullying Manner, but he was really a bully without a bullying manner.

Patrick Arthur Devlin (25 November 1905–9 August 1992), son of an architect, read law at Christ's College of the University of Cambridge, where he was President of the Union. In 1929 he was called to the Bar, having realized that he did not really have a vocation as a Jesuit priest. He built up a large commercial practice, taking silk in 1945. In 1948, at the exceptionally early age in England of 42, he was appointed a judge of the King's Bench Division of the High Court, where he attained a notable reputation.

Sir Patrick Devlin was available to preside over what would clearly be the lengthy jury trial at the Old Bailey once the Lord Chief Justice, Lord Goddard, had decided not to take the case himself owing to his advanced age and the need for him to preside in the Court of Criminal Appeal.

The leader of the defence team was Geoffrey Lawrence QC (1902–67), aged 55, who had been at New College of the University of Oxford, taken silk in 1950 and built up a reputation in the largely unexciting sphere of local-government litigation. He was an unexpected choice for an Old Bailey murder trial, but an inspired one, as it turned out. He proved to be very determined, for all his natural courtesy; very hard-working; deeply versed in all medical aspects of the case; astute to every change in the nature of the trial; a master of strategy and tactics; a brilliant cross-examiner even if inclined to be rather laborious; a counsel who never raised his voice but capable of making his forensic points by quiet eloquence.

In what follows, as in what I have already written, I have had the advantage of having at hand Devlin's account of the trial. One must bear in mind that the judge did not think well of the forensic ability of the Attorney-General. His calling him constantly 'Reggie' in the book, whereas defence counsel was normally 'Mr Lawrence', otherwise Lawrence, was criticized. (It must be pointed out, though, that Devlin occasionally called Lord Goddard LCJ by his first name, 'Rayner'. He was on visiting terms with the Chief Justice, who called him Pat, which could explain his feeling that it was in order to refer to Goddard in this way.)

Manningham-Buller was determined to secure a verdict of guilty. It was not the typical attitude of a prosecutor in those days (nor is it today), which was simply to present the facts in an objective way. To Devlin,[62] it was beyond the imagination of the Attorney-General to present the accused as someone more complex in nature than the standard poisoner who ended the life of a patient lest she might once more remove his legacy: someone who may have been between a mercy-killer and the doctor who prescribed heroin to keep a patient happy, and so likely to leave him a legacy, which led to ever greater doses until the patient succumbed. But then to establish that the doctor murdered his patient would be very difficult.

To prove that Adams had murdered Mrs Morrell, the Crown called the four nurses who had attended her in her last days. Nurse Helen Stronach gave evidence that Adams had given his patient an injection of a substance not known to her. Yes, she said, the nurses always wrote down everything of significance in the nurses' report book. Lawrence, like a conjurer pulling a rabbit out of a top hat, then produced a notebook the contents of which destroyed the credibility of the witness. It was the crucial report book, which normally would have been destroyed on the death of the patient. By chance, when the effects of the late Mrs Morrell were being disposed of, her chauffeur had handed a parcel to Adams 'in case it might be of use'. Adams simply cast the parcel at the back of a steel cabinet, and it then passed out of his mind. The police had failed to find it. But Adams's solicitor did find it. The notebook recorded the treatment of Mrs Morrell from 21 June 1949 to her death. It changed the nature of the trial and struck at the heart of the prosecution. It showed that Adams had himself administered very few of the drugs.

The evidence of the nurses suffered under another devastating blow, what Devlin called a coup de théâtre,[63] when they had to concede that, contrary to an instruction to them by the judge not to discuss the case with one another, they had done so on a train journey from London to Eastbourne. The one nurse had said 'Don't say that or you will get me into trouble'. It was that Nurse Stronach had been wrong in saying there had been no cupboard at all. The drugs had been securely kept. Only years later was Devlin told how the defence discovered what had happened. A good citizen, disgusted at hearing the conversation in the train compartment, informed defence counsel by telephone to the Old Bailey.

The case for the prosecution had become weak by now. Its two medical experts at the preparatory inquiry had committed themselves to the opinion that the administration of 78¾ grains of opiates over the last six days of Mrs Morrell's life would have accelerated death. But the quantity actually administered as shown in the notebooks was very much less — possibly only 30 grains. Devlin expected Manningham-Buller to throw in his hand at this stage. He did not.

Dr Arthur Douthwaite of Harley Street, Senior Physician to Guy's Hospital, a recognized authority on opiates and an eminent specialist medical practitioner, gave evidence. A man of great integrity, he was unfortunately far too decisive, not adaptable in his views. In fine, he believed that Adams had decided on 8 November to end Mrs Morrell's life, and carried this intention into effect over the following five days. In cross-examination he conceded, however, that another doctor, reviewing all the medical evidence, could reach another conclusion. This answer, damning to the Crown's case, was the culmination of two days of quiet, persistent cross-examination. In answer to questions by the judge, Douthwaite changed front, now saying that the execution of the murder had begun on 1 November, starting with the dropping of morphine in order that tolerance to it could be reduced, allowing it to be reverted to later in rapidly increasing doses in combination with large doses of heroin, to deadly effect. It was an extraordinary alteration of view by an expert, and a serious blow to the case of the prosecution, which could now gracefully withdraw. But the Attorney-General would not; it was crucial to his ambition that a prosecution enjoying great public attention should not end in a fiasco; but to continue showed lack of judicial quality, according to the presiding judge.[64] The second medical expert for the Crown was Dr M G C Ashby, whose evidence amounted only to Adams's having acted in a very unorthodox way which fortunately caused no harm, and that he had not done all he should have to keep his patient alive.

Lawrence now asked the judge to withdraw the case from the jury as not proved beyond a reasonable doubt on the medical evidence. But this Devlin could and would not do, no matter he believed the Crown case would ultimately fail; he could not withdraw the case in the face of the view of two eminent doctors that Mrs Morrell had died from a medically unjustified overdose of drugs that Adams must have known would end life prematurely.

To the surprise of the judge and the media, Lawrence then announced he would not call Adams to give evidence. It is a decision that normally is prejudicial to an accused, even though in England the prosecution is not allowed to comment on his or her silence, for a jury could nevertheless draw a very adverse inference. The danger of calling Adams lay in his verbosity and foolishness. For example, he had told Hannam that he had injected nearly all the drugs he had prescribed, which the nurses' notebook showed he had not. In cross-examination, Manningham-Buller would have broken Adams, revealing him as a doctor who was incompetent and with a limited knowledge of drugs. But Devlin[65] was very doubtful if the jury would then conclude that he deliberately killed his patients, all of whom believed he really cared for them.

The defence medical expert witness, Dr John Harman, was as eminent as his colleagues who were called by the Crown. In examination in chief and cross-examination he turned up trumps for the defence.

Devlin was now of the opinion that in the very improbable contingency of the jury finding Adams guilty, the Court of Criminal Appeal would quash the conviction. His summing-up to the jury was correctly regarded as favouring an acquittal, in contrast to the usual summing-up, which finds the prosecution's case the stronger one.

After forty-six minutes the jury returned a verdict of not guilty. That left the indictment for the murder of Mrs Hullett. It was a weak case to start with. The verdict in the Morrell trial made it virtually certain that there would be an acquittal in a trial for the murder of Mrs Hullett.

Manningham-Buller immediately entered a nolle prosequi (literally, 'not to wish to prosecute') on that indictment. This startled all present. The normal procedure is for the Crown to proceed, the accused to plead not guilty, the Crown to offer no evidence, and the judge to then instruct the jury to return a verdict of not guilty. In his book Devlin said he could not remember a nolle prosequi ever being used before to prevent an accused committed for trial from being acquitted; it is not designed for use in court. It would be interpreted as leaving an innocent person still under suspicion of having committed murder.[66]

It is now time to trace what happened to 'two of the most self-righteous men in England', to use the words of Devlin[67] — Adams and Manningham-Buller, and then to Devlin and Lawrence.

Dr Adams's troubles were not yet over, though the remaining ones were not so serious. Before they had to be faced, he benefited the day after his acquittal on 9 April 1957 by ten thousand pounds from giving an account of his unexciting life to the *Daily Express.* In it he recorded his deep thanks to Lawrence QC, his junior counsel Edward Clarke, and his solicitor for saving his life.

On 30 June 1957 Adams resigned from the National Health Service. The next month, on 26 July, he faced charges of medical crimes at the Sussex Assizes, held in Lewes before Mr Justice Pilcher. Those of making false statements on three cremation forms were serious. The judge said had Adams not spent three months in gaol as an awaiting-trial prisoner, he would probably have given him a prison sentence. He was fined £500 for each offence. For attempting to hide dangerous drugs from the police when they were searching his house for them, he was fined £250, and for failing to keep a register £500. For forging the name of a doctor on three occasions so that a private patient could get a National Health certificate resulting in a free prescription, he was fined £150. In all, his fines amounted to £2 400.

But that was not his only punishment. His authority to prescribe under the Dangerous Drugs Act was withdrawn in September 1957, never to be restored. In the following month, because of his convictions before Mr Justice Pilcher, his name was removed from the medical register. Surprisingly to the laity, this did not make it an offence to practise medicine, only to hold oneself out as a qualified person. So Adams went on practising at Eastbourne, and, for all the adverse evidence on his medical competence at his trial for murder, many of his former patients returned to his ministrations. Some left him legacies, though how many did and for what amount and whether he was still a legacy-hunter I cannot say.

In 1961 fortune began to smile on the doctor. First of all, his name was restored to the medical register. Secondly, his suits for libel against several newspapers for repeating incorrect gossip about him came to a head. The major culprit was the *Daily Mail*, which withdrew every allegation it had made, offered deep apologies, and paid a large sum (the amount not revealed) in settlement. Certain other newspapers followed suit.

On 5 July 1983, at the age of eighty-four, Adams died. His funeral, attended by a hundred and fifty friends and patients, was shown on the television screen. There were obituaries in the top-level and tabloid national newspapers, which expressed differing views on whether or not he was a murderous medical man. *The Times* sat on the fence in saying that he was 'the classic enigma in the annals of mass killing'.

Adams left an estate of £402 970, a considerable one for a general practitioner in a seaside town. But he was a bachelor and not a spendthrift. There were many legatees, few receiving bequests over £5 000. Among the legatees were patients who had stood by him in his time of trial. The main beneficiaries were Miss Norah O'Hara, who in the nineteen-twenties had broken off her engagement to Adams, but had remained on friendly terms with him and believed in him; and close relations.[68]

Well, did he or didn't he? Did he merely ease the passing of elderly patients or did he accelerate their deaths? There are those, not only members of the police but also lawyers and journalists, who believed and still believe that Adams was the most cunning mass murderer up to the time of his death.[69] On the other hand, the highly regarded crime reporter of the *Daily Express*, Percy Hoskins, from the start was convinced that Adams was innocent; that he was found guilty in advance by trial by newspaper.[70] Lord Devlin in his book on the trial did not himself comment beyond saying that Adams 'might have murdered — it must be remembered that euthanasia is murder — either as a mercy-killer or perhaps just to finish off a troublesome patient who was dying anyway and for whom he could do no more'.[71] Perhaps he 'eased the death' of a dying patient at the patient's request, far removed from the Crown's allegations. I am inclined to think that this is what he did on many occasions: accelerated death that was imminent. Not truly monstrous in the eyes of some; but at least deplorable if done as a consistent practice.

I turn now to Sir Reginald Manningham-Buller QC MP. The Labour Opposition in Parliament tried to get him to agree to an independent inquiry into the conduct of the Crown case. It was a forlorn hope.

Harold Macmillan, the Prime Minister, would not then contemplate Manningham-Buller's becoming Lord Chief Justice, and asked the aged Goddard to continue for another year, which he agreed to do. On the retirement of Goddard in 1958, the post was offered to Lord Kilmuir, the Lord Chancellor, an able jurist, who, as Sir David Maxwell Fyfe, had done brilliantly at the Nuremberg trials in his cross-examination of Goering after the American counsel, Justice Robert Jackson, had made a hash of it. Kilmuir rejected the offer. Manningham-Buller now hoped, indeed almost expected, that it would be made to him. It was made to Lord Justice Parker (1900–72). Sir Hubert Parker was a highly regarded jurist, and his appointment was universally welcomed. While Manningham-Buller's political services were valued by the Conservative government, his professional standing, it seems, was not high enough; in outlook and behaviour he seemed to be cast in the mould of the tough Goddard, whose replacement, it was widely felt, should be of a mellower nature; and his prosecution of Adams was not to his credit. To Devlin — he was regarded by some as unduly critical of Manningham-Buller, it must be pointed out — the merits of Reggie ('Reggie' was the name he 'was called by friend and foe alike because he was the sort of person who obviously ought to be called Reggie') 'in relation to so great a judicial post could fairly be said to be negligible'.[72] He was like Lord Hewart, a former Attorney-General who became Lord Chief Justice in 1922, clinging on to office until 1940, and proving to be 'the worst chief justice ever': 'neither man had a grain of judicial sense.'[73]

Manningham-Buller carried on as Attorney-General, hiding his deep disappointment with dignity. His only hope now for advancement lay in his succeeding to the Lord Chancellorship held by Kilmuir. In the meantime he had an opportunity of bringing balm to his troubled soul. The Nyasaland Commission of Inquiry under the chairmanship of Mr Justice Devlin reported in 1959. The other three members were prominent men of wide experience, all of whom had been knighted for services to the state and the community. The report exonerated Dr Hastings Banda from allegations of a plot to assassinate the Governor of Nyasaland and all other whites in the colony. In Parliament, Manningham-Buller attacked the report and was supported by the Conservative Party, then in power. Harold Macmillan was delighted with the performance of his Attorney-General. As was to be expected in his book, Lord Devlin was scathing about it. It remains to be said that, after he had become Lord Chancellor, Manningham-Buller had the delightfully ironic task, on behalf of the British Government, of travelling to the now independent Malawi to congratulate Dr Banda on his appointment as its President.

On 13 July 1962, on the famous 'night of the long knives', Macmillan summarily dismissed seven senior ministers, including Lord Kilmuir, the Lord Chancellor, who had held the post for the previous seven years and nine months. Kilmuir met his dismissal with chagrin and bitter resentment, recounted in his memoirs.[74] His place was taken by Manningham-Buller, now elevated to the peerage as Lord Dilhorne. The position of Lord Chancellor is a most anomalous one: head of the judiciary, member of the Cabinet, and 'Speaker' of the House of Lords.

Dilhorne's period of office as Lord Chancellor ended on 17 October 1964 with the defeat of the Conservatives by Labour in the general election. His term of twenty-seven months revealed that he was not a reforming Lord Chancellor, though minor improvements in the law and its content were promoted by him. He was succeeded by quite a different personality, Gerald Gardiner QC, appointed Lord Gardiner, who became the greatest law-reforming Lord Chancellor known to the last century.

Only fifty-nine years of age, Dilhorne had to be content with the pension of a former Lord Chancellor of £5 000 a year. Convention precluded him from practising at the Bar. He now sat far more frequently in the House of Lords in both its judicial capacity (he was ex officio a law lord) and its legislative capacity. When Edward Heath became leader of the Conservatives, Dilhorne, knowing that Heath's views of him made the prospect of his ever becoming Lord Chancellor again remote, devoted himself with exemplary dedication to hearing appeals to the Appellate Committee of the House of Lords and to the Judicial Committee of the Privy Council. Five years after his loss of political office, financial rescue came to him. Lord Pearce had retired as a law lord in late 1969, at the rather early age of sixty-eight. For some time there had been delicate pulls to secure the actual appointment of Dilhorne as a law lord (as I have pointed out, he was one ex officio), which would raise his annual income to £11 000. Lord Gardiner LC saw to it that this was done. While Gardiner was on good terms with Dilhorne, he could not have been more different from him in his political outlook and in his attitude to law reform. And there were more brilliant members of the Court of Appeal who could have been elevated to the Lords. What Gardiner did was typical of his kindheartedness.[75]

Dilhorne sat in two hundred and fifty appeals in his period as an appointed law lord from 1969 to 1980, truly a phenomenal number. His judgments, as Professor R F Heuston rightly wrote, 'will not figure in any anthology of English prose'.[76] Nor did many cut new ground; his view was that such an activity was primarily the function of Parliament. This eminently competent law lord will not go down in history as one of the great judges of England. Professor Robert Stevens labelled him as 'a solid, workmanlike judge, good — sometimes impressive — in ascertaining the facts, but not outstanding in his analysis of the legal authorities and loath to develop the law'.[77]

Dilhorne died unexpectedly on 7 September 1980 just over the age of 75, the age at which the Judicial Pensions Act of 1959 had required him to retire. He had ensured that his last judgment was completed after his retirement.

Mr Justice Devlin's career after the Adams case was a most successful one. In 1959 Macmillan caused him to be elevated to the Court of Appeal and in 1961 to the House of Lords. Lord Devlin was sitting there when the following year Lord Dilhorne joined him on the Bench. As a law lord, Devlin's reputation continued to be extremely high. Then in 1964 at the age of 59 he suddenly resigned. He had had more than the fifteen years of judicial service entitling him to his pension, but this surely could not have been the cause of leaving the highest court at an unheard-of early age. There were many who regretted his departure; and there were many who felt it was a step that did not serve his country well. Some believed that he quit the judiciary as he had grown tired of browsing in what he used to call the meadows of the Appellate Committee of the House of Lords. Lord Devlin did not retire from active life, though. On three occasions he sat on the Appellate Committee of the House of Lords as a supplementary member, and more often on the Judicial Committee of the Privy Council. From 1964 to 1986 he was a judge of the Administrative Tribunal of the International Labour Office. He headed various official commissions of inquiry. From 1964 to 1969 he was chairman of the Press Council; on his retirement *The Times* complimented him on his causing the body to grow in authority. He was President of the British Maritime Association from 1962 to 1976. 'Justice', the English branch of the International Commission of Jurists, benefited from his devoted services. There were a number of other bodies relating to education and the press that enjoyed his keen support. In the last years of his life he worked with Cardinal Hume to ensure the correction of the 'miscarriage of justice' cases, which resulted in the quashing of the convictions of the 'Guildford Four' and the Maguire defendants.

In particular, Devlin engaged in writing further works on the law. It is an activity that very few judges and retired judges engage in. Already in 1956 Devlin had been invited to deliver the highly regarded Hamlyn Lectures, which resulted in the appearance of his book *Trial by Jury*, which met with much praise. A body of other publications followed, in several of which he constructively criticized English civil and criminal procedure and practice. In 1963 he attained the high honour of election as a Fellow of the British Academy. He held a host of honorary doctoral degrees in law from great universities.

To law students of his time, Devlin was best known for his controversy over law and morality with Professor H L A Hart, Professor of Jurisprudence in the University of Oxford, and one of the greatest of legal philosophers. Devlin's attitude was opposed to that of John Stuart Mill and that of Hart. In his view, there was no area of private morality into which the law cannot enter, and the morality the law enforces has to be popular morality.[78]

As a judge, a remarkable tribute was paid to Lord Devlin by Professor Robert Stevens.[79] Despite his professed view that the English judge could not be truly law-creative, he did develop the law in carefully reasoned, lucid judgments, at times written in striking prose. 'Devlin was one of the most powerful minds to sit on the Appellate Bench in the post-1945 period. Within the narrow confines delegated by the British Constitution to the judges, Devlin was a masterful operator. . . . Devlin in fact "developed" the common law with grace and elegance.' On

Lord Devlin's death, the eminent law lord Lord Scarman paid a splendid tribute to him:[80] 'He possessed great technical skill in his profession — witness his mastery of commercial law. But he disdained a life which failed to go beyond a speciality or technical excellence. . . . Practice never held all of his attention. He was also a theorist, a philosopher and a scholar. He was a splendid judge; indeed I believe him to have been a great judge. . . . He was a tranquil man, reflective, very private, devoted to his family, and confident in his religious faith. A very different man, to be sure, from Erasmus and Sir Thomas More, but he reminds me of both. His ever-pressing concern was that the law should be just in practice as well as in theory and principle. In his famous controversy with Professor Hart, he urged forcefully the need for the law to protect moral values.*

It remains for me to go back to 1985 when Devlin's book on the trial of Dr John Bodkin Adams was published. What I have so far written about the book will show that its author was highly critical not only of the forensic performance of Manningham-Buller in the trial but also of his mental adaptability and judicial qualities. The book was widely reviewed, mainly in laudatory terms. One of the reviews was considered by Lord Devlin in a postscript in a supplementary edition of the book published by Faber & Faber, London, in 1986. Two letters criticizing the book were also considered there by Lord Devlin.

The review was in the *Daily Express.* Remember that this newspaper had believed Adams to be innocent. The review said that though Adams had been found not guilty, Devlin in his book tampered with the verdict. In the postscript, Devlin said that he had not questioned the verdict in his book: quite the contrary: he had written that it was 'unquestionably a true verdict'.[81] The *Daily Express* review then denounced the book as damaging beyond repair the reputation of the Bench for impartiality.

The first letter was by a former lord justice of appeal, Sir Robin Dunn. It appeared in *Field.* In it Dunn stated that the book was 'an attack upon the character and ability of the Attorney-General at the trial'. This, among other things, was what it substantially was, replied Devlin. Dunn did not actually support Manningham-Buller's conduct of the trial. 'To

* In March 1969 Lord Devlin spent some time in Johannesburg at the request of the International Press Institute to observe the defence case in the trial of Laurence Gandar, editor-in-chief of the *Rand Daily Mail,* and Benjamin Pogrund, senior reporter on the newspaper, for publishing alleged wrongful information about conditions in prisons. See *The Star* 22 March 1969. The Wits Law School entertained Lord Devlin at a tea party. As I remember — I have no note of the occasion and my memory may be faulty — Lord Devlin was a particularly small man, so round-shouldered that he resembled a hunchback, and he was very quiet and non-committal. It's a pity that my recollections are not clearer.

redress the balance', he referred to Dilhorne's speeches a decade later as a lord of appeal: 'widely acclaimed', 'robust approach . . . clarity and certainty'. Devlin, in typical vein, said he had no quarrel with Dunn's prophecy that 'many of Dilhorne's judgments will be remembered when the more obscure pronouncements of some who regard themselves as his intellectual superiors are forgotten'. Devlin added: 'If he meant to include me, I have started the process myself by forgetting most of mine. They were not addressed to posterity.' A nice touch.

The second letter was a joint one by Lord Scarman and Lord Bridge, both law lords, published in *The Times Literary Supplement.* It was a response to what Devlin called 'an extremely provocative review of the book', the reviewer speaking of the author's 'profound contempt for an obtuse mediocrity as the theme of the book'. This description of Devlin's attitude (not of the subject of it) Lords Scarman and Bridge found to be regrettably true.

Their letter was almost a repetition of Dunn's as to the merits of Dilhorne as a law lord, and was as silent as Dunn's on Dilhorne's conduct of the trial of Adams and Devlin's criticism of it. It complained of an attack that was posthumous, was upon a former judicial colleague, and was made with contempt. To each of these criticisms Devlin made a withering reply. There was a decent margin of five years after the death of Dilhorne. It was impracticable to criticize Dilhorne to his face; his office would hamper him in replying. In any event, Adams had outlived Dilhorne, and the book was defamatory of Adams. The book could only be published after he had died. As for the work being an attack on a former judicial colleague, Devlin wrote that he had never sat in a case with Lord Chancellor Dilhorne, and after both had retired they sat together in the 'supplementary list' perhaps six times. Scarman and Bridge, said Devlin, must have meant 'colleague' in another sense: that they were men of a kind, and dog should not eat dog. But, continued Devlin, this sentiment precluded impartiality, and a judge writing of one of his trials must write impartially. As for the criticism of displaying contempt, Devlin found 'it hardly believable'. Nowhere had he expressed contempt for Dilhorne, and he was not told what passages the two law lords had in mind. True, there 'is a lack of admiration'. But 'Dilhorne's defects, chiefly narrow-mindedness and obstinacy, were not those which excite contempt. Think of General de Gaulle who almost turned them into virtues; no one dreamt of despising him.'

In general, wrote Devlin, the letter by the law lords was wholly irrelevant. 'It is no defence of a man's performance as an advocate to say that a decade later he was an excellent judge.'

His book, commented Devlin, was more than the story of a criminal trial: 'it is also part of the story of how the politicians' grasp of the highest offices in the judiciary was prized loose.' With Dilhorne came the turning point. 'It killed the tradition that political service established a claim for a place in the judiciary.' The 'whim of the gods' made him the first Conservative politician to be selected as a lord of appeal by a Labour government.

The very high claims his friends made for Dilhorne, confessed Devlin, he found rather startling, but 'if Lord Scarman, himself universally regarded as a judge of great distinction, rates him as an outstanding appellate judge, he must at least have been well worth his judicial place in the House of Lords'.

There is an interesting final observation by Devlin about Dilhorne. 'His handicap was that he went through life blinkered. He wished to see only what was in front of him.' He could see only the guilt of Adams. For a trial judge, blinkers are disastrous. But in the final court of appeal the case is already mapped out, and the choice of route is very limited; if the choice is right, blinkers could even be an advantage in eliminating doubts and distractions.

Devlin concludes his sparkling reply by saying that he depicted Dilhorne 'as I saw him in public life, a man of average abilities not then equal to his high ambition, a hungry man fighting for what he thought to be his rightful place at the banquet. The Scarman–Bridge letter is a portrait of a man more than a decade later in the contentment of age, a Samson Agonistes. . . . There is no reason why both should not be true.' If only the Scarman–Bridge letter had pointed out that this picture was not the whole picture; but it amounted to the lamentations of viewers of a portrait that is not a likeness of which they are familiar and who then condemn the painter.[82]

A few words remain to be said about Geoffrey Lawrence. He was knighted in 1963, and in 1965 appointed a judge of the Queen's Bench Division of the High Court. Two years later he died prematurely.

HAROLD FREDERICK SHIPMAN[83] — *the most atrocious English criminal since Palmer?*

The mystery about John Bodkin Adams will never be solved. And the mystery about Harold Frederick Shipman will never be solved. The difference between the two mysteries lies in two simple questions: Did Adams murder? And precisely how many did Shipman murder?

Harold Frederick Shipman (called Fred by relations, friends and colleagues) was born in Nottingham on 14 June 1946 to a working-class family. His father, of the same name and nickname, was a lorry driver. To his mother Vera, of her three children the middle one, Fred, was the clear favourite. She regarded him, as indeed she regarded herself, as a superior person. Yet there was not much in his early life to justify such an attitude. While the short, stocky Fred excelled at school in athletics and rugby, though he was hard-working he was only a little above an average student. Still, he had managed to get a place at the élite High Pavement Grammar School, the best state school in Nottingham. There he remained in the C stream, never demoted to the D one or raised to the A or B one. He made few close friends.

To Vera's joy, young Fred decided to become a medical practitioner, and chose Biology, Physics and Chemistry as A-level subjects. But when he was midway in his studies his mother contracted terminal lung cancer. In those days there was no pump by which a patient could administer morphine to herself. Fred, deeply attached to his mother, would watch the family GP inject morphine to alleviate the increasingly agonizing pain. On 21 June 1963 Vera died at the age of forty-three, leaving Fred disconsolate.

The first attempt by the young Shipman to gain entry to the medical school of the University of Leeds failed: his A-level results were not good enough. After resitting the examinations he was accepted, and started his studies in September 1965 with a full student grant from the local authority.

Shipman passed the five-year course leading to the degree of Bachelor of Medicine and Bachelor of Surgery (MB ChB) with adequate results, but had made little impression on his fellow students, who regarded him as a loner. Early on he met the plain and stout Primrose Oxtoby, aged seventeen, of a working-class family, who had come to Leeds on a grant to study art and design at a college there. The upshot was that Primrose fell pregnant. Towards the end of his first year Shipman, now twenty, married Primrose.

After completing his five-year course in medicine, Shipman served a year as a pre-registration house officer at the General Infirmary in Pontefract before being fully registered in August 1971 with the General Medical Council. He stayed on to take a diploma in child health and a diploma in obstetrics and gynaecology. Then on 1 March 1974 he secured a position in a busy group general practitioner practice in Todmorden, a small town near Manchester and Bradford. Enthusiastic (he persuaded the partners to instal a more up-to-date system of categorizing patient records), knowledgeable (he had recently qualified) and hardworking, after a short probationary period as an assistant GP Shipman was made a junior partner, prior to becoming an equal partner. He got on very well with patients and reasonably well with his medical colleagues, but was prone to be confrontational with and rude to the support staff and call them stupid, a favourite word of his.

In the meantime Shipman began having blackouts. A consultant diagnosed epilepsy of unknown origin. But then a receptionist in the practice discovered that entries in a pharmacist's narcotic register revealed that Shipman had been prescribing frequent large amounts of pethidine for a number of patients and written many prescriptions for the drug on the practice's account, almost all of which, by various devices, he had diverted to his own use. Pethidine (also called meperidine or meperidine hydrochloride) is a synthetic strong opioid analgesic with properties similar to those of morphine. It is frequently used as a painkiller in childbirth. Owing to the risk of undesirable side effects which include addiction, respiratory depression, retention of urine, palpitations and convulsions, pethidine is not generally used for the long-term relief of chronic pain. A medical practice commonly keeps small quantities of the drug on hand for emergencies and treatment in the surgery or on home visits. But the amounts prescribed by Shipman were unaccountably in excess of these needs. At a conservative estimate Shipman had obtained seventy thousand milligrams of the drug. An investigation by Home Office drugs inspectors and the police showed deficiencies in the documentation of controlled drugs. A Home Office inspector saw all the partners in August 1975 and advised them on the institution of a controlled-drugs supply register and the correct procedure for destroying controlled drugs.

In September 1975 Shipman's dismayed partners discovered that he was abusing pethidine, obtained illegally, and insisted that he leave the practice. There was an altercation, but leave he did. A consultant psychiatrist booked Shipman into The Retreat, an outstanding private psychiatric institution in York, where he was successfully withdrawn from pethidine. On his discharge on 30 December 1975 he was advised to continue under psychiatric supervision for several years.

Meanwhile Shipman was interviewed by the police, to whom he admitted that he had been injecting himself on some fourteen occasions a day with six hundred to seven hundred milligrams for the past six months. The veins in his arms and legs were in a state of collapse. He was also interviewed by a Home Office inspector on the forgery of the prescriptions for the drug.

The Penal Cases Committee of the General Medical Council decided not to strike Shipman off the register or suspend or restrict his registration. It acted on favourable reports of the psychiatrists who had treated him and of the Area Medical Officer of the Durham Area Health Authority, where Shipman had taken up employment on 2 February 1976 as a clinical medical officer, having no access to controlled drugs. Nowadays he would at least have had a psychiatric assessment and restrictions on practising. It was the start of his series of escapes from due consequences.

On 13 February 1976 Shipman was charged before the magistrates at Halifax on three counts of obtaining pethidine by deception, three counts of unlawfully possessing pethidine, and two of forging a prescription. He pleaded guilty to the charges and asked that sixty-seven offences of obtaining pethidine by deception and seven of forgery leading to the same result be taken into account. The penalty imposed was a fine of £600 and a compensatory order of some £60 in favour of the National Health Service Practitioners' Committee, which would convert into today's currency at four times those sums. It was a very light sentence. Once more Shipman escaped due consequences. It seems clear that he never again abused drugs.

Shipman held a post as a clinical medical officer in the Durham area in the community child health service at the Newton Aycliffe Health Centre from 2 February 1976 to 30 September 1977. Towards the end of this period he had seen an advertisement in the *British Medical Journal* for a post in a GP practice in Hyde, a town close to Manchester. It was known as the Donneybrook practice. There had been eight members, but one had recently left to work in industry. Shipman applied for the post. He admitted his past addiction to pethidine and his criminal convictions, but said he had had treatment and was now clean. He gave the name of one of the psychiatrists who had treated him. A member of the firm received a favourable report from the psychiatrist. The seven members of the practice were impressed by Shipman and, finding he was not restricted in the use of controlled drugs, admitted him to the firm on 1 October 1977. Shipman was skilled at making himself impressive before and agreeable to those who could serve his ends. Each member was a solo practitioner as far as patients went, but they all shared overheads in proportion to the volume of their work. As Shipman walked into at least part of the practice of the retired member, he was well away. And he built up his practice by hard work, by kindness to and tolerance of patients, by his preparedness to prescribe the best drugs liberally, and by his willingness to pay domiciliary visits. He introduced new ideas to the practice and was active in professional organizations. As a colleague he could be trying and hard, abrasive and unpleasant, and was always sure he knew the answers, believing he attained a standard the others did not attain. To the support staff, as earlier in his career, he could be rude, but he must have been held in esteem by several of them, for they accompanied him to his new practice in 1992. In truth, it must be said that he was an able practitioner — leaving aside the occasions when he was engaged in a murderous mission.

By 1990, at the latest, Shipman was stockpiling morphine or making false prescriptions for patients who did not need or receive the drug or who had died. There were nine pharmacies in or around Hyde from which the supplies derived.

At the start of 1992 Shipman left the Donneybrook practice, though remaining in Donneybrook House until he was able to open his own consulting rooms in Hyde. His decision to go solo was made after he had discovered through a solicitor that he could leave with financial advantage to himself, though commensurate disadvantage to the remaining seven members of the practice, who had to bear the overheads he had borne, about £20 000 a year. They had also to buy out his share of the building, amounting to some £23 000. Finally, Shipman refused to pay his share of the tax bill, the practice being run as a company. This amount of £30 000 the remaining members had to shoulder entirely, as their lawyers advised them that success in suing Shipman for his share of the sum was most uncertain.

On 24 August 1992 Shipman opened up his rooms at 21 Market Street, which he called The Surgery, only three hundred yards from Donneybrook House. His practice flourished. He was in great demand. One woman who was accepted as a patient told her son that she felt 'as though she had won the lottery'. The husband of Dr Linda Reynolds, who, as will be shown, caused alarm bells to ring at the extraordinary number of deaths of patients of Shipman's, said he was regarded as 'the best doctor in Hyde'.[84]

Already the strange deaths of his elderly female patients living alone were mounting up. After this Shipman began killing with abandon. Eventually some observant persons began to be suspicious of the conduct of Shipman, even though it was almost impossible to believe that so competent, respected and well-liked a doctor could do anything so evil as murder patients.

There was John Shaw, a private taxi driver, who was attached to and on friendly terms with some two hundred elderly ladies who were his clients, who became concerned with the number of them who had been Shipman's patients and had died suddenly — thirty in the past six years.

By the time he told the police of his worries, the police investigation was under way. Then Frank Massey, a local undertaker, noticed an odd pattern in the deaths of Shipman's patients: the high number of them; so many being found dead, fully dressed, in an easy chair or on a sofa in their residences; nothing in the residence of the deceased to indicate she had been ill; the great majority being elderly women who lived alone; and so many having died in the presence of Shipman or shortly after he had attended to them.

So worried was Massey that he went to see Shipman, who, quite unconcerned, told him that there was nothing to be concerned about, that anyone who wished to could look at his death certificate book and his patients' records (which in fact he had already doctored to correspond with the false death certificates).

Massey was satisfied with the response, but his daughter Debbie Brambroffe, also a funeral director, was not. After seven of the patients of Shipman had died in February 1998, she conveyed her misgivings to Dr Susan Booth, a member of the so-called Brooke GP local joint practice which had had rooms across the road since 1993. As will be shown in more detail later, according to English law, a doctor from an independent practice has to sign a cremation form — Form C — separate from the form signed by the doctor who attended the deceased. The fee for such a signature is known in medical circles as 'cash for ash'. Dr Booth conveyed what she had been told to a colleague, Dr Linda Reynolds, who already had her suspicions arising out of the extraordinarily high number of deaths of Shipman's patients compared with those of each of the members belonging to her practice. The previous belief had been that the death rate of Shipman's patients was exceptionally high because of the very large proportion of elderly patients, whom he would strive to treat at home. But now it became unacceptable.

She then conveyed these suspicions to John Pollard, the coroner of South Manchester. She told him that she and her colleagues had signed sixteen cremation Forms C for Shipman in the past three months, while for their 9500 patients, over three times Shipman's number, there had been only fourteen deaths in that period. Pollard saw the police. Together they decided to institute a discreet inquiry. The examination of Shipman's records showed that treatment and causes of death matched perfectly. Unknown to Pollard and the police, Shipman, after he had dispatched a patient, altered her (or his) record on his computer to cause the match.

With that evidence before them, after six weeks the police decided that there was no purpose in continuing with their investigation.

Subsequently there was criticism of the police in the press in not checking Shipman's record of drug abuse and forgery.

At least three more elderly female patients were killed by Shipman before his arrest put an end to his homicidal career. The first two were Winifred Mellor, on 11 May, and Joan Melia, on 12 June; of their murder Shipman was to be convicted. The third put an end to the career of Shipman, as will now be shown.

The twenty-fourth day of June 1998 saw the sudden death of Kathleen Grundy. An eighty-one-year-old widow, for her age very well and exceptionally active, she had for long been a patient of Shipman's, of whom she thought highly. Once a mayoress of Hyde, this wealthy woman was regarded by all with esteem. She had been looking forward to a visit to Derbyshire over a weekend. Punctual almost to a fault, Kathleen had failed to turn up at the Age Concern Club, where she served meals to pensioners. Very worried, two of her friends at the club went to her house, where they found her lying on a sofa, fully dressed, dead. They communicated with Shipman, who had visited the house, the last person to do so, a few hours earlier. He came. His purpose, he said, had been to take a blood sample for a study on ageing. A few days earlier he had lured Mrs Grundy into agreeing to participate in a research project into ageing, supposed to be conducted by the University of Manchester. In this way Shipman secured her signature, which he intended to use for a fraudulent purpose; and also to have an ostensible reason to attend her at her home.

After a cursory examination, Shipman said that the cause of death was cardiac arrest. He typed out the death certificate, attributing the death of Kathleen Grundy to 'old age', the last resort of doctors as the only cause, one never used by most doctors.

The police contacted Mrs Grundy's daughter, Angela Woodruff, a skilled solicitor of Harbury, a town a hundred miles from Hyde. Her law firm in Warwick had always looked after her mother's affairs and had possession of a will executed in 1986 leaving her entire estate to her daughter, Angela.

Kathleen Grundy was buried on 1 July 1998 at Hyde Chapel. On the thirteenth of that month Messrs Hamilton Ward & Co, solicitors of Hyde, showed Angela Woodruff two documents they had received. The one, dated 9 June 1998, was completed in typing, save for the signatures of the testator and witnesses, on a printed form obtainable from a stationer, headed 'LAST WILL & TESTAMENT', with a subheading 'RESIDUE TO ADULT'. It purported to be the will of 'Kathleen Grundy' whose address was typed. The executors who were appointed were Hamilton Ward & Co, a firm that had never had dealings with

Kathleen Grundy. The 'will' left 'All my estate, money and house to my doctor. My family are not in need and I want to reward him for all the care he has given to me and the people of Hyde. He is sensible enough to handle any problems this may give him. My doctor is Dr H F Shipman 21 Market St Hyde Cheshire HL14 2AF.' Against printed words reading 'but if he fails to survive me by 28 days or if this gift or any part of it fails for any other reason I give the residue of my estate or the part of it affected to' was typed 'my daughter'. The document stated that the testator wished her body to be cremated. Against 'TESTATOR'S SIGNATURE' appeared the signature 'K. Grundy'. The witnesses' signatures were 'P Spencer' and 'Claire Hutchinson'. The 'will' had been sent to the solicitor together with a letter dated 22 June 1998, purportedly written by Kathleen Grundy, and bearing the same signature 'K. Grundy', saying that she is enclosing a copy of her will; that 'Dr Shipman is to benefit by having my estate but if he dies or cannot accept it, then the estate goes to my daughter. I would like you to be the executor of my will.' The will and this document were received by the solicitors on 24 June. On 30 June day they received a further letter, dated 28 June 1998, and reading: 'Dear Sir, I regret to inform you that Mrs K. Grundy, of 79 Joel Lane, Hyde, died last week. I understand that she lodged a will with you, as I as a friend typed it out for her. Her daughter is at the address and you can contact her there. Yours J [perhaps S] Smith.' Neither Kathleen Grundy nor her daughter ever knew such a person. The typing on the will was very poorly done. Her mother, a most meticulous person and herself a good typist, Angela Woodruff felt sure would never have signed so ill-produced a document. And it spoke of 'my house', whereas she owned two houses. The more Angela looked at her mother's signature on the will the clearer it became that it was a forgery; that the whole document was a forgery.

Indeed it was. How ironic it is that Shipman's downfall and the cessation of his career as a serial murderer would be caused by an atypical action of his. Though he did not shun the making of money, the accumulation of a large fortune was not a major aim of his.

Kathleen Grundy's estate turned out to amount to the tidy sum of £386 000. It is this act of Shipman's that warrants his appearance in these pages. Not only did his run of good fortune now end, but his cocksureness, his arrogance and his stupidity — he who often called others stupid — caused his downfall. Twenty-two years earlier he had been convicted of forgery. Now he tried it on a much larger scale and in an area, the law, the intricacies of which he was ignorant. He was a devil in human guise and up to now he had had the luck of a devil.

Angela Woodruff interviewed the two witnesses to the new will, Paul Spencer and Claire Hutchinson, both of whom were patients of Shipman's. On 10 June, when they were in his waiting room, Shipman had asked them just to 'witness a document', which they did. They saw the name Kathleen Grundy and her signature, but did not see her sign. Their signatures had been forged on the 'will'.

The police were now alerted. It was decided to apply to coroner John Pollard for an exhumation order, the first one ever by the Greater Manchester police. It was done, and at two in the morning of 1 August 1998 the body of Kathleen Grundy was exhumed. That day a postmortem examination was conducted by Dr John Rutherford, a forensic pathologist. He found the body to be in excellent condition for an eighty-one-year-old woman, with no obvious cause of her sudden death. Tissue samples were sent to a laboratory in Chorley, Lancashire. Later that day the police went with a search warrant to The Surgery. It specially mentioned Shipman's typewriter. The police found the doctor his usual arrogant self. On producing an old Brothers manual typewriter he made a revealing comment, not called for in the circumstances, 'Mrs Grundy used to borrow it'. Why bring her name in? Subsequently a forensic laboratory reported that it was the machine used to type the new will. On the word 'will' in the document Shipman's little finger on his left hand had left a print, while there was no print anywhere on the document from the hands of the 'testator'.

On 3 August Detective Superintendent Bernard Postles was put in charge of a major investigation. On 10 August a Home Office inspector informed the police of something they had been quite unaware of: Shipman's criminal record. On the twenty-eighth, Michael Hall, a forensic documents examiner, reported that the signatures in the will had been forged and that the document had probably been typed on the typewriter that had been seized in Shipman's surgery.

The report of Julie Evans, a forensic toxologist, took four weeks to prepare. It arrived on 28 August. There was a level of morphine in the body, it stated, which, according to previous findings, would have caused death within three hours of the administration of the drug.

Shipman had falsified written and computer records to make Kathleen Grundy an abuser of drugs. It was, on the face of it, an incredibly foolish thing to make this deeply respected lady, a pillar of society, to be a client of drug dealers. It was yet another mortal blow to the credibility of Shipman.

After the exhumation of the body of Kathleen Grundy, Shipman on a couple of occasions almost confessed to having caused her death. To a patient he said he could get twelve years. He told Mrs Marion Gilchrist, a district nurse in his surgery, that on the evidence he could be found guilty, but all he had done wrong was not being able to arrange for the cremation of the body of Mrs Grundy.

On 7 September 1998 Shipman was arrested on suspicion of the murder of Kathleen Grundy, and of attempting to obtain property by deception and of forgery. On that day his practice of medicine came to an end for ever. The following day he appeared before the Tameside magistrates' court, and was remanded in custody, where he was to remain.

The police investigation into possible homicidal activities by him produced chilling results.

The question then facing the police and prosecuting authorities was how many counts of murder Shipman should be charged with. It was decided to work on a manageable number where the evidence of guilt was particularly strong. The burial of a patient was naturally regarded as an important factor in favour of prosecution, but cremations were certainly not looked at as precluding it. What was the primary consideration for putting the death of a patient on the list of prosecutions was its slotting into Shipman's system of homicidal activity: seeing a patient almost always during a house call, for a complaint that did not exist, her death in his presence or shortly afterwards, and his immediate fraudulent alteration of the patient's clinical record on computer to correspond with a false death certificate; in the case of a burial, an unexplained presence of morphine in lethal quantities in the body.

Shipman's conduct was a classic illustration of the arrogance of ignorance. The hard drive of his computer program, Micro-Dot, designed especially on 14 October 1996 for general medical practitioners, made a permanent, dated and timed, copy of what was typed. Shipman did not know this. As soon as he was arrested, his computer records were impounded. Detective Sergeant John Ashley of Great Manchester police, an expert on computers, discovered the falsification of the records. When the police revealed this to Shipman, he got a terrible shock.

Shipman's use of morphine to murder patients was irrational, unless, as some psychologists have suggested, all the time he was wanting to be caught, which seems quite unsupportable, however arguable it may be that that desire was the prime cause of his forgery of the will. Almost certainly throughout he believed himself to be invincible, a doctor — a being who is a demigod of the modern world.

Surely Shipman knew of the grave danger of using morphine, which would explain his wish to have his victims cremated. As was pointed out above, morphine is an alkaloid, a narcotic analgesic extracted from the head of the opium poppy, and used as an anaesthetic or a sedative. It blocks the flow of pain signals, causing euphoria. Diacetylmorphine (diamorphine) is double-strength morphine. Morphine never degrades, remaining in a body of a live or dead person for ever. As long as the state of preservation of an exhumed corpse allows it, the drug can provide overwhelming evidence of a death-dealing dose. This danger must be weighed against the relative ease with which a doctor can acquire and accumulate morphine. Less dangerous from the point of view of discovery, though probably more difficult to acquire in quantities, would be a drug such as insulin or potassium. A medical practitioner who conducts a superficial study of murder as a fine art would know that the injection of a large air bubble from a hypodermic syringe can do the trick with little chance of discovery.

One hundred and thirty-six deaths of Shipman's patients were investigated by the police. For those to be selected for prosecution for alleged murder a scale was created, based on patterns. At the head of the list were patients whose deaths followed a house call by Shipman. Those patients who were cremated, where as a consequence there could be no postmortem examination, entered the list mainly on conditions present before death; Shipman's seeing them shortly before death; the false recorded causes of death; the lying by Shipman on the calling and cancellation of an ambulance.

The upshot was the choice of fifteen cases, starting with the death of Marie West on 6 March 1995 and ending with the death of Kathleen Grundy on 24 June 1998.

The remains of six of those believed to have been murdered had been cremated. These six were Maria West, Lizzie Adams, Laura Kathleen Wagstaff, Norah Nuttall, Pamela Marguerite Hillier and Maureen Alice Ward. The Crown prosecution service found that with a burial more than five years back, an exhumation would produce a body from which it would be difficult to adduce clear evidence of poisoning by morphine, even though the drug is ever-lasting. Furthermore, to prove Shipman to be a mass murderer, it was desirable to have cases based on purely circumstantial evidence without forensic evidence: on falsified computer records, or false telephone calls.

Of the fifteen alleged murders, one took place in 1995, one in 1996, six in 1997 and six in 1998. Shipman had murdered many more of his patients during this period — the police had prepared twenty-three further cases, all of patients whose remains had been cremated, and, as a later investigation showed, this was only a small portion of the total killings — so little reliance can be placed on inferences drawn from these figures.

As Shipman was found guilty of murdering all fifteen, it may be helpful to give a synopsis of the evidence at trial on which he was convicted in each case, in order of the deaths of the victims;[85] and also some of the views of Dr John Grenville MD DObstRCOG MRCGP, a highly qualified and experienced general practitioner who gave evidence in 2001, over a year after the trial, before the Shipman Inquiry headed by Dame Janet Smith of the Queen's Bench Division of the High Court of England and Wales, an inquiry that will be dealt with shortly. Suffice it to say that Dr Grenville found most of the explanations of Shipman's quite unacceptable and at times making no sense at all.

Maria (Marie) West. 6 March 1995. Cremated. An eighty-one-year old widow, she had been seen regularly at her house by Shipman for the past two weeks. She had high blood pressure, but it was under control. She complained of pains in her legs and problems with breathing. On the day she died a friend had called, but, hearing a voice in the living room, waited in the kitchen. Then in walked the doctor. He said 'She collapsed over me'. The friend saw Maria dead, sitting in her usual armchair, as she had been when the friend left her for the kitchen. The Medical Certificate of Cause of Death (MCCD) completed by Shipman attributed her death to a stroke. Dr John Grenville, in reviewing the record, said that had she had a stroke she would have fallen to the floor, and Shipman would have tried to resuscitate her and called an ambulance. The jury, wrote Dame Janet Smith, must have inferred that Shipman had injected Maria with diamorphine shortly after he had arrived.

Irene Turner. 11 July 1996. This sixty-seven-year-old widow was in quite good health, apart from suffering from some heart disease. She had had a heart attack in 1994. In answer to a call by Irene saying she had a bad cold, Shipman turned up at her home at a quarter past three in the afternoon. He asked a neighbour to help pack a bag for Irene, as she was to go to hospital. Off went Shipman. On arrival the neighbour found Irene dead on her bed. On his return Shipman said she was 'riddled with diabetes'. As always when asked, he said there was no need for a postmortem examination, and this was accepted by relations and friends. As always, there was no arrangement with a hospital. Shipman killed his patient by injecting a lethal dose of morphine. This was established in all nine murders of patients who were buried. The inference that this was the cause of the murder of the six patients whose bodies were cremated is irresistible.

Lizzie Adams. 28 February 1997. This seventy-seven-year-old widow was in general good health apart from mild diabetes. On 27 February, feeling rather unwell, she obtained a prescription for an antibiotic at Shipman's surgery. That day she and her daughter Doreen went shopping for two and a half hours. At noon the following day, finding the antibiotic not agreeing with her, she arranged for a domestic visit by Shipman. In mid-afternoon a male friend called, to find Shipman admiring Lizzie's collection of Royal Doulton figurines and cut glass. Lizzie was apparently asleep in her chair. Shipman said that Lizzie was very ill and he had called for an ambulance. At 2:30 pm he phoned Doreen to say that her mother was very ill with pneumonia and he was sending her to hospital. On Doreen and her sister Sonia arriving, Shipman said 'She has gone'. It seemed incredible to the daughters, but they accepted his statement that a postmortem examination was unnecessary. As always, Shipman did not call an ambulance and falsified his computer records.

Jean Lilley. 25 April 1997. This fifty-eight-year-old married woman suffered from heart disease, hypertension and respiratory problems. As she had a bad cold, her husband asked Shipman to call. He was with her for forty to fifty minutes. After he had departed, two friends came to see Jean. They found her dead on the couch. Shipman stated the cause of death to be heart failure. Subsequently a forensic pathologist found no evidence of severe heart problems and that the cause of death was morphine poisoning.

Ivy Lomas. 29 May 1997. She was a sixty-three-year-old woman who was the only one to be murdered in Shipman's surgery. Before he told his receptionist of her death he saw three other patients — so as not to keep them waiting, he said. His story was that Ivy had collapsed and he tried for fifteen minutes to revive her with heart massage and mouth-to-mouth resuscitation. There was evidence that he had considered her a 'nuisance' as she consulted him so often. The autopsy revealed death by morphine poisoning. At the trial Shipman could give no explanation for the presence of morphine. As always, Shipman had almost immediately altered her medical record.

Muriel Grimshaw. 14 July 1997. A seventy-six-year-old widow, in very good general health, she had her customary arrangement to go shopping on the fourteenth with a friend at nine in the morning. The friend could get no response from her home, so she telephoned Muriel's daughter. The two gained entry to the house and found Muriel dead on her bed. She had died the previous day. Shipman was called. He gave a certificate that she had died from a stroke. As frequently happened, Shipman did not examine the body of his dead patient even enough to establish that the patient had died, let alone to establish the cause of death. The inference is irresistible that he had murdered his patient and had decided what cause of death he would certify. It was discovered that he had inserted in her computer record the day before a false entry of a stroke. The postmortem examination revealed the presence of morphine in the tissues consistent with the administration of a lethal dose.

Marie Quinn. 24 November 1997. This sixty-seven-year-old widow had been very active. Shipman told her son that she had telephoned him saying she thought she had had a stroke. When he had arrived at her house, she was dead. But phone records showed that no such call had been made. The real cause of death was Shipman's death-creating injection of morphine. The postmortem examination revealed enough morphine in the tissues consistent with the administration of a lethal dose.

Laura Kathleen Wagstaff. 9 December 1997. This eighty-one-year-old widow was well on the morning of her death; she went to her building society. At two in the afternoon, to her surprise Shipman called. Later he knocked at the door of a neighbour to say that Mrs Wagstaff had telephoned him at his surgery to attend to her, that he had at once summoned an ambulance, but when he arrived he found she had died, so he cancelled the call for an ambulance. Investigations showed that none of the three telephone calls had been made, and she had not died of a heart disease as Shipman stated in his death certificate (MCCD) and falsified computer record. As with a number of relatives of his victims, Mrs Wagstaff's daughter believed initially when Shipman was accused of murdering her mother that he was the victim of a witch hunt.

Bianka Pomfret. 10 December 1997. This forty-nine-year-old divorcee (youngest of the victims) had been born in Germany. Even more so than the other victims, she was devoted to Shipman. The afternoon of her death Shipman saw her at her home. At 5 pm her psychiatric support worker (Mrs Pomfret suffered from a depressive illness) found her dead on her chair, fully clothed. Shipman was called and said she had died of coronary thrombosis and ischaemic heart disease. It was discovered, through an 'audit trail', that he had falsified her computer record at 4 pm to show a history of heart disease over nine months. Her son and daughter-in-law had never been told of it. Again, the postmortem examination revealed enough morphine in the tissues consistent with the administration of a lethal dose.

Norah Nuttall. 26 January 1998. A couple of days earlier this sixty-four-year-old widow had seen Shipman for her cough, and had returned home with a bottle of medicine. On the fateful day her son visited her at lunchtime. On returning in the afternoon he found Shipman there, and his mother slumped in a chair. Said the doctor: 'She had chest pains; I have phoned for an ambulance.' And later: 'I have felt her pulse. She has died. I will phone to cancel the ambulance.' Naturally, there was no record of Mrs Nuttall's having asked Shipman to call, or of Shipman's having ordered or cancelled an ambulance. That day Shipman changed her computer record to say she had 'wheezy bronchitis'. Such a chest condition, on top of this very stout woman's having high blood pressure and heart disease, would justify a death certificate recording a sudden heart attack.

Pamela Marguerite Hillier. 9 February 1998. A sixty-eight-year-old widow, she had been a patient for over twenty years. A week before she died she had seen Shipman twice to attend to a hurt knee, and expected a home visit from him on the day of her death. She suffered from high blood pressure, but it was under control and not out of control as her computer record, altered by Shipman after her death, showed, recording the death by a stroke as a result. Up to the end Pamela had been fit and active, engaged in the past week in stripping wallpaper. On 9 February at 1 pm a daughter of Pamela's rang the bell of her home but got no reply. At 4:30, when the same thing happened, she managed to gain entry, to find her mother, fully clothed, lying dead on the floor of the back bedroom, with blood-pressure pills on the bed. Summoned, Shipman told the two children of the deceased that he had called at 1:30, and told Mrs Hillier to take another blood-pressure pill. She had high blood pressure, and had died from a stroke. The children found this hard to accept, and took some persuading — including the unpleasantness of the procedure, a standard argument of Shipman's — not to insist on a postmortem examination. The police found that Shipman had made ten changes to his computer records two hours before Pamela's body had been found — and before he was ostensibly aware of her death — to bear out his diagnosis.

Maureen Alice Ward. 18 February 1998. Died at 5:30 pm. She was a fifty-seven-year-old spinster, a retired teacher. At the time of her death Shipman had already typed out the cause of it in his computer records as tumour of the brain, to back up his intended murder. Maureen had had cancer, but by 1994 it had been cured. On 18 February she had already booked for her holiday. On the morning of that day she had been shopping with a friend. In the afternoon Shipman went to see her at the old-age home where she stayed, saying to the warden that he had come to tell his patient that he had arranged for her to see a consultant at Stepping Hill Hospital. There was no record at the hospital or Shipman's surgery of this appointment. Then Shipman at 5:30 told the warden that Miss Ward had died in her bed of a brain tumour, a result of the spread of her cancer. At the trial of Shipman an oncologist told the court that it was impossible in the circumstances to say Miss Ward had died of a brain tumour.

Winifred Mellor. 11 May 1998. She was a seventy-three-year-old widow with five children, who led a very active life and was in good health. On the day of her death she had a slight chest infection, but had arranged to attend a dance in the evening. She had been visited at her home by Shipman at three in the afternoon. At five he returned, then called two neighbours to open the door, as he could see his patient through the window but she did not answer the bell. The neighbours and Shipman found Winifred dead in her chair, the sleeve on her right arm rolled up. Shipman made only a cursory check of the body and said curtly that she was dead. He telephoned one of the daughters and told her that her mother had died of a heart attack. She had asked him to return at five, he said, but there was no trace of the call. The real cause of the death was a murderous injection of morphine, revealed by the postmortem examination. No evidence emerged of a natural cause of death. There was the usual backdating by Shipman of entries in the records to bear out his diagnosis.

Joan May Melia. 12 June 1998. An attractive widow of seventy-three who was in fairly good health, she saw Shipman at eleven in the morning the day she died, as she had a sore throat and was feeling off colour. She was taken home by a man who, unknown to Shipman, was her lover. As had been arranged, this man returned to Joan's flat at five, opening the door with his key, only to find her in her armchair, dead. He telephoned Shipman, who on arrival said immediately and casually 'She's dead'. He must have paid a visit and injected a lethal dose of morphine intravenously, causing death almost immediately. His death certificate (MCDD) stated the cause to be pneumonia aggravated by emphysema. A postmortem examination revealed no serious lung problem but a high content of morphine consistent with the administration of a lethal dose.

Kathleen Grundy. 14 June 1998. The circumstances surrounding the murder of this lady, which led to the end of the homicidal activities of Shipman, have already been outlined.

From at least December 1990 Shipman had started stockpiling morphine by making out false prescriptions for patients who did not need it or who had died. In all it is estimated he procured 22 000 milligrams of morphine, equal to 1 466 fatal doses.

His patients were very attached to him. He was normally a caring, very competent and hard-working practitioner, who had developed an attractive bedside manner. As before, he prescribed the best drugs liberally. Small wonder that he had built up a patient list of 3 100, far above the national average. He was an excellent doctor by health-authority standards: no registered complaints by patients, a high number of vaccinations and immunizations, and regular surgery audits.

As has been shown, though, in several of the murder cases — and there must have been other instances where he performed his satanic acts but escaped consequences in law — his conduct on the day his victim died was questioned by her relations and friends. Why didn't he send her to hospital? She refused to go, was the routine answer. It was always reluctantly accepted. Why didn't he at least call an ambulance? He did, was the reply, but cancelled the call as she died before the ambulance arrived. Why not ask for a postmortem examination? Because it is a most distressing thing to do, and the cause of death was clear. When questioned on these occasions he could be brusque, assertive and most unsympathetic, showing a lack of compassion for the bereaved.

When Shipman was arrested for the fifteen alleged murders, an application for bail by incredulous friends and supporters who were prepared to stand surety in substantial amounts was naturally rejected. As facts emerged, so support among the patients and the public started to fall away rapidly. The GP from Hyde changed identity from Dr Jekyll to Dr Hyde.

The trial began on 5 October 1999, thirteen months after the arrest of Shipman. It was held in the Crown Court at Preston, the medium-sized town on the west coast some fifty miles away. The defence had successfully claimed that an impartial jury could not be empanelled in Manchester. In his lengthy stay in prison awaiting trial Shipman had lost thirty pounds in weight. Only fifty-three years of age, he looked much older. His beard and moustache were whiter. His wife, daughter and two sons stood steadfastly by him. He was confident he would be acquitted.

The head of the prosecuting team was the redoubtable Richard Henriques QC (55), leader of the Northern Circuit of barristers, of very high reputation (he was appointed a judge of the Queen's Bench Division of the High Court of Justice of England and Wales on 19 April 2000, less than three months after the conclusion of the trial). With him was Peter Wright QC. Both had chambers in Manchester. They were confident of a conviction.

The head of the defence team was Nicola Davies QC (46). With her was Ian Winter. Ms Davies had appeared in a number of highly publicized medical cases, but almost all were of a civil, not a criminal, character.

The presiding judge was Sir Thayne Forbes (61). Mr Justice Forbes had been appointed to the Queen's Bench Division of the High Court of Justice of England and Wales in 1993.*

Ms Davies presented an initial three applications. She contended that Shipman could not receive a fair trial owing to the earlier 'inaccurate and misleading' newspaper reports. Mr Henriques opposed the application, which was rejected in a careful judgment by the judge. She then argued that the trial for the murder of Kathleen Grundy should be tried separately, as only in it was there an alleged motive — greed. The prosecution replied that as all the cases were interrelated they should be tried together. The application was dismissed. Finally, Nicola Davies asked that evidence be disallowed of the accumulation by the accused of morphine from that prescribed to twenty-eight patients, some being already dead and others who never needed it. Once more the application failed.

After this the jury was empanelled. Now came the opening address of Henriques. 'None of those buried — nor indeed cremated — were prescribed morphine or diamorphine. All of them died most unexpectedly. All of them had seen Dr Shipman on the day of their death.' None had a terminal illness, so there was no question of euthanasia — mercy killing.

After giving an outline of his case, Henriques advanced a reason for the apparent irrational fifteen murders. 'The defendant killed those fifteen patients because he enjoyed doing so. He was exercising the ultimate power of controlling life and death, and repeated it so often that he must have found the drama of taking life to his taste.'

The prosecution started with the alleged murder of Kathleen Grundy. As throughout, the defence had an almost impossible task in trying to shake the accuracy of the testimony of witnesses for the Crown or in any way to reduce the force of the Crown's case. For example, the defence tried to bring out that Kathleen's daughter Angela Woodruff was not on good terms with her mother. It was a hopeless effort: when Kathleen's letters were looked at and many witnesses were asked the question, it was clear they were on the best of terms. The attempt to impugn the accuracy of the Crown's expert on fingerprints failed utterly. Again, after one Crown forensic analyst conceded that he could

* He had attended Winchester College and then University College of the University of London, where he took LLB and LLM degrees. He was called to the Bar by the Inner Temple in 1966. In 1984 he was appointed a QC.

not say whether the finding of morphine in a tissue proved single or multiple use, it seemed that the defence could contend that the high level of morphine might result from years of use. But then Dr Karch Steven, an internationally distinguished expert, explained that the test he had done was based on a new, absolutely accurate, technique that had been described in *The Lancet* only a year back, based on analysing hair samples. In every instance long-term use was ruled out.

The case for the prosecution ran on for twenty-five days. Over one hundred and twenty witnesses were called. There was convincing evidence that Shipman had stocks of morphine — the police had found considerable amounts in a bedroom in his house; and that they had come through false prescriptions.

On 25 November 1999 the defence case began. Shipman had made copious notes and given many instructions to his counsel. He was put into the witness box. There he denied murdering any of the fifteen alleged victims and tried to explain why he did what he conceded he did. Some of his explanations were acceptable, but he could not explain the presence of morphine in the bodies. His cross-examination for seven days was deadly. It brought out the falsification of the records of the deceased to make them correspond with the death certificates, for which his explanation was utterly unacceptable; the failure ever to call an ambulance or admit a patient to hospital or to allow a postmortem examination to take place — 'the poisoner fears pathology, ambulances and hospitals'; and all the many other clear indications of guilt.

Only one other witness was called by the defence, to speak on the fingerprints on Kathleen Grundy's will.

On 13 December 1999 the evidence for the defence ended. The trial resumed on 5 January 2000.

Richard Henriques's closing speech for the prosecution followed that outlined in the cross-examination of Shipman. Nicola Davies's closing speech for the defence dwelt on the absence of a clear motive for killing; contended that the toxological evidence for the prosecution was unreliable; but had difficulty in raising any defence to the charge of forging the will.

Mr Justice Forbes commenced his summing-up to the jury on 10 January. For two weeks he carefully analysed the evidence. On 24 January the jury retired to consider its verdict. On 31 January it returned a verdict of guilty of all fifteen charges of murder and guilty of the forgery of the will of Kathleen Grundy.

Nicola Davies asked that sentence be passed immediately.

Mr Justice Forbes said: 'You have finally been brought to justice by the verdict of this jury. I have no doubt whatsoever that these are true verdicts. The time has now come for me to pass sentence upon you for these wicked, wicked crimes. The sheer wickedness of what you have done defies description. It is shocking and beyond belief. You have not shown the slightest remorse or contrition for your evil deeds. Each of your victims was your patient. You murdered each and every one of your victims by a calculated and cold-blooded perversion of your medical skills, for your own evil and wicked purposes. You took advantage of and grossly abused their trust. You were, after all, each victim's doctor. I have little doubt that each of your victims smiled and thanked you as she submitted to your deadly ministrations.'

For each murder the judge imposed a sentence of imprisonment for life; for the forgery of the will a sentence of imprisonment for four years. He went on to say that in the ordinary course he would write to the Secretary for Home Affairs giving his recommendation as to the length of the sentence; but justice demanded he make known his views at the conclusion of the trial. It 'will be that you spend the remainder of your days in prison'.

The trial that had lasted for fifty-seven days was over. But many queries remained and also much grief among surviving spouses and relations of others whose sudden deaths were now the subject of deep suspicion.

On the conclusion of the trial, Shipman was suspended from practice by the General Medical Council's Preliminary Proceedings Committee and on 11 February 2000 his name was erased from the medical register by the Professional Conduct Committee of the General Medical Council.

As has been mentioned, the police had prepared a further twenty-three charges of murder, but on 18 February 2000 the Director of Public Prosecutions, David Calvert-Smith, stated that he had decided not to proceed with them, for two reasons: the one was that the 'enormous publicity' surrounding the first trial would preclude all fair further trials, the other was that further trials might significantly hamper or delay the public inquiry that the government had started the day after Shipman's conviction which would be set afoot in Manchester into why for so long Shipman's murderous activities had remained undetected. The members of the inquiry would consider the role played by all agencies, including coroner, police and health services. In announcing the inquiry, the responsible Minister, the Secretary for Health, Alan Milburn, said that its object was to reform the existing system of audit of medical prescriptions and accountability, to avoid a repetition of such a happening, and to ensure public faith in the medical profession.

By now an important document has been published. It was by Professor Richard Baker OBE MB BS MD FRCGP, Professor of Quality in Health Care and Director of the Health and Clinical Governance and Development Unit, Department of General Practice and Primary Health Care, University of Leicester. He had been commissioned by the Chief Medical Officer, at the request of the Secretary of State for Health, to review Shipman's clinical practice. His report was published by HM Stationery Office, London, in January 2001. It was entitled *Harold Shipman's Clinical Practice 1974–1998.*[86] Professor Baker had identified virtually every death in Todmorden and Hyde for which Shipman had signed the required Medical Certificate of the Cause of Death (MCCD). His investigation concentrated on the patterns of deaths among his patients, in order to identify any excess in their number, their time and their place, and the relationship between the certified cause of death and clinical history. Baker relied mainly on surviving clinical records, surviving cremation certificates, and data gathered from the registration of deaths.

Analysis of the 179 available clinical records of patients (aside from the fifteen Shipman had been convicted as having murdered) in which Shipman had issued the MCCD reflected 102 as highly suspicious of the cause of death and 39 as moderately suspicious.

Cremation forms were also revealing. A cremation in England must be authorized. Among the information required is that of the doctor who attended the patient in his or her last illness. The doctor has to complete a Form B, which includes details of persons present at the death, and the mode, duration and time of death. A Form B is retained for fifteen years, which led to most of those completed by Shipman from 1985 onwards being traced . Baker compared the information Shipman provided in his forms with that provided by a sample of six local GPs who had cared for similar patients and been in practice for about the same period as Shipman. Of the 767 forms available for consideration, 292 were completed by Shipman. The key findings were these: the GP was present at death with 19.5 per cent of Shipman's patients and only 0.8 per cent of the patients of the other GPs; the parallel percentages for no one being present being 40.4 and 19, and for relatives or carers being present 40.1 and 80.2. Deaths within twenty-nine minutes were recorded with 60.4 per cent of Shipman's patients and only 22.7 per cent of the patients of the other GPs.

Next came an analysis of death registrations. Every death has to be notified to the registrar of the district of death, with information about the patient additional to that in the MCCD: date and place of birth, occupation, usual address. A comparison of the deaths of Shipman's patients with those of the patients of other GPs from 1974 to 1998 showed an estimated excess of 236 deaths of Shipman's patients. With all patients for whom Shipman had issued an MCCD, including those who died in hospitals and residential nursing homes, the estimated excess of deaths was 297.

Then a comparison of the numbers of deaths from 1987 to 1998 of Shipman's registered patients, no matter where they occurred or who completed the MCCDs, compared with the number represented by the national death rate, revealed an excess of 197 (among females, of 162); with the number represented by other manufacturing districts, of 176 (153 among females); with the number represented by the local health district of Tameside, of 152 (141 among females). These figures relate to only twelve of the twenty-three years of Shipman's general practice.

Professor Baker concluded that the estimated excess of 236 deaths set out above was the number about which there should be concern within a 95 per cent confidence interval; the number of patients Shipman had probably killed lay between 198 and 277.

On 1 February 2000, the day after the conviction of Shipman, Alan Milburn MP, the Secretary of State for Health, announced the setting-up of an inquiry in terms of section 2 of the National Health Service Act, under the chairmanship of Lord Laming. As it was a private inquiry there were widespread objections by concerned relatives of deceased patients of Shipman. The High Court set aside the appointment of the inquiry. On 21 September 2000 the Secretary of State announced the appointment of a public inquiry under the chairmanship of Dame Janet Smith, a judge of the Queen's Bench Division of the High Court of Justice of England and Wales.*

The instrument of appointment was issued on 31 January 2001, precisely a year after the conviction of Shipman. The Shipman Inquiry was given the powers conferred by the Tribunals of Inquiry (Evidence) Act 1921. The terms of reference covered four matters: first, the extent

* Dame Janet had been born Janet Holt on 29 November 1940 in Stockport, Greater Manchester, but grew up in Bolton, where her father was a bank manager. She attended Bolton School, where her brilliant academic results secured her a place in Girton College, University of Cambridge, to read for a degree in natural science. At the age of nineteen, however, she left her studies in order to marry Edward Smith. Of the marriage two sons and a daughter were born. The union ended in a divorce. In 1984 she married Robin Edward Alexander Mathieson. In her late twenties she began to study for admission to the Bar. She was called by Lincoln's Inn in 1972. Her practice was noted for her appearance in claims for damages for personal injury, for medical negligence and for industrial disease. In 1986 she was appointed a QC and in 1992 a judge.

of Shipman's unlawful activities; secondly, the actions of statutory bodies, authorities, other organizations and responsible individuals concerned in the procedures and investigations following the deaths of Shipman's patients in unlawful or suspicious circumstances; thirdly, with reference to the case of Shipman, the performance of such bodies and individuals with responsibility for monitoring primary-care provision and the use of controlled drugs; and fourthly, following these inquiries, to recommend the steps that should be taken to protect patients in the future.

The inquiry was held at Gateway House, Manchester. Work began immediately on the collection and assessment of available evidence by the legal team, which was soon composed of Caroline Swift QC, Christopher Melton QC, Anthony Mazzag and Michael Jones, these counsel being instructed by Henry Palin, solicitor to the inquiry. Later six further solicitors and nine paralegals joined the legal team, which clearly performed its task praiseworthily. Dr Aneez Esmail LRCP MRCS MFPHM PhD was appointed medical adviser to the inquiry.

Dame Janet decided, in responding to the first of the terms of reference — the extent of Shipman's unlawful activities — to ask the legal team to investigate fully every suspicious or potentially suspicious death in which Shipman may have been involved. She would then reach a decision on each one whether or not he was responsible for the death. These findings were published on 19 July 2002 by HM Stationery Office in Volumes Two to Six of the First Report of the Shipman Inquiry. Together with Volume One: *Death Disguised*, published on the same day, which extended over 335 pages, the total First Report was over two thousand pages long, each page of an average length of 1200 words.

The legal team had available a huge amount of information already collected by the police and the Baker report. In all, the inquiry investigated 887 deaths initially believed to have some connection with Shipman. Dame Janet gave written decisions in 493 of them (and also one incident involving a living person). The inquiries into the remaining 394 deaths resulted in findings of natural causes. In the cases of some deaths, further inquiry revealed that Shipman had no connection at all with them. But otherwise, unless there was compelling evidence that Shipman had not been involved in a particular death, the legal team would investigate every case as fully as possible and refer it to Dame Janet for decision.

An enormous amount of evidence was gathered. There were statements of witnesses, relatives, friends and people who might be able to shed light on investigations. In all there were 3 687 statements of witnesses. There were coroner's documents; documents relating to death registration and cremation, notably MCCDs and cremation Forms B; Shipman's practice records and other medical records; and other contemporaneous documents, such as logs kept by Shipman's deputizing doctor service.

The benefits of modern technology were available. To keep the hearings as paper-free as possible, the 37 500 pages of evidence to be placed before the inquiry were scanned into an image database and made available to legal representatives on CD-ROMs. Dame Janet had given leave to various individuals and organizations to be so represented before the inquiry.

Evidence relating to 65 deaths and the incident involving a living person was submitted orally, but broadcasting and filming of the inquiry into Phase One — Shipman's unlawful activities — was prohibited in order to avoid further distress to relatives of patients whose deaths were under investigation. It was held by Dame Janet Smith that article 10 of the Convention on Human Rights, dealing with the right to freedom of expression, did not give a right to film the proceedings. Evidence relating to a further 428 deaths, where there was no oral hearing, was placed on the Inquiry's website. The oral evidence was made available on laptop computers almost immediately. Documents being discussed were displayed on three large screens. A fourth large screen showed an image of the person speaking. The object to make the inquiry a truly 'public' one seems to have been admirably attained. Furthermore, facilities were made available for family members of deceased patients whose deaths were being investigated to read the relevant evidence on a computer screen.

As it was impracticable for Dame Janet to hear oral evidence relating to all 494 cases requiring a decision, it was decided to confine such evidence to where it was needed for clarification or for some other reason, such as a link with another death. In all there was oral evidence by 179 individuals in 66 cases.

Expert evidence was given by Professor Richard Baker; Dr John Grenville; Professor Helen Whitwell, a forensic pathologist; Professor Henry McQuay; Professor Kevin Park, Head of the Department of Pharmacology and Therapeutics in the University of Liverpool; and Dr Peter Goldblatt, Chief Medical Statistician.

Through his solicitors, Shipman refused to participate in the inquiry. It was in the circumstances purposeless trying to compel him to give evidence, as the punishment for refusal to do so is imprisonment, and he was already in prison for life.

Mrs Shipman eventually gave oral evidence. She was granted immunity from legal consequences flowing from her oral or written evidence or documents she produced, save on a charge of having given false evidence before the inquiry. This type of undertaking is common. She was found to be an honest and co-operative witness. Her evidence proved very damaging to her husband's interests in one case.

Where there was no oral evidence in a case, counsel to the inquiry made a detailed summary of the relevant evidence and submissions as to the appropriate finding. All was put on the inquiry website. Where oral evidence was given, brief written submissions were prepared and made public in the same way. Where the family of a deceased were legally represented, usually written submissions were made by their counsel. The final decision was, of course, made by Dame Janet.

After a review of the working of the procedures for the registration of death and the certification of cremation, Dame Janet concluded[87] that, despite the procedures being intended as a safeguard for the public against concealment of the fact that a person has been unlawfully killed, Shipman had killed (she almost always uses 'kill' when 'murder' would be the standard word) 215 patients (171 being women) in twenty-three years. 'It is clear, therefore, that the existing procedures provided no safeguard at all, either because they were flawed in themselves, or because they were not properly implemented or, possibly, by reason of a combination of both these factors.' Proposals for change were to be the subject of a further report.

Dr Grenville was the principal medical expert on whose evidence Dame Janet drew in making her decisions on the cause of death of Shipman's patients. He said a doctor could expect at most once in his career being called to attend a patient suffering an angina attack and that patient then suffering a heart attack virtually as he or she arrived. Yet Shipman would have us believe it happened to him on a regular basis.[88] If it did happen, the doctor should make a most detailed note. Shipman's notes were brief and sometimes there was not one at all.

Dr Grenville pointed out that it is extremely uncommon for a deceased patient to be found sitting on a chair, appearing to be peaceful and asleep, as so many of Shipman's patients were found. Nor would it be consistent with death from a heart attack, or acute left ventricular failure or bronchopneumonia or lobar pneumonia, all causes advanced by Shipman for the death of patients. It would be entirely consistent with the patient having become drowsy, then unconscious, and finally having slipped into death through the administration of a lethal dose of opiates.

Shipman frequently claimed to have been present when a patient collapsed, but he very rarely attempted cardiopulmonary resuscitation when he should have done so. When he alleged that he had done so, it is clear from his failure to disturb the patient's clothing or to summon an ambulance, which would have had a trained crew, that he had lied. Very often, though, he fobbed off queries by relatives by telling them that resuscitation would have been inappropriate.

If a doctor had seen a patient and shortly afterwards the patient had died, a situation in which Shipman stated he frequently found himself, it was essential to conduct tests to determine that the patient had indeed died. Such tests were rarely conducted by Shipman.

There was a high incidence of the bodies of Shipman's patients being found in overheated rooms, which was likely the result of his efforts to make it difficult for others to estimate the time of death.

Shipman often claimed that a patient with a serious medical condition refused admission to hospital or other necessary treatment. The solution to the problem by Shipman was, at least usually, to leave the patient at home without any immediate care and without seeking the help of relatives to cause a change of mind, telling the patient to let the surgery know of a change of mind or deterioration. According to Dr Grenville, it is 'incredibly rare' for a patient to refuse such admission or treatment; if it happened, the persuasion of a relative, friend or neighbour ought to be sought; if there were still no success, the doctor should make a detailed note of what had happened and ask the patient to sign it as correct. And the doctor should try to see that the patient was continually under observation.

In reality, though, said Dr Grenville, most of Shipman's patients had been registered with him for years, had the utmost confidence in his medical abilities, and trusted him implicitly. It was highly unlikely that they would resist his advice to be admitted to hospital.

Chapter 7 of the report discusses the issue of drugs. Here the inquiry was aided by expert evidence by Professor Henry McQuay MD FRCA, Professor of Pain Relief in the University of Oxford; Professor Kevin Park, Professor of Pharmacology and Therapeutics in the University of Liverpool; and Dr Grenville. The report points out that diamorphine, which is twice as potent as morphine when given by intravenous injection (that is, straight into the bloodstream), changes within thirty seconds into morphine in the body, so toxicological tests cannot establish which type of drug was administered. But the available evidence points to the overwhelming likelihood that, in his years at Hyde, Shipman's choice was diamorphine. Morphine works by binding to the receptors (sensory nerve endings) that carry messages to the brain. It must be transported in the bloodstream to the brain and the spinal cord, where the receptors are situated. Intravenous injection is the quickest mode of transportation. Intramuscular injection is much slower, and oral administration slower still.

The principal effect of morphine is to give relief from pain, but it also causes euphoria (exaggerated elation); vasodilatation (dilation of the walls of blood vessels); and respiratory depression, which can slow the rate of breathing and ultimately breathing altogether.

Morphine injections come ready-mixed as a transparent liquid in various strengths, in little glass pots (ampoules); they are administered by a syringe. When diamorphine is used, the powder containing it has to be mixed with sterile water for it to be available for injection. It dissolves easily, and with an intramuscular injection the smaller the volume used the less uncomfortable it is for the patient.

Ideally, the drug should be used in the smallest quantities to give the required relief from pain or distress; that is, titrated against the patient's problem. With intramuscular injection, titration is not possible, and such injection should not be resorted to except where the patient is in severe pain and has veins which have collapsed.

The nature of a fatal dose of morphine or diamorphine obviously varies according not only to the amount given but other factors, such as the patient's habituation to the drug, age, size, and general state of health. To a fit, normal person, not habituated, Professor McQuay estimated it to be 60 milligrams morphine and 30 milligrams diamorphine administered over a minute; Dr Grenville felt 40 milligrams and 20 milligrams would suffice. With such a person, Professor McQuay expected breathing to stop within one minute and death to follow within five minutes owing to lack of oxygen to the brain.

One can picture the modus operandi of Shipman about to embark on one of numerous expeditions to kill a patient. He would measure out what he believed to be a lethal dose, add sterile water, put the phial in his medical bag, and then embark on his deadly mission. The patient would possibly be told that it was an injection for flu, or one containing an antibiotic or vitamins. She or he would then almost always drift off into a peaceful everlasting sleep in beloved home surroundings. Very occasionally Shipman would underestimate the necessary dosage, and the result could be tragic in another way. Mrs Renate Overton was injected by Shipman on 18 February 1994 with sufficient diamorphine to cause her to become unconscious and survive in a persistent vegetative state for fourteen months.[89] Shipman must have used less of the drug than he usually did or underestimated the amount needed to kill his patient, a robust forty-seven-year-old. She had been kept alive by the intervention of paramedics. He was fortunate in that his treatment of his patient, which even according to his own lying version was very negligent, was not investigated.

Professor McQuay considered that a lethal dose of pethidine would be of the order of five hundred milligrams for a non-habituated person. In the nineteen-seventies this would have entailed the injection of five ampules. The conclusion reached at the inquiry was that it was unlikely that Shipman used that drug to kill.[90]

In his Hyde years Shipman certainly injected chlorpromazine (Largactil), an antipsychotic drug used to manage agitated states and pain in patients with terminal illness. A lethal dose would have required a large, very painful intramuscular injection. The conclusion reached by the inquiry was that Shipman could not have resorted to this mode of murder. But, as with morphine, he could have administered a sublethal dose which might have contributed to the death of a particular frail patient.

Dame Janet Smith, in deciding on individual cases of possible murder of a patient,[91] had in the vast majority of instances statements of witnesses taken by the inquiry team, death-registration documents, and at least some surgery records. Many files contained statements by witnesses taken during the police investigation, cremation certificates, medical records, and expert evidence. There were also a variety of documents, such as records of nursing homes, telephone billings, and police and ambulance records. There were very few medical records before 1992 but many after then. In general, the older the case, the fewer the documents and the less detailed the recollection of witnesses. In some cases Dame Janet obtained oral evidence; in most she had to base her decision on written statements and documentary evidence.

Apart from those among the fifteen whom Shipman had been convicted of murdering, the police could point to only three patients in whose body tissues traces of morphine had been found. Shipman would not give evidence. Dame Janet decided that she would have to make decisions very largely based on inferences from circumstantial evidence; and that her confidence in drawing such inferences would be greatly increased if she found that a patient had died in circumstances strikingly similar to those in which the jury had found that Shipman had murdered his patients. She wrote: 'It is universally recognised that people do tend to repeat their patterns of conduct, good, bad and indifferent. We all have propensities to behave in certain ways, just as we have traits of personality. In a civil action, a judge is allowed to take a person's propensities into account rather more freely than is permitted in a criminal trial. A public inquiry is neither a criminal trial nor a civil action. My task in this Phase of the Inquiry has been to find out what

Shipman has done. . . . If I formed the view that he carried out a killing in a particular way on one occasion, I felt free to infer that he might have done something similar on other occasions, either before or after that occasion. I began by analysing the circumstances of the 15 cases in which Shipman had been convicted of murder.'[92]

The jury had found that Shipman had given a large injection of opiate to each victim, whose death was not imminent, not for therapeutic purposes. It must therefore have inferred that Shipman had in every case intended to kill. She, Dame Janet, would therefore properly infer the same intention in similar circumstances.

The striking features of the circumstances surrounding the convictions, she concluded, were the proximity of Shipman, physically and in time, to the death of the victim; the victim's appearance in death; and the sudden and unexpected nature of the death. Only with Joan Melia did the Crown not show a close association between Shipman's contact with the victim and her death. Many of the victims were found dead, sitting peacefully in a chair or on a sofa, or lying on a sofa or in bed, as if asleep. None of the patients was terminally ill. In no case had Shipman been summoned through a sudden and serious deterioration in the health of the patient. All the deaths were sudden and not expected by family and friends. The positions the deceased were found in, according to Dr Grenville, were one might expect as the consequence of a lethal dose of a strong opiate administered intravenously. In cases considered at the Inquiry the positions were regarded as indicative, though not strongly probative, of guilt.

It is very rare for a patient who is not terminally ill or threatened by a sudden, life-threatening illness to die during a general practitioner's visit. Yet six of the fifteen Shipman murdered did so in the course of three years. The jury must have concluded that he had killed them. Dame Janet found a large number of sudden and unexpected deaths of Shipman's patients when he was present. It was reasonable to infer that he probably killed them, unless other evidence suggested the contrary.

It is also most unusual, the report continues, for a patient, not terminally ill, to be found dead shortly after the visit by her or his doctor. Were death to be imminent, the doctor would arrange for the admission of the patient to hospital. An occasional death in these circumstances might not be suspicious; frequent such deaths, such as the seven among the fifteen whom Shipman at his trial was found to have murdered, justifies a finding that the doctor probably killed the patient. Many of the deaths probed in the Inquiry were of this nature.

It is quite unusual, though it could occasionally happen, for a doctor to find a patient dead at home. According to Shipman, it happened to

25 Sir Alexander Cockburn

26 Dr Marcel Pettiot: a modern Bluebeard

27 Lord Chief Baron Pollock

28 George Henry Lamson

(From a drawing by P B Whelpley)

29 Inside the Old Bailey at the trial of Dr George Henry Lamson, 1882

30 Sir Henry Hawkins and his dog Jack

31 Lord Herschell, out of office

32 Montagu Williams

33 Dr John Bodkin Adams: the classic enigma

34 Mr Justice (later Lord) Patrick Devlin, the presiding judge

35 Sir Reginald Manningham-Buller, the Attorney-General

36 Geoffrey Lawrence QC, leading counsel for the defence

37 Lord Scarman

38 Dr Harold Shipman: apparently liked to kill his victims – mostly elderly women – on Mondays, Tuesdays and Fridays between 1pm and 7pm *(Picture: PictureNET Africa)*

39 Dr Harold Shipman's victims.
Top row (from left) Winnifred Mellor, Kathleen Grundy, Irene Turner, Jean Lilley
Middle row (from left) Laura Kathleen Wagster, Lizzie Adams, Bianka Pomfret, Joan Melia
Bottom row (from left) Marie West, Maureen Alice Ward, Norah Nuttall and Pamela Hillier
(Picture: Reuters)

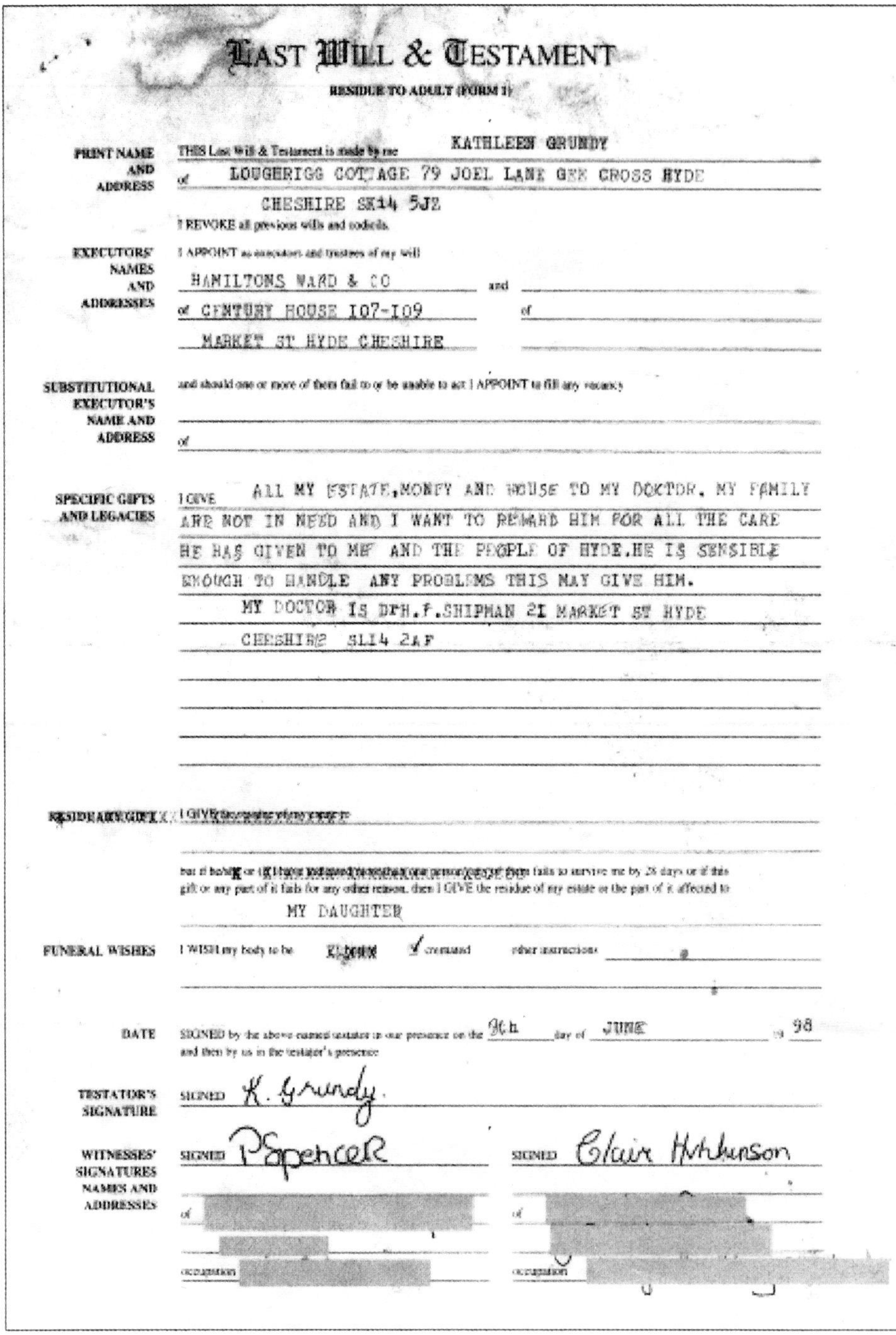

LAST WILL & TESTAMENT

RESIDUE TO ADULT (FORM 1)

PRINT NAME AND ADDRESS
THIS Last Will & Testament is made by me KATHLEEN GRUNDY
of LOUGHRIGG COTTAGE 79 JOEL LANE GEE CROSS HYDE
CHESHIRE SK14 5JZ
I REVOKE all previous wills and codicils.

EXECUTORS' NAMES AND ADDRESSES
I APPOINT as executors and trustees of my will
HAMILTONS WARD & CO and
of CENTURY HOUSE 107-109 of
MARKET ST HYDE CHESHIRE

SUBSTITUTIONAL EXECUTOR'S NAME AND ADDRESS
and should one or more of them fail to or be unable to act I APPOINT to fill any vacancy
of

SPECIFIC GIFTS AND LEGACIES
I GIVE ALL MY ESTATE,MONEY AND HOUSE TO MY DOCTOR. MY FAMILY
ARE NOT IN NEED AND I WANT TO REWARD HIM FOR ALL THE CARE
HE HAS GIVEN TO ME AND THE PEOPLE OF HYDE.HE IS SENSIBLE
ENOUGH TO HANDLE ANY PROBLEMS THIS MAY GIVE HIM.
MY DOCTOR IS DR H.F.SHIPMAN 21 MARKET ST HYDE
CHESHIRE SL14 2AF

RESIDUARY GIFT I GIVE

but if he/she or (if I have indicated more than one person) any of them fails to survive me by 28 days or if this gift or any part of it fails for any other reason, then I GIVE the residue of my estate or the part of it affected to
MY DAUGHTER

FUNERAL WISHES I WISH my body to be ✓ cremated other instructions

DATE SIGNED by the above named testator in our presence on the 9th day of JUNE 19 98
and then by us in the testator's presence

TESTATOR'S SIGNATURE SIGNED K. Grundy.

WITNESSES' SIGNATURES NAMES AND ADDRESSES
SIGNED P Spencer SIGNED Claire Hutchinson
of [redacted] of [redacted]
occupation [redacted] occupation [redacted]

40 The forged will in the name of Kathleen Grundy, leaving her entire estate to Shipman

41 Margaret Elizabeth Rheeder: her husband died a slow death

42 Lord Russell of Killowen
(From the painting by J S Sargent RA in the National Portrait Gallery. Copyright photograph: National Portrait Gallery.)

43 Lord Alverstone

him quite frequently. This was regarded by the Inquiry as highly suspicious.

Dame Janet found that 'Shipman became a plausible and accomplished liar'.[93] One of his most common lies was found to be for him to state on a cremation form that a person had been present at the moment of death in addition to, or instead of, himself. This would be to avoid any suspicion of unlawful conduct by him. Another of his frequent lies was that he saw a patient within fourteen days before death. It could have been to deter the registrar of deaths from questioning Shipman's capacity to certify the cause of death, which could lead to a reference to the coroner and a postmortem examination. Such a lie, Dame Janet found, could be caused for other, non-suspicious reasons too; so only if it fitted in with other signs of suspicious death should it be regarded as adding a little weight to the evidence.

Shipman had a number of ploys, the report states, to discourage relatives from insisting there be a postmortem examination where the law and common sense demanded there be one.

As has been shown, to avert suspicion over the sudden and unexpected deaths of the vast majority of his victims, Shipman lied about their state of health. The inquiry concluded that backdating entries on the computer was highly probative of guilt. So, too, with the many fabricated handwritten records.

There were a number of cases in which there was no distinct evidence of Shipman's presence at the home of a patient at the time of her or his death, and no evidence of morphine in the tissues of the body. In some instances there were such remarkable changes to the medical records or lies on the cremation Form B that Dame Janet concluded that Shipman had murdered the patient. In other instances, all she could conclude was that there was a real suspicion that he had done so. She made her decisions without imposing any onus of proof or requiring any standard of proof, such as that of beyond a reasonable doubt as in criminal cases or on a balance of probabilities as in civil cases.

Decisions were made with almost five hundred deaths. In some cases, particularly more recent ones, the quality of the evidence was so high that a clear conclusion could be reached. In others, Dame Janet said that she felt sure Shipman had killed. In yet others, she said that he probably had. Relatives who sought compensation from the Criminal Injuries Compensation Authority had only to satisfy it on the civil-law standard of balance of probabilities.

There were many cases where the death of the patient was found to be natural; some in which it was very likely or at least likely it was natural.

Finally, there were cases in which no conclusion could be reached one way or the other.

When it came to terminally ill patients receiving injections of morphine or diamorphine for the relief of pain, suspicion arose if death occurred shortly after an injection. A lethal dose of opiate, if given intravenously, will kill within a few minutes; if given intramuscularly, it will kill within an hour. A drug may lawfully be given to relieve pain even though it might shorten life. And it can be very difficult to assess the right amount to give to a patient with intractable pain. The conclusion reached in the inquiry was that if the drug did hasten the death of a patient of Shipman's, the inference should not be drawn, without other supporting evidence, that he had intended to kill. All that could be said was that there was a suspicion that he might have. The hope was expressed that relatives would find some consolation in knowing that if he did hasten death, it was not for long.

Distressed relatives of a murdered patient on several occasions complained to the police that money and other property, particularly jewellery, was missing from the patient's home. A belief that Shipman stole it could not be substantiated, however.

Professor Baker's statistical analysis referred to above was not used by Dame Janet to reach her findings, but his views, though based on very limited information, were regarded as an item of expert evidence. She reached this striking conclusion, though: 'I must acknowledge that Professor Baker's overall conclusion about the number of deaths attributable to Shipman gave me some reassurance, as I found more and more cases of murder. Had it not been his statistical analysis, I might have doubted the validity of my own conclusions. They might have seemed unthinkable. As it has turned out, our conclusions are broadly compatible, despite the fact that the processes by which we reached our conclusions were very different.'[94]

In chapters 10, 11 and 12 of the report there is a detailed analysis of Shipman's unlawful activities during his medical career. His period as a medical officer at the Pontefract General Infirmary from August 1971 to February 1974 yielded no evidence of his killing a patient.

Then came his time as a general practitioner in Todmorden that ended with his partners insisting he leave the practice for abusing pethidine, which he had obtained illegally, and his convictions by the magistrates in Halifax on 13 February 1976. There was no suspicion of his having killed a patient in 1974, but he committed a serious crime on 21 August by unlawfully injecting Mrs (now Professor) Elaine Oswald with a drug, probably pethidine. She collapsed. Shipman gave cardiac massage and the 'kiss of life' and summoned an ambulance. While he had not intended to kill his patient, possibly he had wished to involve the unwilling patient in some sexual activity. Probably Shipman got a very nasty shock. There was no evidence of his having embarked on such a venture again.

In 1975 and in 1976 until Shipman became a clinical medical officer in the Durham area there were twenty-one deaths with which he had some association. In only one was the conclusion reached that he was responsible. The patient was suffering from terminal cancer, and the intravenous injection that was given was probably with the primary intention of ending her life. There were a further six deaths, three occurring on the same day, in which suspicion was aroused that Shipman might have caused them.

In the following career of Shipman at Newton Aycliffe Health Centre in the Durham area from 2 February 1976 to 30 September 1977 there was no suggestion of concern over his conduct. In any event, he had no access to controlled drugs.

When one turns to the Donneybrook years (1977–91), however, one encounters thirteen years of chilling murderous activities. The report states that on his arrival at Hyde Shipman was probably extremely cautious about the ways in which he initially obtained controlled drugs. Very likely he used the method least vulnerable to detection — to take drugs left after a cancer death, if need be saying he was removing them for destruction. The Inquiry revealed a remarkably close correlation between opportunities to obtain drugs prescribed for the terminally ill and his murders.

In the three months of 1977 covering the opening of Shipman's practice in Hyde there was no cause to believe he indulged in his homicidal activities. He was found to have murdered four patients in 1978. The early part of 1979 was devoid of killings. He was suspected of causing four deaths in the rest of that year. Towards the end of 1979 he killed Jack Shelmerdine by an intramuscular injection of an opiate. In 1980 there was a suspicion of one murder. The next murder the Inquiry actually found Shipman committed was in April 1981, that of Mary Slater (84), who lived in sheltered accommodation. It was followed by that of Elizabeth Ashworth, who was in pretty good health, in August 1981, significantly the day after the natural death of a patient from cancer. There were suspicions about three deaths in September and October that year and four in 1982, but the only positive finding of the next killing was as late as January 1983. It was of Percy Ward (80), who was extremely ill and near to his end: a pretty 'safe' dispatch.

There was a suspected murder in May 1983. It was followed by a clear one in June, that of Moira Fox (77), who lived in sheltered accommodation. This was the first recorded case of Shipman's subsequent common practice of disguising the intravenous administration of a deadly dose of a drug as the taking of a blood sample.

The period from 1984 to 1989 reflected a change from sporadic murders to regular ones of eight to twelve a year, with no long intervals between them at least until 1988.

The killing of Miss Fox was followed by that on 7 January 1984 of Dorothy Tucker (51), obese and hardly able to walk. This was one of the very rare cases where Shipman apparently used the slowly working intramuscular injection on a patient not ill in bed. Possibly he could not find a vein in his overweight patient; he took a chance. An active patient might raise an alarm before the drug did its deadly work. There was no risk with a bedridden patient. It is possible, though, that Shipman actually tried to give an intravenous injection, but the needle slipped out of the vein and the drug entered Mrs Tucker's system subcutaneously — beneath the skin. This was also the first of the number of cases in which Shipman ensured that the room of death was at a very high temperature. Possibly the object was to make it difficult for a pathologist to make a reliable estimate of the time the patient died.

On 8 February 1984 came the killing of Gladys Roberts (78), who lived alone. It was an early example of a very common ploy for Shipman: to say he had called an ambulance and was arranging admission to a hospital, but the death of the patient resulted in the cancellation of the arrangement.

There are so many subsequent findings of murder of patients by Shipman that I must confine myself to a mere mention of the number unless there was something of special significance in what he did. On 15 April 1984 Joseph Bardsley (83) was killed and on 24 April Winifred Arrowsmith (70). On 21 September came the murder of Mary Winterbottom (76), one of many cases in which Shipman lied in saying he tried unsuccessfully to resuscitate a patient who was having a heart attack. It was one of several instances where Shipman had removed the dentures of a patient who had not died naturally. The possible explanation of this odd conduct given by Dr Grenville was that the deep sleep caused by a lethal dose of opiate might cause the dentures to become dislodged, resulting in the patient gagging and struggling, so interfering with the intended smooth progress towards death.

Ada Ashworth (87) was murdered on 27 November 1984. She had been well, but was found dead, seated upright in her chair.

In the Christmas period of 1982 came three killings: those of Joseph Everall (80) on 17 December, Edith Wibberley (76) on 18 December and Eileen Cox (72) on 24 December.

There were eleven murders of patients in 1985, eight in 1986 and eight in 1987. In 1988 there were eleven. After six patients had been murdered by 16 February, there was no further killing until 18 September. Possibly Shipman had been worried that the sudden deaths of four of his patients dispatched in one week in February might have aroused suspicions.

In 1989 Shipman killed twelve patients, the last on 6 November, when his victim was Joseph Wilcockson (85). He had a varicose ulcer that was dressed periodically by the district nurse. When she called in around noon to dress it, she found him sitting in his usual chair, dead. He was still warm. Shipman had visited his patient, almost certainly after 10.30 am. He had probably only narrowly avoided being caught red-handed by the district nurse. Very likely Shipman had had a bad scare, for ten months went by before he resumed his malign activities.

The next victim, Dorothy Rowarth, hastened on her way on 18 September 1990, was terminally ill with cancer, and so was a 'safe' candidate for elimination. The final murder for the year was a little more dangerous, for Mary Dudley was only sixty-nine, but she did have heart trouble. Shipman created a false medical record showing chest pain during the prior fortnight.

The last year at the Donneybrook practice, 1991, was homicide-free. Shipman's tally of murders in his thirteen years in the practice was seventy-one, and there were an additional thirty suspected ones.

Finally came the period between January 1992 and the arrest of Shipman on 7 September 1998, a period when he was a sole practitioner, up to 23 August 1992 in Donneybrook House and after that in his own rooms in Market Street, Hyde, immediately adjacent to the large Norwest Co-op Pharmacy. The tally of murders in these six and three-quarter years was the staggering one hundred and forty-three, with a further ten suspected ones. The first victim was Monica Sparkes (72), on 7 October 1992. In February 1993 Shipman resumed his regular pattern of killing, in much the same way as before. Almost surely he now felt free of the constraints imposed by practice at the Donneybrook surgery. It was clear that he was using thirty milligram ampoules of diamorphine, which he was able to obtain freely in the names of patients, mostly those he murdered. 1993 witnessed sixteen killings.

Every now and then Shipman had a close shave, causing him to desist from his diabolic behaviour for a while. The case of Renate Overton, injected ineffectually on 18 February 1994, discussed above, must have left him feeling vulnerable. He had his usual extraordinary luck when the coroner issued a certificate of cremation.

In 1994 there were eleven murders, in 1995 thirty, and in 1996 also thirty. On 6 June 1996 Shipman had obtained an incredibly large haul of 12 000 milligrams of diamorphine from a pharmacy in the name of Keith Harrison, a cancer sufferer who had died a natural death that day. It was enough to end the lives of some three hundred and sixty healthy adults. Small wonder that in the following two months Shipman murdered eleven patients. His techniques of concealing his criminal conduct became more sophisticated around this time.

The number of murders in 1997 reached the astounding figure of thirty-seven. In the first three months of 1998 another fifteen were killed, seven in February alone. What happened after that, leading to Shipman's arrest on 7 September 1998 and eventual conviction of murdering fifteen patients, has already been recounted.

In chapter 13 of her brilliant, engrossing report on a splendid investigation, written in a way that readers not trained in law or medicine can easily follow, Dame Janet Smith analysed Shipman's character and motives in committing his almost unbelievable number of murders. She would have wished to obtain thorough psychological and psychiatric assessments, but Shipman's refusal to participate in the Inquiry, and his continued denial of responsibility for deaths of patients in the face of overwhelming evidence of guilt, forced recourse to only such materials as were otherwise available.

What you and I would have liked to know is why Shipman committed these dreadful deeds that harrow the soul and freeze the blood. What caused him to take the constant time-consuming detailed care to despatch his victims?

A team of experienced forensic psychiatrists from the Institute of Psychiatry, King's College, University of London was consulted: Professor John Gunn, Professor of Forensic Psychiatry; Professor Pamela Taylor, Professor of Special Hospital Psychiatry; Dr Clive Meux, Honorary Senior Lecturer in Forensic Psychiatry; and Dr Alec Buchanan, Clinical Senior Lecturer in Forensic Psychiatry. They were unable to carry out the examinations that normally precede the preparation of a full psychiatric assessment, but they read the relevant material assembled by the inquiry team and had a full discussion with Dame Janet, Dr Esmail and counsel to the inquiry.

The psychiatrists, with the available materials, were unable to reach any conclusions on the explanation for Shipman's conduct. All that Dame Janet herself felt able to do was to draw attention to aspects of his behaviour that might throw some light on his personality and motivation. Her views were reached by drawing common-sense inferences from evidence.

Only with Mrs Kathleen Grundy was there any evidence that Shipman was moved by monetary gain. Very few patients left him money, and then it was always a modest sum. On the other hand, he was acquisitive, and at times asked for an item of property that had belonged to a patient he had just killed. There had been much suspicion that Shipman had pilfered money and property from the homes of victims, but the evidence was inconclusive, and in any event it could not have been a reason for murder.

The murder of Kathleen Grundy by Shipman on 24 June 1998, the forging of her will and the typing of various related documents by him have already been related. How did the report of the Inquiry view these matters? It is pointed out there by Dame Janet Smith[95] that Shipman knew Kathleen Grundy quite well, for not only had she been his patient for many years but both had been involved in local affairs. 'Mrs Grundy was very proud of her daughter and grandchildren and Shipman must have known that Mrs Woodruff [her daughter] was a solicitor.' The report continues: 'The forging of Mrs Grundy's will led directly to Shipman's downfall. I have little doubt that his killing of her would not have been detected but for his forgery of her will. However, the will was so obvious a forgery and so entirely uncharacteristic of Mrs Grundy that Mrs Woodruff was bound to investigate it. In fact, she reported her suspicions about the will to the police. The forgery was soon uncovered and the rest is history.'[96]

Dame Janet and the forensic psychiatrists who had been consulted considered that Shipman could not rationally have thought he would get away with Kathleen Grundy's estate. Discovery was inevitable. While it seems that Shipman planned the forgery of the will in advance of the murder, his intention was more complex than simply to get the money. The psychiatrists said that it is not uncommon for serial killers to be discovered because they draw attention to themselves in an obvious way: the pressure becomes too great and some means must be found to bring the crimes to a halt or of relieving guilt. The absence of a confession is not inconsistent with a desire to be stopped from killing. But the psychiatrists stressed that this was only one of several possible explanations for Shipman's actions; too little was known of his psyche. To Dame Janet, Shipman was raising a flag to his conduct. The conflict between whatever drove him to kill and his fear of detection must have driven him to the edge of breakdown. 'No longer in touch with reality, I think he might then have devised a fantasy plan, by which he could obtain Mrs Grundy's money, run away and stop being a doctor. The plan, rationally considered, was bound to fail, but it would offer him a fantasy future and a way to stop himself from killing.'[97]

The report states[98] that there did not appear any overtly sadistic or erotic cause for Shipman's crimes. There was not one of the features that commonly actuate murderers. To find an explanation one must look within his personality, as revealed by his actions and descriptions by people who knew him.

In Hyde, the report runs,[99] Shipman had the reputation of being a good and caring doctor, and was respected by his fellow medical practitioners; he was held in very high esteem by the overwhelming majority of his patients, who appear to have regarded him as the best doctor in the town; his register was always full and there was a constant waiting list. Many patients said he 'always had time for them', including words of a personal nature — he never hurried them out, even if it meant his surgeries overran. Paticularly elderly patients and their families were grateful for his willingness to pay visits at home when other doctors might insist that patients be brought to the surgery. This preparedness to conduct domiciliary consultations could facilitate the commission of his nefarious activities, but there must also have been many occasions when this consideration for his patients was not a cover for these activities. Still, there was a 'deeply sinister aspect' to the way Shipman created his reputation of 'an old-fashioned family doctor' who willingly paid professional visits at the homes of patients and even called unexpectedly when in the area of a patient; and who let it be known that he preferred an elderly patient to die 'with dignity' at home instead of amid the 'hustle and bustle' of a hospital ward. In these ways many opportunities to kill with apparent impunity arose.

Shipman was most industrious. By 1998 he had a list of 3 046 patients, far greater than the average of under 2 500 of single-handed GPs in Tameside. He was a regular attender at continuing education sessions. Seldom did he fail to visit a patient on the day of request. Several members of the Donneybrook staff moved with him to his new premises at Market Street.

Shipman's one professional failure was to keep his records well — except entries associated with a murder.

While Shipman was involved in many local activities in Todmorden and later in Hyde, worked with the St John Ambulance Brigade in Hyde, was active in medical politics and was a school governor, he nevertheless had very few friends.

Many patients described him as having a wonderful bedside manner, especially with the elderly. He made many feel he was a real friend — 'yet he would kill them'.[100] Many of the families of his victims said that his usually kind and sympathetic attitude disappeared on the death of their relative, and he would then be curt and sometimes make hurtful remarks.

'Other well-masked traits of Shipman's personality were aggression, conceit, arrogance and contempt for those whom he considered to be his intellectual inferiors.'[101] He took delight in humiliating those he felt were not doing their job properly. These traits caused many to dislike him. Still, a great number of his patients accorded him adulation.

An important trait of Shipman's was his 'profound dishonesty', shown by his obtaining drugs by illegal means; he was also 'an accomplished and inventive liar'.[102]

Dame Janet Smith concluded, though, that this 'unattractive constellation of traits' is 'not particularly uncommon'.[103] They cannot of themselves explain why Shipman became a serial killer. If he had unresolved grief over the death of his mother this would not account for it. The psychiatrists thought that his conduct was that of a diseased mind, but his refusal to speak to them made it impossible to say what it was. Tentatively, Dame Janet concluded that there was some evidence that Shipman had a morbid interest in death or derived pleasure from killing or felt compelled to search for a victim. 'There is some evidence that he is an addictive personality and it is possible that killing was a form of addiction. I do not think he can have had any concept of the value or sanctity of human life. I regret to say that I can shed very little light on why Shipman killed his patients. I do, however, think that it is possible to gain some insight into his thinking from an examination of which patients he chose to kill.'*

The report goes on to point out that Shipman killed mainly elderly women living alone and some men, most elderly and living alone. In general, his victims were in poor health. He seemed to think he knew when a patient ought to die. As most of his early murders were of patients close to death or very ill, perhaps he persuaded himself that these actions were justifiable. Certainly there was little risk of detection of such homicides.

Shipman continued to kill terminally ill patients and also those suffering from acute life-threatening conditions possibly justifying his conduct. So too with his murders of patients who said they did not want

* § 13.57. Dr Thomas Stuttaford, medical correspondent of *The Times*, wrote on 20 July 2002: 'medically, his disturbed and heartless behaviour could be more accurately described as a manifestation of an impulse control disorder, of the same group of personality disorders as repetitive arson, and kleptomania. . . . Shipman was certainly impulsive, without conscience, indifferent to the suffering caused to others, had neither guilt, nor compassion, and has expressed no regret. In this respect he had all the features of what most people describe as a psychopath.'

'to go on'. But he was also particularly willing to kill the bereaved and patients with chronic conditions requiring much medical attention or whom he seemed to regard as a nuisance or who annoyed him.

While the murders which were initially not frequent increased in frequency, there were interruptions apparently dictated by Shipman's fear of detection. When he resumed killing, he did so gradually. This conduct suggests he was able to restrain himself from murdering. After 1994 his rate of killing gradually increased, reaching its peak in 1997 and early 1998, which is consistent with the hypothesis he had become addicted to the conduct. Then came his downfall flowing from the death of Kathleen Grundy.

The conclusion reached in the report was that of the 493 patients whose deaths were investigated 200 had been murdered. To this number, the fifteen of which Shipman had been convicted had to be added. Of the 215 victims, 171 were women. His first victim was Eva Lyons, murdered in March 1975 on the eve of her seventy-first birthday. The oldest victim was the ninety-three-year-old Anne Cooper and the youngest the forty-one-year-old Peter Lewis. There were also 45 cases, mostly in the early years of his practice, in which there was real cause to suspect he might have murdered the patient, but there was insufficient evidence for a definite conclusion. A further two hundred deaths were 'highly suspicious'. Dame Janet Smith found that the similarity between her estimate of the number of killings and that of Professor Baker was truly remarkable, bearing in mind that his inquiry was a statistical one, whereas hers was without regard to statistical information.[104]

To Dame Janet it was deeply disturbing that the systems that should have safeguarded Shipman's patients or at least detected misconduct failed to operate satisfactorily; that his murders did not arouse suspicion for so many years; and that, had it not been for his grossly incompetent forgery of Kathleen Grundy's will, it was not clear whether his crimes would ever have been detected. Shipman had damaged the good name of the medical profession and led many people to distrust their family doctor. In the next stage of the inquiry the reasons for the failure of existing procedures to reveal homicide would have to be considered; ways should be found to ensure that unexpected or unexplained deaths are reported and properly investigated; measures should be found for improving the ways of ensuring control of drugs; effective systems should be identified for monitoring death rates and for encouraging those genuinely concerned about possible medical misconduct to express their concerns to proper quarters. Already by the time the report was published certain reforms had taken place.[105] It is necessary for me to say, however, that to keep Shipman's terrible tally of homicides in proper perspective it is impossible to believe that a medical mass murderer of this dimension ever existed previously (other than, possibly, in the Nazi concentration camps) or will ever exist again. There have been notorious medical mass murderers. Save for Mariel Petiot, who admitted to killing sixty-three would-be fugitives from the Nazis in his surgery in Paris from 1941 to 1944 in order to collect their belongings,[106] those I have come across, such as William Palmer, Neill Cream, Edward William Pritchard and Arthur Waite, contented themselves with but a handful of victims.

Shipman had betrayed the trust of patients and their families 'to an extent . . . unparalleled in history. . . . The way in which Shipman could kill, face the relatives and walk away unsuspected would be dismissed as fanciful if described in a work of fiction.'[107]

On the day of publication of *Death Disguised*, in which Dame Janet Smith found that at least 215 patients had been murdered by Harold Shipman, church bells were rung 215 times in the town of Hyde in their memory.*

* Helen Carter and David Ward in *The Guardian* 20 July 2002. According to early reports in the press (I have benefited from those by Richard Ford) in July 2002 Shipman was imprisoned in Frankland maximum security prison in the county of Durham, one of the some six hundred dangerous offenders there. He was a model prisoner whose main duty was to work as an orderly in the hospital wing. He had learned braille and translated almost all the Harry Potter books into braille. He still denied committing his crimes. On 15 May 2003 the English tabloid *Daily Mail* reported that Shipman was attending elderly patients in the gaol hospital as a porter, pusher of trolleys and collector of meals, and that he was said to be arrogant, sarcastic and in total denial of his crimes. There was an outcry by relatives of his victims on receiving this information. Shipman is one of twenty-three prisoners who have been told they will never be released from prison because of their heinous crimes. Among them are Ian Brady, the 'Moors' murderer; Rosemary West who murdered ten girls; Peter Sutcliffe, the 'Yorkshire Ripper', convicted of murdering thirteen women; and Denis Wilson, who murdered at least fifteen homosexual men. Myra Hindley, the other 'Moors' murderer, died on 15 November 2002 at the age of sixty, having been thirty-six years behind bars. While Shipman's number of victims seems not to have been the greatest among those recorded in the world, it is by far the greatest in the history of Britain.

Murder to benefit from an insurance policy

MARGARET ELIZABETH RHEEDER — *slow death for Ben*

The call of patriotism dictates that I start with the South African Margaret Elizabeth Rheeder. She was hanged in 1958 for the murder of her husband Ben through the administration of poison. (I am unable to find a word, parallel to uxoricide, to describe the murder of a husband. There is the adjective (rare, according to the *Oxford English Dictionary*) mariticidal, meaning husband-slaying.) She was the third woman to suffer this fate in our country for homicide by poisoning, the earlier ones being Daisy de Melker (of whom more has appeared earlier) and Maria Lee.

Margaret's given names and her maiden name Harker — and those of her siblings — were misleading, for she was of Afrikaner stock and her home language was always Afrikaans. Born on 6 September 1922 to Grace Maud Harker, who was married to her cousin, Clarence Wilfred Harker, Margaret had an early life of unremitting hardship. Grace bore eight children to Clarence. On the death of Clarence she married Cornelius Share, and bore him five children. But for all the grinding poverty of her family, Margaret was neat and clean, and always remained so. On her father's death when she was twelve she and her sisters Gwen and Olga were sent to an orphanage. At sixteen she had reached standard four at school and was engaged by a kind Paarl couple as a sort of maid-housekeeper. From this post she moved on turning twenty-one, ending as housekeeper in a Knysna hotel. Then she met a young barman, married him, and had a daughter by him. During his periods of incarceration in gaol, she enjoyed sexual relations with other men. Unlike Daisy de Melker, she liked men. The birth of a second daughter caused greater poverty for the family and the dread by Margaret of her children being sent to an orphanage. She divorced her errant husband and cast her eyes around. Soon she met Ben Rheeder, in the throes of a divorce action, who also had two young daughters. He was a checker at the Railways at the Port Elizabeth docks and was occupying a double-storied house at 24 Dyke Road, Algoa Park. To Margaret he looked a good catch: a sound man in sound employment, healthy and only nine years older than her. They were married on 6 September 1952. Initially a happy union, it soon degenerated into one characterized by incessant quarrels. One evening Rheeder assaulted his wife seriously; it was generally believed that he had caught her in a compromising situation with a lodger. At this stage Margaret became a woman who spoke too much, a sufferer from logorrhoea, one whose tongue, as Benjamin Bennett put it in his analysis of her conduct that led to her trial, helped her hang.[108] To her sister Gwen Strydom and Gwen's husband Willem, and also to her brother Kenneth, she said again and again she wanted to give Ben a 'slow death': she needed a husband who was not 'ou afgelekte bene' (old licked-off bones). She attempted to entice a young lodger. When she told the lodger that she had tried to get rid of Ben by putting rat poison in his sandwiches, but Ben had found them tasting odd and thrown them away, he asked her why she did not simply divorce Ben. The answer was she would not let another woman have her things and her being left penniless. Margaret told the lodger that if Ben died she wanted to marry him. But it takes two to entwine. The young man rejected her.

Margaret told others too that she wanted to give Ben 'a slow death'. She believed that when he died she would benefit from his life insurance with the South African Trade Union Assurance Society and a Railway pension and allowance. On 27 April 1957 she did a very foolish thing: she went to Kempston Pharmacy, some two miles away, to buy poison to rid her house of 'swarms of ants'. Now the pharmacist, A I Redhouse, recognized her as a fairly frequent cash customer. Once Margaret realized this she should have bought something innocuous. But she persisted in her original intention, probably as she was tight-fisted. So she walked out with a bottle of the then popular but highly poisonous Antexit (pronounced as two words). Redhouse warned her that it contained arsenic. She gave her correct name and address for the register of poisons and signed her name. Had she gone to a pharmacist far distant who did not know her and given a false name and address, it is possible that he might not have recognized a photograph of her and she would have got away with her crime.

On Monday 27 April Ben Rheeder became ill at work, vomiting. The next day he visited the Railway doctor, Dr Edmund Bloch, complaining of a sore shoulder. Dr Bloch diagnosed fibrositis and prescribed some pills. In the evening Ben was in greater pain. Dr Bloch now prescribed pethedine. On 2 May he was summoned to Ben's house, where his patient was complaining of vague pains in his limbs and nausea. He was given a prescription for nausea. Margaret knew that Dr Block didn't imagine she was poisoning her husband. The short trial run was successful, and now it was time for the real thing.

At four in the afternoon of 7 May, in response to Ben's desperate pleading before witnesses for medical help, Margaret asked Dr Bloch to call to attend to Ben's diarrhoea and vomiting. A careful examination disclosed nothing other than a slightly raised pulse rate. After giving Ben an injection of largital, an innocuous drug, Dr Bloch said he must go to hospital that evening, or at the latest the following morning for observation. Margaret knew she had to take a decisive step immediately. When kind neighbours called, they found Ben moaning of a burning pain and in a dreadful state. Margaret all the while showed no concern. She managed to get Ben to drink some Oxo. About ten in the evening Kenneth saw his sister give Ben some dark-coloured liquid. Soon after that he was dead. Dr Bloch was shocked at the unexpected death of his patient. He diagnosed the cause as acute gastroenteritis, fully understandable from Ben's symptoms. The coast seemed clear. Margaret, however, could not resist embroidering things with an incredible and disgraceful allegation before several friends that Dr Bloch had given Ben a deadly injection because he had his knife into him and all members of the National Party. But naturally she completely rejected the suggestion by concerned friends of 'exposing' the doctor by asking for a postmortem examination.

The benefits Margaret stood to gain from her husband's death amounted to £351 from superannuation and sick funds, and a widow's pension of £17 a month. (Her hopes of obtaining £135 from the insurance policy were dashed: it turned out to be in favour of Ben's first wife.) The benefits, small as they were, would help her en route to a third marriage. Talk of foul play, however, became incessant: the alleged rat poison in the sandwiches; the sudden fatal illness; her lack of concern over her husband's distress; the repeated desire to give him a slow death. The police investigated. They traced the pharmacist Redhouse. They then caused Ben's body to be exhumed for a postmortem examination. At the government chemical laboratories in Johannesburg Dr B W Marloch found in the viscera amounts of arsenic sufficient to cause several persons to die.

The trial of Margaret Rheeder for the murder of her husband began on 2 November 1957 in Port Elizabeth before Mr Justice A G Jennett and a jury of nine white males between the ages of twenty-five and sixty-five (as juries were then composed). For the Crown (the prosecution) appeared the Attorney-General of the Eastern Cape Division of the Supreme Court, Mr Lawrence C Barrett QC, with him Mr Michael Imber (later SC and Attorney-General of the Natal Provincial Division). For the defence appeared Mr J A F Nel, whose task was an unenviable one, as the case against the accused was overwhelming. In the witness box Margaret showed during the six hours of cross-examination that she had an innate shrewdness but some of her replies to questions made the prosecution's case even stronger. The expert evidence of Dr Reuben Turner, senior government pathologist, was damning. He explained to the jurors that samples of the deceased's hair showed that arsenic had started being administered eight or nine days before his death. The 1.11 grains in the liver must have come from an administration of the poison within twenty-four hours of death, possibly within six hours of it at the time Kenneth Harker saw his sister giving Ben a drink of Oxo.

Some of the evidence of the accused woman was preposterous, such as that her brother and sister and her sister's husband had lied in saying that she wanted to cause Ben a slow death, since 'they had no time' for her and wished to do her great harm.

The jurors returned a unanimous verdict of guilty of murder. Then came the question whether they found that there were extenuating circumstances. While the nature of these circumstances were not defined by legislation, there was general acceptance by the judges that they reduced the moral culpability of the accused. The jurors found that they existed, on the ground of the accused having endured 'a hellish life from her young days'. A judge was not required to accept a finding of extenuating circumstances and Mr Justice Jennett did not in this case of a cold, premeditated, excruciatingly painful murder by the administration of poison. Before she was hanged on 6 May 1958 Margaret Rheeder confessed her guilt.

Eugene Marie Chantrelle — *cultivated and learned linguist*

From Britain I select a few famous murders for gain from an insurance policy. Eugene Marie Chantrelle is still a reviled name in Scotland even though he left it for ever on 31 May 1878.[109] He was born in 1834 in Nantes, France, where he attended the local medical school. His father's financial collapse caused him to break his studies and adopt an aimless existence. Later he attended medical schools in Strasburg and Paris but failed to apply himself enough to qualify. In 1862 he emigrated to Britain to teach French, finally settling in Edinburgh in 1866. A cultivated and learned person, fluent as well in German and skilled in Latin and Greek, he taught mainly French but also these three languages. When teaching French at a private school, Newington Academy, in Edinburgh, he met a girl of fifteen years, Elizabeth Cullen Dyer. Chantrelle seduced her, resulting in her becoming pregnant and agreeing to marry him on 11 August 1868, two months before the birth of her child. Chantrelle turned out to be a drunken, debauched man who frequently assaulted his wife and threatened to kill her by poisoning her. The immoral life of Chantrelle resulted in his professional work diminishing greatly. On 18 October 1877 he took out an insurance policy on Elizabeth's life for a thousand pounds in the event of her accidental death. The insurance policy was against the expressed wish of Elizabeth, who told her mother that her life would now soon end. So it did. On 1 January 1878 Elizabeth, who had been well, went to bed early as she began to feel off colour. When her maid returned from her leave at about ten o'clock that night, Elizabeth complained that she was ill. At her mistress's request she gave her some lemonade and a piece of orange. The maid then left. On her return the next morning, she found her employer unconscious and moaning loudly. The gas heater was out and there was no smell of gas anywhere in the house. When the maid summoned Chantrelle, he asked her if she did not smell gas. Shortly afterwards there was a strong smell of it. Chantrelle called for Dr James Carmichael, who sent for the medical officer of the city, Dr Henry Littlejohn, to whom Chantrelle said that gas had escaped in his wife's bedroom. At the Royal Infirmary, where she had been taken, Elizabeth died that afternoon, the second of January 1878, without regaining consciousness. Then Professor Douglas Maclagan was summoned. After a careful examination he concluded that the deceased woman had died not from gas poisoning but from narcotic poisoning. A postmortem examination the next day by Maclagan and Littlejohn made it clear that death had not been caused by gas poisoning, but did not establish the presence of narcotic poison. The maid and Dr Carmichael, however, had noticed vomit on the nightdress and bedclothes of Elizabeth at her house. Examination of it showed clear evidence of opium.

On 7 May 1878 Chantrelle was tried for murder before Lord Justice-Clerk Moncreiff, the highest judge in criminal trials in Scotland. The prosecution team was headed by the Lord Advocate, William Watson (the Lord Advocate is the senior law officer of the Crown), who later became a great law lord. The defence was a powerful one, headed by John Trayner, who became a Scottish judge, Lord Trayner. But its task was a hopeless one. The trial, which lasted up to 10 May, resulted in the jury, after deliberating for just over an hour, returning a unanimous verdict of murder. On 31 May that year, 1878, Chantrelle was hanged, the first not to be executed in private, a result of the Capital Punishment Amendment Act 1868. Four young children, one a baby, were now orphans.

SIDNEY HARRY FOX — *truly a dreadful fellow*

To turn from this case of uxoricide to one of matricide: Sidney Harry Fox, a work-shy swindler, made out that his mother's death in her room in a hotel that had caught alight was due to suffocation and heart failure.[110] The famous forensic pathologist Sir Bernard Spilsbury, however, was satisfied that she had been strangled before the fire had started. Fox had insured his mother's life against accidental death. Clearly he had started the fire. He was convicted of the murder of his mother and executed in April 1930. Two years earlier he had tried unsuccessfully to cause the death of a Mrs Morse by turning on the gas in her room in her flat, having persuaded her to make a will and insure her life for a large amount, both in his favour. Truly a dreadful fellow.

ALICE HEWITT — *her tongue dug her grave*

Another case of matricide, not well known but of much interest, is that committed by Alice Hewitt on 26 March 1863 in Stockport, in the county of Cheshire.[111] Alice Hewitt (born Bailey), a widow, was living with one Holt as his apparent wife at 43 Great Egerton Street in the borough of Stockport. Residing with them was Alice's mother, Mary Bailey, also a widow. All were very poor, and Alice and Holt found Mary to be an encumbrance. Alice devised a plan to get rid of her mother with benefit to herself. The Wesleyan and General Assurance Company at Stockport insured for very small sums. Sixpence a week yielded life insurance of £28. On 18 February 1863 Alice decided to take out a policy for this amount on the life of her mother. At the time Mary was ill with bronchitis, but one Garlick, the canvasser for the insurer, told Alice that anyone would do to pass the medical examiner. So Alice approached a lodger, Ann Bailey (no relation), to make out to the medical examiner that she was Mary Bailey. Ann would have nothing to do with the deception. Alice then got the co-operation of Elizabeth Wells, who passed the medical examination under her assumed name of Mary Bailey. The insurance was effected on 6 March. Before then Mary was improving in health, but after that she became very ill, with great pain in her stomach. Around this time Ann Bailey was on several occasions sent to buy meat pies, which were always warmed by Alice. Anyone who by chance ate a piece of one of them became ill, vomiting violently. Of course, the intention was that Mary should eat them, which she did. Her sufferings were diagnosed by a medical practitioner as bronchitis. A few weeks before Mary's death on 27 March Alice had bought some arsenic from a druggist, one Davenport. On the fateful twenty-sixth day of May, Alice (yet another woman who spoke too much and whose tongue dug her own grave) said to Ann: 'You mustn't say anything about this arsenic.' Later, around nine in the evening, Alice gave her mother a drink of brandy and water. There was something else in the mixture: when the cup was examined some days after the death of Mary Bailey, which took place early the following morning, it was found to be strongly impregnated with arsenic.

After the old woman died, Alice, still suffering from logorrhoea, went to the room of Ann Bailey and remarked, 'Well, Ann, I am very glad my mother's dead. I've all my clothes fast [pawned] and I wanted this money to release them.' She added that if she had not got it, Holt would have beaten her.

On 8 April the insurance company paid Alice the insured sum. But soon rumours of criminal conduct by her began spreading widely. An investigation by the insurer disclosed the fraud she had committed. And a court order was obtained for the disinterring of the body of Mary Bailey. An examination of it on 12 June revealed 130 grains of arsenic, enough to kill twenty-six souls. On 10 December 1863 Alice Hewitt was tried for the murder of her mother. The jury took only twenty minutes to return a verdict of guilty. It added an odd recommendation of mercy, which was of no avail. On the court dispersing after the judge had sentenced the accused to death, some members of the public outside the court looked for Holt to give him a beating, but on being told of this by certain gallant members of the prosecution team he escaped through a side door and, putting on another hat, got safely to the railway station.

Public hanging was still to take place for the next five years, and an enormous crowd of morbidly curious spectators was expected to witness the end of Alice; but only a few thousand turned up on the Monday after Christmas 1863 to the grim scene.

AMY ARCHER-GILLIGAN — *'there will soon be a vacancy'*

A variant on life insurance is illustrated by the activities of Amy Archer-Gilligan.[112] She ran the Archer Home for Elderly People in Hartford, Connecticut, United States. It had been founded in 1907 by Amy and her then husband James Archer. He died in 1910 just as the business was becoming profitable and was succeeded by Amy's second husband in 1913, Michael Gilligan, but he lived only a further four months before succumbing to a strange illness. The death of a patient,

Franklin Andrews, on 30 May 1914 caused some people to be concerned. He had been well until dinner when he said he was feeling ill and went to bed. Amy telephoned Andrews's sister, saying he was unwell. Before midnight he was dead. Dr H F King, called to his bedside, diagnosed his death as caused by gastric ulcers, and assured worried citizens that there had been no foul play. Nevertheless a number of them became increasingly concerned about the continuing large number of deaths at the home, shown by constant visits by undertakers. The police were alerted and several women detectives infiltrated the home. The police discovered not only that Amy had been owing money to Andrews but that between 1911 and 1916 there had been forty-eight deaths at the home. The number of inmates at any time was at most only fourteen. The death rate was over six times the death rate in other old-age homes in the area. Each inmate paid on admission for lifetime care a sum between $1 000 and $1 500, depending on age and financial circumstances. The sooner an inmate died, the more profitable it was because of this payment. One prospective client had been told 'there will soon be a vacancy'. There was, and later the successful applicant left a further vacancy. The bodies of Andrews and Gilligan were exhumed. They showed the presence of arsenic. Further exhumations followed, showing the same results. It was ascertained that arsenic had been bought by inmates on behalf of Archer-Gilligan, and that in 1914 alone she had accumulated over a pound of it. A protracted trial for first degree murder of five inmates followed, which resulted in Amy being found guilty and sentenced to lifelong imprisonment. At a new trial following an appeal, she pleaded guilty to murdering Andrews and the sentence was reimposed. In 1928 she died at the age of fifty-nine.

A further farrago of homicidal females

Catherine Wilson[113] — *'very ingenious, sir, but . . .'*

Catherine Wilson was in one way like Daisy de Melker: pitiless, a woman who, without compunction, caused the death of her victims through the administration of poison that gave rise to excruciating pain, in order to obtain some small financial gain. Unlike that of Daisy, however, the background of Catherine Wilson was little known: not her parents, not her schooling, not whether she was married or a widow or a spinster (her calling herself Mrs Wilson did not signify). All that is known is that she was born in 1821, acted as a nurse or housekeeper in England (mainly in London), and over some nine years committed a series of murders.

The first death at her hands took place in 1853. She was then the housekeeper of Peter Mawer, a retired sea captain, in Boston, Lincolnshire. Mawer suffered from gout, and, to get relief, took doses of colchicine, a crystalline alkaloid extracted from seeds or corms of the autumn crocus (also called meadow saffron), a plant easily obtainable. An overdose of the drug can cause an agonizing death. This Wilson discovered. She ingratiated herself with Mawer, who in April 1854 executed a will making her his heir. That sealed his fate. In October he began suffering from severe internal pain, retching and purging, indicative of cholera or the ingestion of an irritant poison. Death followed. His doctor did not suspect foul play.

Catherine Wilson took her inheritance and moved to London. She began living with a young man by the name of Dixon at 27 Alfred Street, Bedford Square, a boarding house run by a Mrs Maria Soames. Dixon became very ill, in agony, with violent vomiting and retching. He died. Wilson informed the attending doctor that he had suffered from consumption, which a postmortem examination years later showed was not so. Then Mrs Soames, the day after her half-brother had given her nine pounds in cash, was afflicted with the same symptoms as Dixon. The doctor who had attended Dixon prescribed some medicine. As administered by Wilson, who professed to be a devoted nurse of Maria Soames, far from doing the patient good, the medicine led to her dying in agony within half an hour. The doctor insisted on a postmortem examination. An inquest must take place, he stated.

Wilson said that Mrs Soames had taken poison to escape the blackmail of a married man. But the autopsy revealed no poison in her body, and the doctor who had demanded it concluded that her death resulted from natural causes.

Wilson took the nine pounds and obtained a further ten pounds from the half-brother by showing him a document supposedly signed by Mrs Soames in which she promised to repay that sum, which had been lent to her.

Three murders had taken place in two years; the next known one came four years later. Wilson visited a friend, Mrs Jackson, in Boston. The friend died in excruciating pain two days later, with the same symptoms as Mawer, Dixon and Soames. The attending doctor did not suspect anything amiss, and signed a certificate attributing the death to a bilious complaint. Wilson got away with £120 obtained from the forgery of a cheque on a form taken from Mrs Jackson's chequebook.

Next came the death of another friend, Mrs Allison, who was staying in London to buy material for her milliner's business in Westmorland, and was residing with Wilson. Allison had left home in good health, with most of her money sewn into her stays. Four days later her husband received a telegram from Wilson saying that his wife was dangerously ill. On his arrival, Mr Allison found a doctor in attendance on his wife, who was in agony, vomiting violently and purging. Nothing could save her. In answer to Mr Allison's query about the disappearance of his wife's money, Catherine Wilson said that she had remarked that it had been stolen in Rugby. Wilson was not suspected of the theft of it, or causing the death of Mrs Allison. The doctor certified the death as being the result of natural causes, and Mrs Allison was buried.

Then followed an attempt by Wilson to poison a man by the name of Taylor, with whom she was living. The attempt failed, as the doctor who was summoned to attend to the same symptoms as were present in the five victims of Wilson applied effective remedies. Catherine Wilson then decided to attack easier game. She chose Mrs Sarah Carnell, whose husband, from whom she was living apart, was a friend of Taylor's.

She arranged to have tea with Mrs Carnell at her house in Marylebone on 13 February 1862 to discuss a possible reconciliation by her with her husband. Soon afterwards Mrs Carnell became very ill. She asked Wilson to get a rhubarb draught from the nearby pharmacist. Wilson returned with a mixture, which she poured into a glass. The glass became very hot. When Sarah Carnell protested, Wilson said, 'Drink it down, love, it will warm you'. On Mrs Carnell drinking some of the mixture, her mouth became blistered, and what she spat out burned through the counterpane.

Soon the police caused the arrest of Catherine Wilson for the attempted murder of Mrs Carnell. They had made other inquiries, too, and were armed with warrants for her arrest on six charges of murder.

The charge of attempted murder came before Baron Bramwell. It was alleged that the accused had administered an ounce of sulphuric acid to the complainant. The defence was conducted by Montagu Williams, the barrister we have already met. He argued that, the pharmacist being absent when Catherine Wilson called, the medicine was supplied by a fifteen-year-old in temporary charge, who may well have dispensed the wrong medicine.

In his summing up to the jury, the presiding judge demolished this defence, saying that had the bottle contained sulphuric acid when it was handed to the accused, it would have become red hot and burst before she reached the bed of the invalid.

To the surprise of Montagu Williams, who thought the Crown case and the judge's summing up were deadly, despite the absence of apparent motive for the deed, the jury asked leave to retire. While he was waiting, Williams was approached by a stranger who said: 'Very ingenious, sir, but if you succeed in getting that woman off, you will be doing her the worst turn anyone ever did her.' Astonished, Williams found out that the stranger was a member of the police with instructions, if the accused were acquitted, to take her into custody on six charges of murder. If, however, she were convicted, the authorities would be satisfied with the lengthy term of imprisonment that would be imposed and would not proceed with a murder charge.[114]

After two hours, the jury returned with a verdict of not guilty, to the astonishment of almost all.[115] But the delight of Catherine Wilson soon changed, as she was arrested.

The cause of the arrest of Wilson was the reading by the coroner of the district where Captain Mawer had died of the preliminary hearing in the case. He caused the body of Mawer to be exhumed. The viscera were sent to the renowned Dr Alfred Swaine Taylor, Professor of Medical Jurisprudence at Guy's Hospital. The bodies of the other five alleged victims of poisoning by Wilson were also exhumed. All had exhibited the same symptoms. In none of the bodies was poison found. But, as in the trials of Dr William Palmer and Dr Thomas Smethurst, the prosecution did not have to rely on proof of poisoning by a particular poison. The death of others who had died with similar symptoms could show that the accused had pursued a system of poisoning for gain. On 25 September 1862 Catherine Wilson was tried at the Central Criminal Court in London before Mr Justice Byles and a jury on a charge of murdering Maria Soames in October 1856. Once more she was defended by Montagu Williams, but this time he did not meet with success. The doctor who had certified that Maria Soames had died through natural causes said that he was now convinced it was due to an overdose of colchicine or some other vegetable irritant poison. Professor Taylor was even more definite in his opinion: the death of Mrs Soames was caused through poisoning by colchicine, no matter that a trace of it could not be found in her body.

Mr Justice Byles delivered a damning summing-up, and on 27 September the jury found Catherine Wilson guilty. In sentencing her to death, Mr Justice Byles delivered a long condemnation of her deed in the strongest terms. Montagu Williams[116] recorded that on the conclusion of the trial the judge asked him to come to his chambers. Wilson found the judge 'walking up and down like a lion in its cage. "You did the case remarkably well", he said, "But it was no good; the facts were too strong. If it will be of any satisfaction to you, I may tell you that in my opinion you have today defended the greatest criminal that ever lived." '

Catherine Wilson was in due course hanged outside Newgate before a crowd of twenty thousand spectators. She died utterly calm, without contrition or confession.

LOUISA MERRIFIELD[117] — *the residue on the teaspoon*

Sarah Ann Ricketts, a seventy-nine-year-old widow who lived in a house in Blackpool, advertised in the press on 12 March 1953 for a housekeeper. The successful applicant was the forty-nine-year-old Louisa Merrifield, then sporting her third husband, seventy-four-year-old Alfred Edward Merrifield. The two performed their duties so well that on the thirty-first day of that very March month Mrs Ricketts made a will in which they were appointed her heirs. When Louisa met a friend, Mrs Brewer, on 11 April, she said to her: 'We are loaded. We were staying with an old lady and she has died leaving us a bungalow worth £4 000.' In fact Mrs Ricketts died only three days later. Her medical adviser, Dr Wood, had examined her the day before and found her to be in quite good health. Louisa tried to get the undertaker to cremate the body of Mrs Ricketts 'at once', but a postmortem examination had been ordered. The finding was death through the taking of yellow phosphorus, which is found in some rat poisons. Louisa had bought a tin containing such a poison. A teaspoon was found in her handbag containing a suspicious gritty, sweetish substance.

Louisa Merrifield and her husband were tried before Mr Justice Glyn-Jones and a jury at the Manchester Assizes in August 1953. The Crown team, as was customary, was led by the Attorney-General, who was Sir Lionel Heald QC. The trial ran for eleven days.

An expert witness testified that the residue on the teaspoon would form through yellow phosphorus being mixed with rum. Louisa admitted offering the deceased rum the night before she died. She had a bad time when cross-examined by the Attorney-General. For instance, she was asked why she did not call a doctor before Mrs Ricketts died at 3:15 am, and waited until two on the following afternoon before doing so. She gave the lame explanation that it was 'not such a nice time' to call a doctor. To which the Attorney-General put it to her that she did nothing, as she 'saw the old lady was going, and wanted her to go'.

The jury found Louisa guilty, but was split on a finding on the charge against her husband. The judge ordered his retrial, but the Attorney-General decided not to proceed with it. Louisa's appeal against the verdict failed, and she was executed on 18 September 1953.

DOROTHEA NANCY WADDINGHAM[118] — '. . . *my relatives shall not know of my death*'

She called herself Nurse Waddingham, but she was not a qualified nurse, only a thirty-six-year-old former factory worker and thereafter attendant at Burton-on-Trent workhouse, with a host of convictions for theft and fraud. Waddingham was her maiden name; she was the widow of Thomas Leech, by whom she had three children. At the time she committed her capital crime, she was running a nursing home for the aged and infirm at 32 Devon Drive, Sherwood, Nottingham. Assisting her was her lover, thirty-nine-year-old Ronald Joseph Sullivan, who had been awarded the Military Cross for gallantry in the Great War. What he saw in this most unattractive woman with buck teeth only he knew; but then Thomas Leech had also found something in her appearance to attract him. The couple appear to have run their nursing home adequately, for in early January 1935 the County Nursing Association asked them to admit Mrs Baguley, a ninety-year-old senile lady, and her daughter, Miss Ada Baguley, aged fifty, crippled by disseminated sclerosis, and obese, weighing some 260 pounds.

The two ladies moved to the home on the twelfth of that month for a trial period of three weeks. Finding everything satisfactory, they decided to stay permanently. The proprietors of the home, however, were not content with the amount of care they had to devote to their patients and in particular not with the approved payment of three pounds a week each, compared with five guineas charged by a hospital.

Financial negotiations took place. The upshot was that Ada asked her solicitor to draw up a new will for her, which was to state that, in return for lifelong care of her and her mother, Nurse Waddingham was to be her sole heir. The solicitor was not happy with the request, but he complied with it on 4 May. The estate was modest, consisting of a small business and about £1 500 in funds.

On 6 May the inhabitants of the home were given a treat of tinned salmon to celebrate Royal Silver Jubilee day. From then on Mrs Baguley's health suddenly declined sharply, and on the twelfth of the month she died and was buried. The attending doctor attributed her death to natural causes.

Ada Baguley continued living at the home. On 10 September she suddenly fell into a coma and the next day she died. Her doctor was surprised at her collapse, but, on hearing of his late patient's symptoms from Waddingham, he signed the death certificate, stating that the cause of Ada's demise was cerebral haemorrhage.

Waddingham was anxious that Ada's body should be cremated. As no mention of her wishes was made in her will, the consent of the Medical Officer of Health for Nottingham, Dr Cyril Banks, was needed. An odd document was shown him headed 'Miss Ada Baguley, 32 Devon Drive, Sherwood, Notts', dated 29 August 1935 and addressed to her doctor. It read: 'I desire to be cremated at my death for health's sake and it is my wish to remain with Nurse until I die. It is my final wish that my relatives shall not know of my death.' Although Ada's signature appeared, the contents were clearly not in her hand; and the strange last sentence was crushed into a small space.

Dr Banks was worried about what he read. He ordered relatives to be traced and consulted. Lawrence Baguley, a cousin who was found, said that Ada had always been opposed to cremation; it was more likely that she wished to be buried alongside her mother. When he had called to see Mrs Baguley and Ada earlier in the year, he was told by Nurse Waddingham and her 'male assistant' that they refused to see him.

These and other suspicious bits of evidence resulted in the coroner's ordering a postmortem examination of the body of Ada and the remains of her mother. The report showed 3.192 grains of morphine in the body of Ada, and in the remains of her mother the presence of an alkaloid into which morphine or heroin could have been converted, in 'a quantity in excess of a medicinal dose'.

Inquiries by the police revealed that two other elderly inmates of the home had died in February and March that year. Their doctors had prescribed morphine to alleviate their pain, but both, according to relations, had died in prolonged agony. That could be a source of the morphine in the bodies of the Baguleys.

Waddingham and Sullivan were tried on 24 February 1935 at Nottingham Assizes for the murder of Ada Baguley before Mr Justice Goddard, who was to become a law lord and then Lord Chief Justice. The prosecuting team was under the leadership of the brilliant Norman Birkett KC, later a lord justice of appeal. (Why a barrister in private practice, and not, as was the custom, the Attorney-General, prosecuted in a case of murder by poisoning I have not discovered.)

How did morphine get into the viscera of Ada? The prosecution contended that it had been administered from morphine tablets prescribed for other patients.

To the police and then in evidence before court, Dorothy Waddingham denied that she had ever given Ada Baguley morphine — she said that Ada's physician, Dr H H Mansfield, had given her pills that must have contained the drug. But Dr Mansfield denied this; there was nothing in her condition to justify the prescription of a narcotic.

The judge found there was no case against Sullivan, and ordered his discharge. The case against Waddingham went to the jury. It found her guilty. For some inexplicable reason the jury made a strong recommendation for the extension of mercy. But murder by poisoning had always been looked on with great abhorrence by the British government, and the sentence of death was carried out on 16 April 1936.

MARY STONEMUIR — *so engaging a housekeeper*

She murdered two men who were brothers in order to inherit from one of them, but she was never brought to trial.[119]

In 1981 Edward Hoskins, a retired civil engineer, sixty-six years of age, who lived in a large luxurious house in the village of Barnwell, near Cambridge, took into his service a housekeeper by the name of Mary Stonemuir. She was a forty-two-year-old single woman, who hailed from Edinburgh so she said. To outward appearances she was most attractive, with amber eyes, striking auburn hair and a soft voice with a Scottish accent. Those living in the village were surprised that Eddie Hoskins, a lifelong bachelor who had had virtually nothing to do with women all his years, should hire so engaging a housekeeper. It certainly appeared to be too lowly a position for a person with her qualities and charm, who had told her employer that she had been housekeeper to the Earl of

Aykerbridge until his daughter returned from America to take the position.

Within two months of her arrival, her employer fell ill. His general practitioner, Dr Michaels, who had attended him for the past twenty-two years, was asked to see him. Eddie Hoskins's doctor had never found his patient really ill in the past, but now he complained of headaches, dizziness, nausea and drowsiness. Believing that Eddie had contracted a low-grade viral infection, Dr Michaels advised him to stay in bed for a few days.

Three days later Eddie Hoskins took a turn for the worse, becoming feverish and suffering from hallucinations. His brother Jack, who had come from London to see him, summoned Dr Michaels, who found his patient groaning, rubbing his stomach and speaking nonsense. Concerned, the doctor took a blood test and sent it to a haematology laboratory for analysis. The report was that there was an unidentifiable foreign element in the blood and that a biopsy to check the patient's liver and spleen was advisable.

Eddie was taken to a hospital for the procedure, but before it could be done he had a violent seizure similar to an epileptic fit and died.

Convinced that the housekeeper had caused the life of his extremely fit brother to suddenly end, and letting people know this, Jack went to his late brother's house, opened the desk in the study with the keys Eddie had left, and found a copy of his will. It left a monetary bequest to Jack, and the rest of the valuable estate to Mary Stonemuir.

In his investigation of his suspicions, Jack Hoskins secured the co-operation of Detective-Superintendent Ralph Gillett through his friendship with one of Gillett's superior officers. Gillett interviewed Mary Stonemuir in the kitchen of the house. Calm and self-possessed, she was asked about her relationship with Edward Hoskins. The surprising reply was 'We were lovers'. They had met a couple of years back in France where both had been on holiday; there they became lovers; and when Eddie retired, he persuaded her to move in as his housekeeper, neither desiring to get married. Against her wishes, she said, he insisted on making her his heir, since she had made him so happy.

Later Gillett told Jack what she had said. The reaction of Jack was that he was more convinced than ever that Mary Stonemuir had murdered his brother.

They awaited the results of the autopsy. It was inconclusive, all untoward that was found being severe irritation of the internal tract. But the forensic pathologist still felt that there was something strange about the state of the body. He contacted a forensic toxicologist,

Desmond Stuart, who examined blood samples, the contents of the stomach and some samples of tissue. In his report four days later, Stuart stated that there were present poisonous elements found in the vegetable species Datura, which contains the alkaloids levohyoscamine, atropine, and hyoscine (scopolamine). A fatal dose is one grain and the action is slow, producing symptoms identical to those shown by the deceased just before his death. Also present were poisons found in the vegetable species Hyoscyamus (henbane) and the plant woody nightshade. (Hyoscine was the poison Hawley Harvey Crippen used to murder his wife in the famous case in 1910.) The conclusion reached by Stuart was that these poisons were the primary cause of the death of Edward Hoskins. Stuart told Gillett that a more skilled poisoner would have administered poisons of this type more slowly, ensuring that they were eliminated from the victim's body before death.

A search warrant was obtained, but a very careful inspection of the house left by the deceased revealed nothing of significance.

Gillett had not seen Jack for two days. Inquiries at the public house where Jack was lodging revealed that, after telling the landlord that his brother Eddie had never been to France, he said he was going to the house to have it out with the housekeeper. He had not been seen since he left; his bags were still in his room; and he had paid for the room for two days after the day fixed for his brother's funeral.

Mary Stonemuir was uncooperative when questioned by the police. Gillett was now convinced she had murdered Eddie Hoskins and was beginning to think she had also murdered Jack. But there was no proof that any of the poisons had been in the house or that she had used poison at all. A check on Stonemuir's background resulted in a complete blank: there was no record of her in Edinburgh, which she had claimed as her home town; her references on her curriculum vitae did not exist; there was no Earl of Aykerbridge.

Gillett engaged a forensic psychologist to accompany him when he interviewed the woman. The psychologist concluded that nothing would make her crack; and that she was capable of doing anything that produced what she desired.

Day by day small plastic bags of minced human flesh and bone now appeared in nearby rivers. Eventually there were thirty bags of them. The police were sure that the contents came from Jack's body but could not prove anything. It was an exasperating situation.

Then fortune smiled on the police. A service engineer had come to fit a new garbage disposal unit, the previous one having been disposed of by Stonemuir. Inside a drain twenty feet behind the house the engineer came across a pair of hands of a human being. They were badly decomposed and had no skin. This was very disappointing, for the fingerprints of Jack Hoskins had been recorded when he had been arrested on a charge of assaulting a politician years ago. Desmond Stuart was called in again. The hands had been boiled, he considered. Had they been fairly intact when they were discarded, the skin would have slipped off. A search of the drain by torchlight, Stonemuir watching from a window, yielded a pair of what appeared to be gloves. They were, however, the skin of Jack's hands.

Mary Stonemuir was arrested. As she was being told of her legal rights, she quietly drank a cup of tea. Then she got into the police car. On her way to the police station, she died.

An examination of the teacup showed that the contents had been laced with deadly aconite.

Every attempt was made to find out who Mary Stonemuir was. Nothing emerged. Her photograph was not recognized by anyone. There was no record of her fingerprints, nor was any dental record found. Where she obtained the poisons from was a mystery. It was as though she had never been.

DIRTY WORK WITH A WILL

Failure to destroy a will

LADY M — *a very strange tale*

A strange tale is told by Sir Ellis Hume-Williams KC in his autobiography,[120] one that is hard to believe. The author regarded it as 'the most dramatic case with which I have been connected'. It happened in 1897, and concerned Lady M, the widow of a distinguished diplomat, and her son Cyril. Cyril was heir to a fortune, but, being an alcoholic, was fair game for a designing female. Such a female turned out to be a demi-mondaine with the name of Olga. Cyril fell helplessly in love with her, and the pathetic pleas of his mother to end the liaison met with no success. Desperate, Lady M approached Captain X, a good friend of Cyril's and apparently a man of standing; he had been in a leading regiment and ADC to the governor of a colony. Imploring the captain to persuade Cyril to break with Olga, Lady M gave him a large sum to cover the expenses he would incur in his mission. Captain X was only too happy to undertake the task. He joined Cyril and Olga at Monte Carlo, participating in their riotous life there, and followed them to their next venue, Paris. According to Captain X, Olga was making strenuous efforts to cause Cyril, whose health was rapidly going downhill, to make a will in her favour. To avoid this happening the captain induced Cyril to make a will in his, the captain's, favour. His intention then, so he explained later, was to destroy the will once Olga's malign influence had come to an end. The danger was that she might discover the existence of the will and prevail upon Cyril to make a new will, one in her favour. So Captain X persuaded Cyril to bolt with him to London, there to catch a boat for New York. As Cyril said that he suffered from seasickness, Captain X bought a mixture to combat it from Pope Roach, a pharmacist in St James's Street, London. At the same time he bought from the firm a bottle of cyanide of potassium, explaining that he wanted it to clean his jewellery. It happened to be a deadly poison. On the ship the two men had separate cabins. In his cabin Captain X, so he explained later, had placed the two bottles on the shelf above the washstand. On the third day the sea turned very rough. According to Captain X, in the middle of the night Cyril, intoxicated, entered his cabin and asked for the seasickness mixture. Half asleep, the captain said that the bottle was on the shelf. Unfortunately, it appeared that Cyril took the wrong bottle, and in the morning was found stone dead in his cabin.

Then Captain X propounded the will in the Probate Registry. The family of the departed testator challenged the validity of the will. The beneficiary resisted the challenge. For him appeared the eminent Sir Edward Clarke QC, former Solicitor-General, with him as junior counsel the young Hume-Williams. Leading counsel for the plaintiffs was the redoubtable Sir Edward Carson QC. Sir Ellis Hume-Williams put the position thus:[121] 'They were in a quandary, for they dared not, and indeed could not, suggest murder, and there was practically no other defence; so the matter was settled by a substantial payment to Captain X.' (One wonders whether a defence of unworthiness or even undue influence or fraud might not have availed. It is a pity that more detail is not available. But Sir Ellis wrote that he had kept no diary and no papers, so that in his account of this unreported case some thirty years earlier he must have had to rely on his memory.)

Within a year or two after his success with the will Captain X was sentenced to a stiff sentence of imprisonment for buying jewellery on credit and immediately pawning it. But he seems finally to have found his feet, for Sir Ellis, shortly before he wrote his book, 'saw him at Ascot, where he strolled past me beautifully dressed and with the air of a Rothschild'.[122]

The mysterious Olga was befriended by the bereaved Lady M, who 'provided her with a house and means of livelihood, and ultimately reclaimed the woman from the life she had been leading. Great is the power of love.'[123]

Concealment of a will

ALBERT HEYER — *'the missing Hertzog will'*

In two of his many books on South African personalities and events, Eric Rosenthal told the tale of 'The Missing Hertzog Will'.[124] William Frederick Hertzog was the son of an early Cape Surveyor-General and a cousin of General J B M Hertzog, for many years Prime Minister of South Africa. In early life William was a land surveyor, but after inheriting wealth he lived a life of leisure, buying books to be housed in his library in his home in Constantia valley and travelling. In his late fifties his health started declining and he decided to make a will. He was a bachelor with no close relations. Albert Heyer called on him one day in 1902. Heyer was then a private detective; earlier in life he had been in the secret service of the Transvaal. Hertzog asked Heyer to read from a certain book. Then he asked Heyer to take down words he would dictate. Heyer did so. The words constituted a home-made will. (The document set out by Rosenthal by no means is a clear disposition of the house and its contents, including the valuable library, to the beneficiary, Michael Hiddingh, a well-to-do landowner in the Cape, but let that be.) Hertzog signed the document, and Heyer and another visitor (not aware of the contents of the document) signed as witnesses. That visitor then left, but Heyer was asked to remain on to write on a sheet of paper that he swore not to tell the beneficiary of the contents of the will until Hertzog died. That happened soon. The estate was worth some £100 000. No will was found, and for the time being Hertzog was regarded as having died intestate. Heyer planned to profit from his sole knowledge of the existence of the will. He told Hiddingh that he believed that Hertzog had left his estate to him. Hiddingh was incredulous, but did say that he would give Heyer a thousand pounds if he could locate the will. Heyer went to the house of Hertzog, found the book he had read aloud, and in it he saw the will and document he had signed, which no longer bound him morally. Now he behaved foolishly, for he told a friend of his possession of the will; the friend, horrified, told Casper van Zyl, the prominent Cape attorney, who told the Master of the Supreme Court. In the result Heyer was arrested. For two months he remained in prison until he was tried for concealing a will for fraudulent purposes in contravention of section 4 of Ordinance 104 of 1833 (Cape). He was sentenced to a fine of two hundred pounds or, in default of payment, a year's imprisonment. It could have been worse.

Doctored will

AN IRISH BACHELOR — *and the fussing farmer's wife*

Maurice Healy's *The Old Munster Circuit: A Book of Memories and Traditions,* published in 1939,[125] has been said by discerning readers to be the most amusing book of legal reminiscences ever written. I have a copy, bought, I believe, from a bookshop in legal London, which contains this barely legible inscription: 'My dear William, this book would be more amusing if your name appeared in it — but it could not have been printed! Yours ever Maurice Healy 6.3.39.' Who was William and why did this, now valuable, work leave his hands? I shall never know. In the book[126] one reads a story which Healy says 'should have been told by Guy de Maupassant'. It concerns an Irishman who had left for America, made his money there and came home to die in his native land. A bachelor, he lived in rural Kerry for his last seven or eight years with a farmer and his wife. The wife, a calculating person, who looked after her paying guest well, feared that he would see a solicitor who would persuade him to make a will leaving his estate to his relations. But he did not, and on his deathbed was without a will. After he had given him the last rites, a priest found out that he would die intestate. So, pushing the fussing farmer's wife out of the room, the priest drew up the will the dying man wished to leave, and then called in a servant girl to witness the document with him. No sooner had they gone than the wife searched for and found the will. It was all she wished: everything to her and her husband. But she still felt unsafe, so she added her name as a third witness. Thereby, wrote Healy, ensuring that she 'signed away the inheritance of herself and her husband to the relatives the testator had declined to benefit'. In a footnote Healy explained that 'neither a witness nor the spouse of a witness can receive anything under the will he or she attests'. Now in those days Kerry, today in the Republic of Ireland, was part of the United Kingdom, and English law prevailed there. Healy, who by the time he wrote his book was practising at the London Bar, and after the war took silk, should have known better than to write what he did. As Sir Robert Megarry, then a judge of the Chancery Division of the High Court of Justice of England and Wales, pointed out in his *A Second Miscellany-at-Law,*[127] for long it had been held by the courts in England that if, after a will had been duly signed by the testator and two witnesses, a further person signs it not with the intention of attesting it but for a different reason, such as a belief that otherwise it would be invalid or in order to show agreement with its content, the signature is regarded as superfluous and a bequest to the signatory will be valid.[128] In 1968 the Wills Act of that year made it clear that a third or still further signature is disregarded if there are two other unimpugnable signatures.

I cannot locate any reported case in South Africa to the same effect as the cases in England, but I should think that our courts would have decided in the same way. Today the question is no longer a practical one, for our Wills Act 1953, section 5 of which originally provided that a person or spouse of a person who attests the execution of a will is incapable of taking any benefit under it, was amended in 1992,[129] section 5 being repealed and a section 4A(1) and (2) added, allowing such a woman or her husband to succeed, if there were two other competent witnesses who did not receive any benefit under the will. (It could not be argued, so it seems, that a signatory such as the farmer's wife 'damages' the will in contravention of section 102(1)*(a)* of our Administration of Estates Act 1965.)

Forgery and falsification of a will

Apart from the common-law crime of forgery, section 102(1)*(a)* of the Administration of Estates Act 1965[130] makes it an offence for a person to steal or wilfully destroy, conceal, falsify or damage any document purporting to be a will. This is virtually a repetition of s 111 of the Administration of Estates Act 1913.[131] The Appellate Division held in *State v Van Zyl*[132] that 'falsify' covered both altering an existing document and manufacturing a false one.

Is forgery or falsification of a will a widespread and largely undiscovered crime? Basically, our will[133] is the underhand will of England created by the Wills Act of 1837, so simple in form and so easy to falsify. All that are really needed are the apparent signatures of the testator and two witnesses. If a plot is considered desirable, well, as Mr Justice Jacob de Villiers put it in his dissenting judgment in *Kunz v Swart,*[134] 'what is easier than for a person . . . to conspire with one or more persons to make a false will without a trace of such a conspiracy coming out?' If a conspiracy is too difficult to arrange, witnesses can be led to believe they are witnessing another document, as Mary Mason did in Anthony Trollope's novel *Orley Farm.* Not that witnesses need even know they are witnessing a will at all. We have no register of wills in any form, with the consequence that it is possible for the existence of a will by a deceased person to be unknown or kept secret by the person or persons who alone know of it and who would benefit from this absence of knowledge. Whether this situation should continue to exist has been considered by several writers[135] and by the South African Law Commission, which concluded that things should be left as they are.[136] The ease and possible cheapness of making an underhand will are advantages that outweigh any consequent risk of illicit actions. That seems to be the opinion of most commentators.

It is generally believed that falsifying a will, and, indeed, any other dirty work with a will such as destroying or hiding it, are very uncommon. Statistics furnished by the police to the Law Commission for the three years ending in October 1984 show four convictions for falsification of wills, with three prosecutions pending; one conviction for unlawful destruction of a will; one conviction for fraud, with two prosecutions pending; and no prosecution for contravention of s 102(1)*(a)* of the Administration of Estates Act.[137] How much crime was not discovered cannot be ascertained.

The number of relevant cases, civil and criminal, in our law reports, on falsification and forgery concerned with a will, apart from several bringing no success to the plaintiff or prosecution, of course is no reflection of the extent of the problem. Still, a few are interesting, if only as showing that there is nowt so queer as folks — or, I would add, so crooked, at times.

TSHONA v WAUCHOPE — another beneficiary?

Earliest of those in the law reports is *Tshona v Wauchope.*[138] Bobi Tshona and his wife Sarah, who were Africans, had made a joint will in which each appointed the survivor as heir and the Rev Isaac Wauchope who, for all his Christian given name and old English surname was described by Mr Justice Kotzé in his judgment as 'a very intelligent and an educated' African man, as executor. Bobi died, and the affairs of Sarah were then managed by Wauchope. On 23 June 1905 Sarah died. Her children asked Wauchope whether their mother had left a will. In October the following year, they claimed, he had told them at a meeting that she had not. Certainly no will had been filed with the Master of the Supreme Court by then, as it long since should have been had it existed. But lo! on 6 December that year Wauchope did file a will which he proved and under which he was appointed executor, which was followed by his taking out letters of administration. Why had he filed it so late when he admitted he knew the practice regarding filing? The children were not made sole heirs under the supposed will (its exact content, unfortunately, is not stated) and contended that it was a forgery. From the evidence it became clear that the signatories as witnesses never existed — indeed, expert evidence established that the signatures were in Wauchope's handwriting. The court set aside the will and the letters of administration and ordered Wauchope to render an account and pay the costs. Whether he was subsequently tried for forgery I do not know. Nor do I know why he did what he did, but I suspect he was paid for his trouble by a beneficiary under the will who was not a child of Sarah's.

KUNZ v SWART — brilliant analysis

Next came a leading decision, never challenged and consistently applied, that of the majority of a panel of three in the Appellate Division in 1924 in *Kunz v Swart.*[139] They held that the person who contended that a will fell to the ground through forgery bore the onus of proving it. Mr Justice Jacob de Villiers protested vigorously: '[A] presumption in law that an underhand document purporting to be a will is genuine, as long as the document appears to be in order and there is no flaw on the face of it, is a proposition to my mind utterly at variance with principle and authority and fraught with the gravest possibilities for injustice.'[140] Now Jacob de Villiers was a most learned jurist, as the analysis of the legal authority in his judgment shows, and one must pay tribute to any of his several dissenting (usually conservative) judgments in the highest court. But Mr Justice Solomon and Mr Justice Kotzé, the majority judges, were also of the highest calibre, and their judgments were equally impressive.

The facts of the case were extraordinarily complex and defy attempts at a condensation. Suffice it to say that those involved were a melange of characters constituting a microcosm of society: an alleged testator nominally a bachelor but who sported for many years a mistress who had borne him children; a solitary sibling, a married sister, who would be his heir on intestacy; a handyman — a very handy man, in Mr Justice Solomon's grim words — who was a liar and scoundrel; two utterly reliable attorneys; honest witnesses whose memories were faulty; dishonest witnesses who remembered things too well; and a host of others. After an exhaustive — to many a reader, exhausting — analysis of the evidence in a judgment running to thirty-nine pages, the bulk devoted to carving the facts at the joint, Mr Justice Solomon found the scales evenly balanced, forgery on the one pan and genuineness on the other. The onus tilted the latter and caused the plaintiff to fail. So Mr Justice Solomon upheld the judgment of Mr Justice E F Watermeyer in the Cape Provincial Division. Although Billy Watermeyer was a highly regarded judge who was to become Chief Justice and must have been happy to have his judgment upheld, he surely writhed on reading Mr Justice Solomon's scathing criticism of parts of it. Mr Justice Kotzé agreed overall with Mr Justice Solomon but expressed some further views on the facts and penned a brilliant analysis of the law. Mr Justice De Villiers, as will have been gathered, disagreed politely but very strongly with his judicial brethren on both facts and the law. A perusal of the three judgments would give any lawyers here or abroad a measure of the high standing of our highest court.

'J. A. JOURDAIN' — *or was it?*

In his autobiography, *Not the Whole Truth,*[141] Mr Justice F N Broome told an amusing story. It concerned a contested case that was heard by Mr Justice Carter and Mr Justice Matthews. Though at that time a single judge in every province was competent to sit alone in any civil trial, it was apparently customary for such a court in Natal to be that of two or three judges. Broome was still at the Bar, and his side was arguing that the signature 'J. A. Jourdain' at the foot of a will was not that of the supposed testator, but a forgery traced from his signature at the back of a cheque made payable to 'J. A. Jourdain', his signature otherwise always being 'Jno. A. Jourdain'. Expert evidence on the validity of the handwriting was conflicting. At the close of the evidence it appeared that the decision depended on who bore the onus of proof. Broome wrote: 'Notwithstanding the (at the time) leading Appellate Division judgment on this point, the question was by no means simple in the circumstances surrounding this particular will.' It would have been helpful to know why this was so. Just before having to argue the point, Broome saw that the court clock had reached one o'clock and that Carter was asleep so it was necessary to push a pile of books to the floor to awaken him to adjourn the court. During the lunch period Broome was in a fog as to his argument on the onus of proof. It being a very hot February, he lunched on two pints of iced beer. As he began to argue the fog lifted, and the solution appeared with crystal clarity. His argument seemed to be convincing Mr Justice Matthews. The court reserved its judgment. Weeks later it was announced that no decision was arrived at, as the judges were in disagreement. (This does not surprise me. Carter had no legal training and was apt to go wrong in civil matters, though he never had any doubts. Matthews had legal training (but no court experience), could go wrong and had doubts.) Funds had run out, so the case was abandoned. Broome could not recall his argument, and I would like to know what it could have been. All he could say was that he did not recommend alcohol as a forensic aid. With that most lawyers would agree.

GROBLER v DORFLING'S ESTATE — nothing too strange

Reported cases after *Kunz v Swart,* as I have said, all applied the majority ruling in that case.[142] One of these cases, *Grobler v Dorfling's Estate,*[143] if the plaintiff's allegations in it were true, which they may have been, illustrates Thomas Hardy's remark that 'though a good deal is too strange to be believed, nothing is too strange to have happened'.[144] The plaintiff stated that in 1903 she had signed the name of her mother (who died only in 1936) to her alleged will, on the forceful persuasion of her brother, who had induced her to sign in the belief that it was for her mother's benefit and that there was a pact between the nominated heirs that when her mother died the false will would be abandoned. She asked the court to declare the will invalid. The other beneficiaries under the will opposed the action, and asked for absolution from the instance on the ground that the plaintiff sought relief from her own criminal acts, and that in any event she should be debarred on the equitable doctrine of laches (delay). The court rejected the first contention, on the grounds that it could raise the issues of par delictum (equal guilt) and possibly giving operation to an invalid will. Secondly, assuming the existence of the doctrine of laches in our law, on the allegations of the plaintiff there was no undue delay. I am baffled by the cogency of the alleged persuasion of the brother. What possible benefit to the mother? What happened between 1903 and 1936? Did the mother never raise the question of making a will?

ISADORE LIONDORE'S WILL — *the charge of forging and uttering*

The story of the mysterious appearance of a later will by Isadore Liondore was recounted by my good friend for many years, the late Mr Justice Cecil Margo, in his absorbing autobiography, *Final Postponement: Reminiscences of a Crowded Life.*[145] The supposed testator had been a very wealthy man of (landed) property. In 1937 he died, leaving a widow, Leah, and a sole blood relation, Jack Ryder, a nephew. A will had been lodged with Liondore's attorney, Maurice Porter, in which the estate had been left in equal shares to Leah and Ryder. Shortly after Liondore died, Cecil Margo, a recently admitted advocate, was briefed by an attorney to attend a consultation arranged for Ryder. At the consultation appeared, too, a woman, Mrs Patricia Kennedy. She said that she was seventy-eight years of age and a devout Catholic, whose conscience told her, now that her life was coming to a close, that she must disclose certain information which could prevent Ryder being cheated out of his birthright. As a caretaker for many years of a building owned by Liondore, she had become a confidante of Leah's, who had insisted, after her husband's will had been produced, that he had made a later will leaving all to her. Porter did not know of it, and a careful search of the home of the Liondores had revealed nothing. One Sunday afternoon at a tea party at her home, widow Leah was entertaining

Mrs Kennedy; Leah's brother, one Pickover; and a Johannesburg advocate, Max Stein, who was not doing well in his practice. After serving tea, Leah excused herself and after a short while returned very excited, saying 'I have found it — it was at the back of the wardrobe!' *It* was a later will, leaving the whole estate to her. Pickover and Stein identified the signatures of the witnesses as being theirs. Subsequently, said Mrs Kennedy, Leah told her in the utmost confidence that Pickover had drafted the document and forged Liondore's signature to it. Later Pickover obtained Stein's signature as a second witness, feeling that the signature of an advocate would not be questioned. For this service Stein was paid a handsome sum, which he used to buy a fine Packard motor car. Maurice Porter, in good faith winding up the estate on the forged will, read in *The Star* newspaper that a person, whose surname also began with L but was not Liondore, had applied from his residence in the Pretoria Central Gaol to have both wills set aside. He claimed that he was the brother of the late Isadore Liondore. It turned out that he really was and that he was serving an indeterminate prison sentence. His family had long since made out that he had been killed in the Great War. Of course, if both wills were set aside the emergent brother would inherit a great part of the estate as an heir on intestacy. Unfortunately for him, the first will was upheld, but according to Porter he was happy to be released from gaol very soon. Cecil and Porter managed to make a photocopy of the second 'will', from which it was clear from the opinion of a handwriting expert that the signature of Liondore had been forged.

Prior to suing to have the document set aside, Ryder obtained an interdict preventing the assets in the estate from being dissipated. On learning of the application, Stein had a nervous breakdown. He told Ryder's legal advisers that he had not been paid anything, but had signed a blank space as a witness to get rid of Liondore, who had a racking cough. Of course, he knew that such a signature in the absence of the testator and the other witness was inoperative. For this signature Stein was later disbarred.[146]

There was a preparatory criminal examination against Leah, Pickover and Stein on a charge of forging and uttering a document bearing the date 16 November 1936, purporting to be the last will of one Isadore Liondore who died on 19 December 1936. The accused were defended by two heavyweight counsel, and were discharged, the magistrate finding that the evidence of the Crown witnesses had been most unsatisfactory.

What happened after that to Leah and Pickover is not known to me. All that I can say is that will number one prevailed.

THE LITHUANIAN WILL — *an unnecessary piece of play-acting*

A somewhat similar tale was told by H H (Harry) Morris QC, the famous defender of criminals and noted wit, in his book *In My Anecdotage.*[147] Husband and wife were immigrants from Lithuania. They were childless. After years of hard work they had acquired fairly substantial wealth, which they invested in a block of flats. 'Then came the awakening. They found according to the laws of Lithuania that the marriage was out of community and that the building belonged to him alone. He decided to make a will entirely in her favour and thus cut out from participation in his estate an entirely useless nephew and niece.' Unfortunately, his sense of economy caused him to persuade the estate agent who managed his block of flats to draw up and supervise the signing of his will. It was not properly attested and so, on the death of the testator, it was found to be invalid. On intestacy in those days the wife obtained very little, and the bulk of the estate would go to the nephew and niece. 'In such circumstances a decent person would have waived all claim to any share of the estate. Few people are built that way. There was no doubt that morally the estate was hers and that it had been her husband's wish that she should have it. Something had to be done about this.' Regrettably she went about it the wrong way. She could have forged a properly executed will and lodged it with the Master of the Supreme Court with considerable hopes of success. But she felt that 'a full-blooded play was necessary. She invited some friends to her house and in their presence went through her husband's wardrobe in order to give to them what she did not require. During the search she came across a sealed envelope. Suddenly she said: "Good God, here is my husband's will", and promptly fainted. . . . The envelope was then unsealed and it was found that the widow's prediction of the contents of the envelope was correct. Unfortunately she made it before the envelope was opened.' The upshot was that the nephew and niece threatened litigation; '. . . in the end everything was settled, mainly in favour of the niece and nephew, and that was the end of an unnecessary piece of play-acting'.

REX v FOREMAN (1) — two purported wills

The accused in *Rex v Foreman (1)*[148] was charged with having forged not only one document but two documents purporting to be the wills of one deceased James. James had left an undoubtedly valid will drawn by Barclays Bank in the usual legal form. Then appeared two manuscript documents, not couched in the usual legal language associated with wills. One was undated and the other purported to have been executed on 6 August 1950 in a particular ward of the Bulawayo General Hospital. In the case Mr Justice Beadle allowed evidence to be given of statements by James which tended to show that his state of mind just before his death was consistent with his regarding the Barclay's Bank will as his valid and only will. I venture to predict that the outcome of the various proceedings relating to James's estate was that this will was found to be the only valid one.

STATE v VAN ZYL — justice was done

Certainly the impugned document in *State v Van Zyl*[149] was found not to be a will. Erasmus Johannes van Zyl had died in an old-age home in Keetmanshoop on 18 June 1981. He was a bachelor, had lived in the home since 1974, and had left a net estate of over eighty-five thousand rand. In a will executed on 30 October 1975 he had left his entire estate to his sister. She had died on 1 July 1981, shortly after her brother. But on the day of the death of the brother, the accused, one J M van Zyl, lodged with the Master a typed document purporting to be a will executed by the deceased on 12 May 1978 in which he revoked all previous wills and instituted — naturally — the accused as his sole heir. One of the heirs of the sister contested the validity of this alleged later will. Expert evidence established that the signature of the testator to it was not that of the deceased and that the document had been typed on the typewriter of the accused. The fraudster was sentenced to three years' imprisonment, half suspended on certain conditions. Justice was done.

PILLAY v NAGAN — a fitting punishment

The latest case on a forged will in the law reports, *Pillay v Nagan*,[150] is of legal significance in that for the first time in South Africa a court held that a person who had forged a will was disqualified from inheriting on intestacy, a rule that is really self-evident. Here a son had forged a will purporting to be that of his mother. In it he was instituted, in convincing legal language, as sole heir (subject to certain conditions attached to his inheriting a piece of land, if he were to sell it). Through this document the fraudster would have deprived his brothers and sisters of their rights of succession ab intestato. The forgery was established, and as a consequence the deceased mother was held to have died intestate and the peccant son was declared unworthy to succeed, a fitting punishment for his fraud.

Two unreported South African instances of forged wills deserve mention.

ERIC STAFFORD — *the financial consultant's forgery*

On 30 December 1991 Ernest Williston Stanton, aged eighty-nine, died in Durban, leaving an estate worth some two million rand. His son Lacon believed that he was sole heir of his father's estate in terms of a will made in 1971. But within forty-five minutes of his father's death Lacon Stanton was told by one Eric Stafford, who had advised his father on investments and his financial affairs generally, that his father had made a new will in 1990, leaving a hundred thousand rand to each of his three grandchildren, a hundred and ten thousand rand among nine charitable organizations, and the balance of the estate to Stafford, so disinheriting his sole child. Deeply suspicious of the authenticity of the alleged new will, Lacon soon secured an interdict freezing the assets of the estate, and set about establishing that the new will had been forged by Stafford, which he did through a handwriting expert, Mr Cecil Greenfield, scrutinizing copies of his father's signatures to documents going back to 1926. Stanton also discovered other documents that led him to allege that Stafford had defrauded his father in many other respects, including the sale of investments. Stafford had meantime gone insolvent, his estate being sequestrated on 29 June 1993, and was the subject of a string of charges of fraud, forgery and theft amounting to many millions of rand. On 8 June 1993 he had been arrested on these charges. At least Stanton had the satisfaction of having the Natal Court on 22 October 1993 declare that the new will was a forgery and so restoring the original will making him sole heir.[151]

That left the criminal consequences of Stafford's forgery of the will to be decided on, among the other charges against him. The trial came before Mr J J Augustyn in Durban in the regional court of Natal, Stafford, insolvent, having been refused legal aid, appearing for himself. It ran for sixty court days, starting on 15 November 1993. There were 151 counts, which involved forgery, fraud, theft and statutory offences under the Insolvency Act and Banks Act. The accused was found guilty on over a hundred of them, including forging the will of Ernest Stanton, and was sentenced to an effective twelve years' imprisonment.

Who was Eric Albert Edgar Thomas Guattary Stafford? He was a person in his mid-forties who had started his career working in Rhodesia for important financial firms such as Syfrets. In 1977 he emigrated to South Africa, where, after serving such leading institutions as Barclays Bank and the United Building Society, he set off on his own in 1982 as a financial consultant, using companies that were his alter egos. One was tailored to place funds he collected in destinations abroad. By offering high interest rates and exercising charm he attracted loans. The trustees of his insolvent estate found that 120 creditors had proved claims amounting to twenty million rand, with another five million rand in claims anticipated. But thirteen million rand he had had from clients was unaccounted for. Many elderly people had suffered grievous losses, among them Ernest Stanton. Several, having lost all their savings, committed suicide.

MOOSA v THE MASTER OF THE SUPREME COURT — 13 forged signatures?

A dispute among handwriting experts was decided by Mr Justice McCreath in an impressive judgment in *Moosa v The Master of the Supreme Court.*[152] Jacoob Adam died a bachelor on 9 September 1992. There was a sharp conflict among Adam's sisters and brothers over whether a document purporting to be his will and bearing his signature and the signatures of two witnesses on 21 August 1992 was valid. The benefits of these relations varied according as Adam died testate or intestate. Adam had suffered from rheumatoid arthritis, increasing in severity over the months prior to his death. The degree of the disability was disputed. A nephew of Adam's, one Mohammed, an attorney, testified that he had prepared the will and saw Adam and the two witnesses sign all thirteen pages in the presence of one another. Adam had signed with some difficulty, clasping the pen with all fingers and thumbs, pausing from time to time, even while signing. The court found that Mohammed was an impressive witness and patently honest. It was highly improbable that he would make himself party to a fraud in asserting that the will had been properly signed by Adam and the two witnesses. There was no evidence to suggest that the signatures of the witnesses had been forged or that they had anything to gain from attesting to a forged signature of Adam. Finally, Mr Justice McCreath considered the evidence of handwriting experts. Messrs Fourie and Bam, called by the plaintiffs, and Mr Cecil Greenfield, called by the defendants, conceded that there was a relative paucity of specimen signatures and handwriting of Adam's closer to the time of his death.

Fourie and Bam considered that the signatures of Adam's were forged. Mr Justice McCreath preferred the views of Greenfield. To the judge the differences between the signatures on the will and the specimens available for comparison that were concentrated on by Fourie and Bam paid insufficient regard to what would be expected of a man with Adam's disabilities called on to sign thirteen times; it was not something to be expected of a forger. The judge preferred the views of Greenfield, who concluded that, bearing in mind Adam's physical condition and the fact that all the signatures were governed by the same basic model patterns, the differences between the questioned signatures were natural variations and, paradoxically, pointed to genuineness. A forger would find it very difficult to produce a set of flaws and irregularities in such thirteen signatures and simultaneously maintain consistency with the basic model patterns shown in the specimens; and to maintain the deception without introducing entirely alien elements. I must say that, looking at the photocopy of the will, I am struck by the force of the observations of Greenfield.

CRESWELL v JACKSON — a codicil in a pickle jar

Several notable instances of forgery of wills abroad call for attention. Sir Robert Megarry in his most entertaining book, *A Second Miscellany-at-Law*,[153] deals with the protracted litigation in the eighteen-fifties and -sixties in *Creswell v Jackson*.[154] The deceased estate involved was worth £50 000, probably around £2 500 000 in present-day money. The will left the estate to a relation of the testator; but three codicils that were alleged by the plaintiff to amend it would give most of it to an employee and some other persons. The codicils were all in the same handwriting as the will and they contained grave misspellings of words that were correctly spelled in the will and always so by the testator, but Else, one of the claimants under the codicils, habitually misspelled the words that way. The employee said he had found them; but the discoveries were very strange. One codicil was in a penny memorandum book; the second was in a pickle jar in a hole in the wall under the sill of a window of an outhouse; and the third was in that hole. The second and third had been found nine months after the first. Serjeant Hayes, alleging that the codicils were spurious, argued satirically that if the proceedings had not been started, after the gestation period of nine months a fourth codicil would surely have emerged. And to find two codicils in a hole in a wall over which was screwed a sixty-pound vice, requiring the testator, suffering from a gravely injured back, to unscrew it, deposit the documents, and then rescrew it! All this to prevent anyone from finding the documents!

In 1859 the Master of the Rolls, Sir John Romilly, ordered the validity of the codicils to be decided by a jury. A jury before Chief Justice Erle found them to be valid; but the Master of the Rolls was not satisfied and ordered a retrial. It came before Chief Baron Pollock the following year; this time the jury found them to be invalid. Ultimately the House of Lords ordered a retrial, and in 1864 a jury under Chief Justice Cockburn also found for invalidity. Believe it or not, a fourth codicil was now produced, which would have ratified the first three. But the Master of the Rolls threw it out without even calling on Serjeant Hayes.

THE WHALLEY WILL CASE — *a near failure of justice*

Two decades later an important case of a forgery of a will was heard in England. It was dealt with by Viscount Alverstone in his *Recollections of Bar and Bench.*[155] Alverstone, then Sir Richard Webster, had been Attorney-General during the periods 1885–92 and 1895–1900, and now, Baron Alverstone, was Lord Chief Justice from 1900 to 1915, when he died at the age of seventy-three. He said that 'the Whalley Will Case in the year 1884 [was] one of the most remarkable cases ever tried in a Court of Law, and which very nearly resulted in a gross failure of justice'. James Whalley died on 7 May 1881, a bachelor, leaving an illegitimate son, Henry Priestman, whom he called his nephew, and an illegitimate daughter, Emma, whom he called his niece. At the time of his death Whalley had been lodging with a railway porter, Charles Thomas. It was known that Whalley had said that he would leave his estate to Priestman, of whom he was very fond. According to Priestman, Whalley, a few days before he died, displayed to his 'nephew' a piece of blue foolscap paper, saying it was his will and in it he had left Priestman most of his property. But Priestman was not shown the paper in order to read its contents. On Whalley's death, he was found to be worth £100 000. The piece of blue paper was not discovered, but another document purporting to be a will was. It left Priestman £5 000, a wine merchant, Edward Gunnell, £100, and the residue to Charles Thomas.

Priestman, represented by the renowned Sir Charles Russell, and the next of kin, represented by Webster, attacked the validity of the supposed will. There was no doubt about the validity of the testator's signature, below which appeared the date (that had been spelt out in the body of the will, 'twenty-first day of March one thousand eight hundred and eighty-one') ' March 21/81'. It was known that when he wrote a letter, Whalley used to put the date just below his signature.

Russell and Webster felt compelled to agree to a compromise, under which a third of the estate was to go according to the will, a third to Priestman, and a third to the next of kin.

Priestman, celebrating his good fortune, went in a brake past the house of Thomas, who, out of bravado, displayed in the window a sheet of blue foolscap paper. The 'nephew' was now convinced that this was the true will. Inquiries led to the emergence of the following facts at the subsequent trial to set aside the compromise: The signature in ink by Whalley had been initially to a letter in pencil written for him by a scribe to Priestman, saying that he was very ill and asking Priestman to see him. The letter had ended half way down the page. Thomas, Gunnell and a solicitor's clerk named Nash had obtained the letter. Nash had written a will in ink on the paper and rubbed out the writing in pencil.

The will looked peculiar in its spacing. Half way down the drafter apparently feared that he was running out of space, so for several lines he had cramped the words together. Then, finding he had too much space, he widened the gap between words.

Counsel caused the original 'will' to be obtained and very good photographs made of it (one is to be found in Alverstone's book) in which some of the original pencil writing had partly reappeared. (It is fascinating to see how advanced photography was around 1883.) Counsel also produced in court the scribe of the original letter, establishing that the pencil writing that had reappeared was in his hand.

In the upshot the court set aside the compromise. Priestman allowed the next of kin to retain the third originally allocated to him; the balance Priestman kept. Some of those who committed the fraud were later convicted at the Old Bailey.

'AND I PUT IT TO YE, WITNESS . . .' — *Daniel O'Connell's wit*

The following captivating story is told by Edward Abinger in his autobiographical work, *Forty Years at the Bar.*[156] To attempt to summarize it or even to recount it in different words would cause it to lose its fragrance:

'Daniel O'Connell, probably one of the greatest counsel who ever practised at the English or Irish Bar, was opposing probate of a will. His case was that after the testator's death his hand was guided by the plaintiff into making the deceased man's signature. The following dialogue ensued:

' "I put it to ye, witness," said O'Connell, "that when the man's name was written at the bottom of the will he was dead."

' "And I tell ye, Mr Counsellor, there was loife in him."

' "And I put it to ye, witness," said O'Connell, "by the oath that ye have taken, that the man was dead."

' "And I tell ye, Mr Counsellor," replied the witness, "by the name of the Holy Virgin, there was loife in him."

'O'Connell, noticing the strained manner in which the witness had repeated the words "there was loife in him," put the following question which may have been induced by previous experience:

' "And I put it to ye, witness, that ye caught a floi (fly) upon the dead man's mouth and put it in and then took his hand and made his signature."

'The witness immediately broke down.'

WILLIAM COOPER HOBBS — *lawyer and rogue*

One of the most disreputable lawyers who ever lived, William Cooper Hobbs, had among his several unsuccessful crimes the forgery of a will. Hobbs, until he was struck off the roll of solicitors of England, ran a practice in London after World War I. A principal activity of his was discovering the identity of, and then blackmailing, wealthy homosexuals. One homosexual, though, he befriended, the well-known theatrical wigmaker of Wardour Street, William ('Willie') Berry Clarkson. A decade after Hobbs had spent seven years of imprisonment for involvement in the celebrated blackmailing of Sir Hari Singh, nephew of the Maharaj of Kashmir, for alleged adultery, he faced a most tempting opportunity of unearned gain when Clarkson died on 13 October 1934. The will of the deceased, on a printed form, appointed Hobbs as executor, but merely made a few simple bequests and named no heir. Hobbs asked Edmund O'Connor, a former practising but now disbarred solicitor who had acted for him in various actions for libel that he had brought, and had acted also for Clarkson, to seek a later will. It was found. In it Hobbs was appointed residuary heir. It was proved to have been forged. For the forgery O'Connor was rewarded with seven years' imprisonment and Hobbs with five. After his release, Hobbs until his death in June 1945 continued with his long-time activity of threatening newspapers with actions for libel, sometimes obtaining a handsome settlement.[157]

THOMAS PATRICK MORRIS — *forger of note*

The story of a forged marriage certificate as well as a forged will is told by Robert S Menchin in his book *Where There's a Will.*[158] In 1931 Miss Ella Wendel, a recluse, died, leaving the bulk of her estate of about forty million dollars to charity. Some 2 303 claims were made to the part of the estate that went on intestacy, mostly by distant relatives. A claimant to everything was Thomas Patrick Morris, who in the witness box contended that he was the son of Ella's late brother. He told a detailed story of his mother's secret marriage, produced the 'marriage certificate', and also a 'will' making him sole heir. All went well until it was discovered that the Bible in which the 'marriage certificate' was inserted was printed twenty-four years after the certificate. Further inquiries revealed that the will was a forgery. Morris's reward was three years' imprisonment.

RONALD SHULMAN — *and a wife in the nude*

A delightful story of a forged will is told by the well-known writer Fenton Bresler in his *Second-Best Bed: A Diversion on Wills.*[159] In March 1971 Clive Raphael was killed in the crash of an aeroplane in France. He left an estate worth £500 000 and no will. The situation was too tempting to an English barrister, Ronald Shulman. He composed a fine-looking will, signed it with a passable imitation of Raphael's signature, got two accomplices to sign as witnesses, and, save for a small legacy, made himself the sole beneficiary. The legacy was to Raphael's estranged widow, a spirited, attractive young model. It was of one shilling and four photographs of herself in the nude. She was not satisfied and instituted proceedings that resulted in the 'will' being set aside, Shulman disappearing to some foreign country, and the two witnesses being sentenced to imprisonment.

BILLIONAIRE HOWARD HUGHES — *was there a will?*

Was there a will left by the billionaire Howard Hughes, who died at 1:27 pm on 5 April 1976[160] aboard a Lear jet aeroplane over Texas en route from Acapulco, Mexico to Methodist Hospital in Houston (his long abandoned place of birth) for treatment after he apparently had had a stroke?

Hughes was seventy years of age when he died, his six foot two inches frame weighing only ninety-two pounds. At the end of his life he was very eccentric, paranoid, and suffering from drug addiction (broken needles were embedded in his arms) and medical neglect. One of the wealthiest persons in the world, and once a handsome Texan tycoon, darling of Hollywood female stars, Hughes had not been seen by those outside his immediate entourage for the past twenty years. The US Internal Revenue Service, very interested in estate tax, took fingerprints of the corpse to establish that it was that of Hughes.

Though he was childless and his two marriages had each ended in a divorce, it was generally believed that Hughes must have left a will. His investments were still vast, though estimates of its size varied greatly — from under one and a half billion dollars, according to Lawrence B Gibbs, a Washington tax attorney representing a large number of Hughes's maternal relations claiming the right to his estate,[161] to over six billion dollars according to Phelan and Chester in their book on the Hughes estate.[162] After years of wrangling in the probate courts, his personal estate alone at the time of his death was valued at a billion dollars.

The closest surviving blood relation of Hughes was his maternal aunt, Annette Gano Lummis, of Houston, where her son, William Rice Lummis, was a practising attorney. Neither he nor his mother had seen Hughes for thirty-nine years. Will Lummis was to play a major and successful role in the unravelling of the deceased estate, in the avoidance of estate taxes consuming all the assets, in securing an agreement among potential intestate heirs to avoid costly and time-consuming litigation, and in procuring an eventual steady distribution of money from the estate among them.

Over the next five years after the death of Hughes forty-one 'wills' were discovered, but all save four were almost immediately found unacceptable — either they were not properly executed or were rejected out of hand by the probate authorities. Four went before the courts. The first one was the so-called handwritten (holograph) Mormon will, said to have been pushed twenty-five days after the death of Hughes under the door of the headquarters of the Mormon Church at Salt Lake City. One of the bequests was a sixteenth of the estate to Melvin Dummar, a Mormon filling-station attendant. His story was that some years earlier he had picked up a dishevelled man in the Nevada desert and had given him a lift to Las Vegas. The will turned out to be by that very man — none other than Howard Hughes. The court didn't fall for the story. While the handwriting resembled that of Hughes, the will was peppered with striking spelling and grammatical errors, which

Hughes was incapable of committing; and it contained the oddest incongruities. As for the handwriting, it was discovered that Dummar had removed a page from a book in a college library that had contained a photograph of a handwritten letter by Hughes. Dummar's fingerprints were found on the book. Furthermore, a thumbprint of his was discovered on the envelope that had contained the 'will'.

More plausible was the alleged will put forward by the most respectable Howard Hughes Medical Institute, which Hughes had often said, finally as late as 1973, that he wished to be the beneficiary of the whole of his personal estate. The difficulty was that if there had been such a will, it had disappeared. The case was reported in the American law reports as *Howard Hughes Medical Institute v Neff.*[163] The Institute alleged that it was the principal beneficiary of a last will made by Hughes some time between 1953 and 1963, or else it was the intended beneficiary of a last will executed on 30 May 1925. The Court of Appeals of Texas, Houston (14th District) found against the Institute, holding that there was insufficient evidence to show due execution of a will or its contents.

Slightly earlier there was a brave attempt by Terry Moore (also known as Helen Cramer) to prove that she was an heir. Undoubtedly the claimant in 1949, when she was eighteen and an aspirant Hollywood star, had had an affair with Hughes, then a womanizer specializing in leading and would-be leading screen actresses. She now alleged that she had married Hughes in a ceremony at sea, aboard a yacht that left San Diego in 1949.[164] The ceremony, so she said, was performed by Captain C B Flynn, (conveniently) now deceased, in the presence of the claimant's mother and certain relatives, of whom her mother alone was still alive, and the couple were still married at the time of Hughes's death. Accordingly, she inherited his estate.[165] Unfortunately, Terry could not give the name of the vessel or the date of the marriage ceremony. No marriage certificate had ever been issued, nor could she produce any other document in support of her claim. The ship's log had disappeared years ago. Worse still, before Hughes died Terry had been married and divorced thrice, the men being, in order, Glen Davis (an all-American football player), Eugene McGrath and Stewart Cramer. In the marriage licence of her union with Davis, she stated that she had not been married before. Furthermore, in the divorce proceedings brought against her by Cramer in 1970 in the Supreme Court of California she stated that she was married to him on 28 June 1959 and asked for the award of custody of the children of the union, child and spouse support, and community property. In the circumstances she could not say (in legal language, she was estopped from saying) that at the time she was married to Hughes. And that is what Judge Pat Gregory held in the Probate Court No 2, Harris County, Texas on 27 June 1981; an appeal to the Court of Appeals of Texas, Houston, was dismissed. A similar judgment was delivered by a Nevada court. Terry's attorney lodged an appeal against both judgments. The settlement of the Hughes estate was then threatened by a delay of several years. Lummis and his advisers offered Terry a confidential sum in settlement, which would be substantially reduced each day it was not accepted. It was accepted almost at once. Later the sum paid was revealed: 390 000 dollars. Privately, Judge Gregory called it 'go away money'.

The fourth failed attempt to establish a claim in the Hughes estate took place in 1981.[166] It had its own distinctive charm. In mid-1981 Martha Jo Graves produced a five-page document drawn in precise legal language with impeccable spelling and witnessed by two most respectable citizens. Martha Graves, in her early fifties, claimed to have worked for several attorneys in Los Angeles and to have founded a number of mining and oil-drilling companies. The will, which was dated 24 July 1960, when Hughes was staying at the Beverly Hills Hotel, was on its stationery. Martha Jo asserted that she came across the will only now, as it had been housed amid the papers of a Los Angeles attorney, a former FBI agent, for whom she had worked for ten years. In 1979 he had died in a plane crash, and she had stored his papers. Only in 1981 did she start sorting them. There was a metal security box; the combination lock numbers of its dial lock she eventually solved. Within it was the will, the witnesses to which, to her astonishment, were her own doctor, Dr Stanley DuBrin, and a businessman she knew, Harold W Mallet. Both were to swear that they had seen Hughes some twenty-one years ago sign two copies of this will. It left 80 per cent of his personal estate to the Howard Hughes Medical Institute, William Lummis to be the sole trustee (but only for as long as he did not challenge the will), and 20 per cent to the Acme Mining Company, of which Martha Jo was president and major stockholder. Martha Jo telephoned an attorney friend in Houston, who said she should bring the will by plane to him. She photocopied the will twice, leaving the copies in her apartment, and then caught a plane to Houston. Unfortunately, she continued, the airline lost her briefcase containing the original will. But the photocopies, she had been advised, were legally acceptable in the circumstances. To Lummis it was clear that Martha Jo had concocted a clever plan to get the will she had forged to be accepted. He had been virtually unknown to Hughes in 1960.

At a deposition the two witnesses came out very badly. The Acme Mining Company, now called the Acme International Corporation, was proved to be an inactive shell whose property consisted of two filing cabinets in Martha Jo's apartment. The two witnesses confessed that they had signed the will, which Martha had drafted. While they were not prosecuted, Martha Jo was. She received the modest prison sentence of a year, the only one of the several forgers of wills of Hughes and the many who committed perjury about the disposition of his estate to land up in gaol.

SUSAN, BARONESS DE STEMPEL — *a will to succeed*

In 1989 and 1990 the press had a field day with the trials of Susan, Baroness de Stempel (born Wilberforce).[167] This lady and her aunt, the then Margaret Wilberforce (called Aunt Puss), had grown up in Markington Hall, Yorkshire, the family home of the Wilberforce family, its best known member being the great William Wilberforce (1759–1833), leader of the movement to abolish the slave trade and subsequently slavery itself. In 1931 Margaret, then thirty-one, not well to do, married the wealthy Lord Illingworth, thirty-five years older than her. In 1942 he died, and Margaret now embarked on a grand social life. Susan had a standard upper-class childhood with largely absent parents. They were shocked when in 1957 at the age of twenty-three she decided to marry Simon Dale, a six-foot-three-inches, two-hundred-and-forty-pound, thirty-eight-year-old half-blind architect who did not hail from the aristocracy. Two years later Susan made the fateful purchase of the fine mansion Heath House. Within six years of her marriage she bore Simon five children. But the union was already breaking up. Susan had to get her aunt Margaret to pay her children's school fees. Simon was behaving bizarrely, holding that the house was on the site of Camelot. And he was beating Susan. In 1973 she obtained a divorce and returned to the surname of Wilberforce. She tried unsuccessfully for fourteen years to get Simon to vacate Heath House. Anyone wishing to view it was confronted with Simon's shot gun. To house herself and her children Susan bought a modest semidetached cottage with the grandiose name of Forresters Hall.

The mental state of Margaret, Lady Illingworth, had deteriorated greatly. She had been suffering from Alzheimer's disease from the late seventies. Suddenly in February 1984 Susan, who had not seen her aunt for years, invited her to stay at Forresters Hall, already hopelessly crowded. That gave Susan the opportunity to forge Margaret's will, which left almost the whole of her very large estate to Susan. Susan now began leading a luxurious life, funded even before Margaret's death by forged cheques, the sale of her aunt's valuable antiques and other money-raising activities. She married Michael de Stempel on 11 September 1984, but that union ended with a divorce decree in 1986. In November 1986 at the age of eighty-six Margaret died in a state nursing home, apparently destitute, virtually abandoned by her niece, on whose instructions she was given a pauper's funeral despite her wish to be buried next to her husband's grave.

Susan, Baroness de Stempel now renewed her efforts to get her former husband Simon Dale to vacate Heath House. They were in vain. Then in the evening of 11 September 1987 a person was admitted through the kitchen door, who proceeded to bludgeon the very large man to his death. It turned out that Susan and some of her children had been working on the exterior of the mansion shortly before. The police believed she had done the deed. In July 1989 she was tried for the murder of Dale, but an eleven-day trial resulted in her acquittal. The police, however, had been mystified on how Susan's bank accounts some time before had unaccountably swollen and how she had acquired some valuable antique furniture and expensive motor cars. In 1990 she was tried for and found guilty of forging her aunt's will and stealing over half a million pounds from her. She was sentenced to seven years' imprisonment. Her former husband, De Stempel, and her children Sophia and Marcus were tried for and found guilty of conspiring to steal, he receiving a prison sentence of four years, Sophia of thirty months and Marcus of eighteen months.

DAVID SPILLMAN — *and the persistent solicitor*

An intriguing case[168] involved the falsification of the will of Annie Kay, who died at the age of eighty-seven in March 1997 at Leigh-on-Sea in Essex. She never married, but lived with her mother until her mother's death in the sixties. A gifted pianist, during the war she used to play at ENSA parties in London for the entertainment of members of the armed forces. It was generally believed that she was a pensioner with limited means, but she was a very wealthy person who left an estate of some £1.8 million, which had reached this sum through her clever investment of several inheritances.

For some years Patrick Wedd shared her bungalow in Dawlish Drive. They were spotted as possible prey by David Spillman, his wife Annette and her mother Annette Russill. Spillman was a lorry driver with convictions for petty crime who persuaded his wife to keep an eye out for a possibly rich, elderly woman whose days were numbered and who had few close relations and friends. Mrs Spillman became a home help in 1996 at Miss Kay's bungalow and ingratiated herself with the old lady. The police believed that she went through the papers of Miss Kay, including her eight bank and building society accounts that amounted to over £500 000.

Within a fortnight Annette Spillman had persuaded Miss Kay and Wedd to move into the Spillmans' house in Guildford Road, Southend, several miles away. Mrs Spillman had once held a licence to run her house as a nursing home for the aged, but the licence had been withdrawn two years back. By this time Annie Kay was housebound with ulcerated legs and Wedd was very frail. In January 1997 Wedd, aged eighty-three, died, leaving Miss Kay his entire estate, amounting to £165 000.

Miss Kay's solicitor, Peter Boardman, called to discuss her tax affairs and her will. Annette Spillman listened to the interview over the baby monitor which she had put on. To her delight she discovered that Miss Kay possessed an estate of some £1.8 million. The main beneficiaries were Scope (previously known as the Spastics Society) and a local charity for the blind. It was arranged that Mr Boardman would return in a few days to update the will.

Now it was time for the Spillmans and Russill to put their plan into operation. First of all Russill, who had a criminal record, was induced (she claimed intimidated) by her son-in-law into practising Miss Kay's signature. In a television programme on Channel 4 on the case, the police showed pages of paper they had found in the Spillmans' house covered with trial bogus signatures. Finally Spillman was satisfied with the product.

Next Spillman, professing to speak on behalf of Miss Kay, informed Boardman that she was changing solicitors. As Annie Kay had been a loyal, if rather trying, client for the past fifteen years, Boardman was nonplussed.

John Twitchen, another Southend solicitor, was engaged to draft a new will for Miss Kay. Russill impersonated the old lady, looking very frail, wearing a wig, padding and heavy make-up. She pretended to reside at the former house in Leigh-on-Sea. Twitchen sent his qualified clerk, Mark Goodson, to take instructions. He found 'Miss Annie Kay' wrapped in a blanket, sitting on a chair in the lounge. She told him that she wanted to make a new will, leaving her estate in equal shares to David and Annette Spillman for the care, love and kindness they had shown her, apart from a bequest of £10 000, which was to go to her good friend Annette Russill.

Goodson drew up the will and returned in a few days with it, bringing his mother with him to be one of the witnesses.

Within two months the real Miss Kay was dead. She had been under sedation for a long time.

When the new will was produced, Boardman became very suspicious, particularly as he had been denied access to an old client. Initially he thought the Spillmans might have exercised undue influence on Annie Kay. Accordingly, he notified Scope, and Scope instructed a solicitor specializing in charity law, Peter Jeffreys of the firm of solicitors Henmans in Oxfordshire, to investigate the matter. (Henmans was founded by the father of the tennis star Tim Henman. Jeffreys appeared in the television production.)

Jeffreys placed a caveat on the will preventing any moneys being paid to the legatees. (Such a caveat in English law is entered in the Probate Registry prohibiting a grant of representation issuing in respect of the estate without reference to the person who gave the notice, the caveator.) Thereafter Jeffreys got into touch with Goodson, who showed him his detailed notes and said that the lady who executed the will was clearly of sound mind, had acted of her own free will without any appearance of pressure by anyone, and definitely wished to benefit the Spillmans and Annette Russill.

Still not satisfied that all was in order, Jeffreys (a devotee of the detective novels of Dorothy Sayers) interviewed former neighbours of Miss Kay when she was still living in her bungalow. One informed him that the old lady had not ever returned there after she had departed with the Spillmans. In the middle of that night Jeffreys woke up realizing what must have happened: someone had impersonated Annie Kay.

Looking at copies of certain documents the real Annie had signed and a copy of the alleged new will, Jeffreys became convinced that the signature of Annie Kay on the new will had been forged. This was confirmed by a handwriting expert.

For almost a year Jeffreys built up a case to have the new will set aside. In addition, he informed the police of his findings. The police obtained an order permitting them to exhume the bodies of Annie Kay and Patrick Wedd, the first such order ever obtained by the Essex police. The bodies had been buried in the same grave at Sutton Road cemetery in Southend. Postmortem examinations were conducted, which revealed that both bodies contained large amounts of thioridazine, a sedative used to calm the senile. Unfortunately, there had been no research on the properties of the drug and whether reliable conclusions could be arrived at from bodies buried for a year or more. The coroner had to record deaths from unascertainable causes.

When Twitchen, who was acting for the legatees in putting forward their claims, was told by the police of their belief that the will had been forged, his immediate unbelieving reaction was that it sounded like a story by Agatha Christie. When he was confronted with the opinion of his own handwriting expert that Miss Kay's signature had been forged, he changed his tune and ceased to appear for the Spillmans and Russill.

The police arrested the three for conspiracy to defraud. Their trial took place in the Basildon Crown Court in July 1999. The two women pleaded guilty. Annette Spillman (47) was sentenced to two years' imprisonment and Annette Russill (65) to three years'. David Spillman (45) pleaded not guilty but was found guilty and sentenced to seven years'. The estate of Annie Kay was distributed in accordance with her real will. The two solicitors who pursued their suspicions out of a determination to see that justice was done caused two most worthy charities to receive what the testator intended them to receive and deserve public approbation.

NINA WANG — *billionaire beyond dreams of avarice*

The last case of a forged will, decided near the closing date of the survey conducted in this opusculum, is a fascinating one concerned with wealth, in Dr Samuel Johnson's immortal words, beyond the dreams of avarice.[169]

The story starts with a will executed by a Hong Kong billionaire in 1968, Teddy Wang, disinheriting his billionaire wife, Nina Wang, and leaving his estate to his father, Wang Dinshin. The cause of the disherison, so claimed Wang Sr, was his son's discovery of his wife's adultery, which led him in his fury to say that he would beat her paramour to death. But he did not do that; nor was there a divorce. In 1983 Teddy Wang was kidnapped, but he survived. The next kidnap, however, was fatal. It was in April 1990. The kidnappers, holding their victim in their speedboat in the South China Sea, were pursued by a Chinese naval vessel. It was concluded that Teddy Wang, who was never seen again, had been thrown overboard. In 1999 Teddy was declared to be dead by the High Court of Hong Kong. Later Nina Wang produced an alleged will, executed a month before the disappearance of her husband. It had been witnessed by the family butler and his wife. In it the testator purported to have stated: 'My beloved wife is the one I love most on earth. My parents have been disappointing to me.' Nina's family, who were thought to have been on good terms with Teddy, were excluded from any benefits on the ground that they were 'all obnoxious'. Nina was instituted as sole heir.

The new will led to an action before Mr Justice David Yam of the High Court of Hong Kong that extended over 172 court days, starting early in 2001 and ending with his judgment, 558 pages long, on 21 November 2002. The case aroused enormous interest in the territory. It was more exciting than any TV soap-opera — better even than 'The Bold and the Beautiful' at its most spine-tingling episodes. After all, Nina Wang, aged sixty-four, in her own right was the richest woman in Asia, her estate, according to *Forbes* magazine, amounting to 2.4 billion US dollars. And Nina was renowned for her love of pigtailed dolls modelled on herself, leading to her being labelled 'Little Sweetie' by the local media. Her father-in-law, ninety-one-year-old Wang Sr, aroused much public sympathy when he shambled into court with his head covered in a woollen cap to shield him from the freezing airconditioning.

Four documents in Chinese were presented to the court as constituting the new will. The judge found that they contained 'convoluted, unreasonable and untrue expressions'. Each document was embellished by the strange words in English, 'one life, one love'. Teddy Wang, said the judge, was 'not a romantic person at all', according to the evidence. He used to handle legal documents with great care, and these words in English seemed suspiciously out of place. They appeared to have been written by Nina Wang. The contention of the defence that the 1990 will was executed by Teddy as a result of a light fall from his horse could not be accepted; he had not changed his will after his kidnapping in 1983. In any event, Mr Justice Yam concluded, after carefully analysing the evidence of handwriting experts: 'I have no doubt that the questioned signatures are forged signatures and the 1990 documents are forged documents.'

One of the four documents, found the judge, was probably composed by Nina Wang.

The court found in favour of the 1968 will.

The legal costs of the case, amounting to 54 million Hong Kong dollars, equivalent to 6.9 million US dollars and 4.4 million pounds, had to be borne mainly by Nina Wang. The amount seems to be a mere bagatelle to her, particularly as she had bought more shares in Chinachem, the city's largest property company, enabling her to buttress her control of it.

The legal representatives of Nina Wang said that they would appeal against the judgment. The Hong Kong police stated that they would study the judgment and get legal advice before deciding on whether to institute a prosecution.

The public as a whole were regaled by the court's reference to a modern version of Psalm 39:6, reading:

'Man is a mere phantom as he goes to and fro.
He bustles about, but only in vain;
He heaps up wealth, not knowing who will get it.'[170]

With this elevating sentiment I close my book.

Notes

[1] For example, Glanville Williams *Textbook of Criminal Law* (London: Stevens and Sons 1978) 93 note 3 and *Learning the Law* 11th ed (1982) (London: Stevens and Sons 1982) 3, especially note 3. See also Bryan A Garner *A Dictionary of Modern Legal Usage* 2nd ed (New York and Oxford: Oxford University Press 1995) 17.

[2] For the life of Daisy de Melker and her trial I have made use of the judgment of Mr Justice Greenberg printed in *The First Forty Years, Being the Memoirs of H. H. Morris K.C.* (Cape Town & Johannesburg: Juta & Co Ltd 1948) 257–95 and Morris's account in chapter XXV of his book. I have also consulted the lengthy account by the leading South African author on criminal trials, Benjamin Bennett, in his biography of Morris, *Genius for the Defence* (Cape Town: Howard Timmins 1959) chapter VII, which I found most useful. I also consulted Napier Devitt's *Memoirs of a Magistrate* (London: H F & G Witherby) 1935 edition.

[3] Morris op cit note 2 at 227.

[4] *The Night is Long* (London: Faber and Faber Ltd 1941) 316.

[5] Op cit note 2 at 220.

[6] *Forty Years of Murder: An Autobiography* (London: George G. Harrap & Co Ltd 1978) Granada Publishing Ltd 1980 reprint pp 268–9.

[7] On his retirement Watt held the qualifications of ED MB ChB (Edin) FRCPE FRSE FRSSAf. In 1972, as one of the founders of Wits, which was celebrating its fiftieth birthday, the university conferred the degree of LLD honoris causa on him. I cannot help pointing out that he seems to have had a sense of fun, usually hidden behind his grave exterior. A student of his studying medicine in the late forties recollected that on one soporific afternoon Watt was demonstrating the function of adrenaline to a large class of sleepy students. In order to illustrate the point he was making, Watt fired a revolver. So dramatic was the effect that almost every student stood up and one even tried to get to the door for safety. When Watt shouted 'Catch that man!' the startled students realized that it was a joke, leaving Watt pleasantly satisfied with the effect of his illustration.

[8] Op cit note 2 at 230.

[9] Op cit note 2 at 241.

[10] The judgment on this point is reported in *Rex v De Melker* 1933 WLD 37.

[11] Op cit note 2 at 240.

[12] Op cit note 2 at 220.

[13] Op cit note 2 at 231.

[14] Johannesburg: Jonathan Ball Publishers 1989 pp 182–3.

[15] Ordinance 14 of 1903.

[16] Op cit note 2 at 221.

[17] Op cit note 2 at 237.

[18] Published in Johannesburg by Mr Nortje in 1992. See page 27.

[19] *The Night is Long* op cit note 6 at 316.

[20] Op cit note 2 at 219.

[21] Op cit note 2 at 217.

[22] Alan Hardy *Some Famous Rhodesian Trials* (Bulawayo: Books of Zimbabwe 1981) chapter 9. I am indebted to the writer for details of the case.

[23] *Leaves of a Life: Being the Reminiscences of Montagu Williams QC* (London: Macmillan and Co 1890) 208–12. I have obtained further facts from J H H Gaute & Robin Odell *Murder Whereabouts* (London: Harrap Ltd 1986) 178–9.

[24] Williams op cit note 23 at 212.

[25] (Notable British Trials Series) London: William Hodge & Co Ltd 1922, reprinted in 1949. See pp vii and 1. There is an interesting account of Smith and his trial in Douglas G Browne & E V Tullett *Bernard Spilsbury: His Life and Cases* (London: George G Harrap & Co Ltd 1951) at 75–92.

[26] On Palmer, see below.

[27] [1894] AC 57 (PC).

[28] *Rex v Smith* (1915) 11 Cr App R 229, 25 Cox CC 271, 31 TLR 617, 84 LJKB 2153.

[29] See Browne & Tullett *Bernard Spilsbury* op cit note 25 at 91.

[30] London: Victor Gollancz Ltd 1929 p 341.

[31] See *Trial of H. R. Armstrong* edited by Filson Young (Notable British Trials Series) London: William Hodge & Co Ltd 1927; Browne & Tullett *Bernard Spilsbury* op cit note 25 chapter 7; Colin Wilson & Patricia Pitman *Encyclopaedia of Murder* (London: Arthur Barker Ltd 1961) Pan Books edition 1964 pp 59–61; Edgar Wallace 'The Armstrong Case' in Nigel Morland (ed) *Crime & Detection* (Oxford: Tallis Press 1966) 71–89.

[32] See *Trial of Harold Greenwood* edited by Winifred Duke (Notable British Trials Series) Edinburgh & London: William Hodge & Co Ltd 1930; Edward Marjoribanks *The Life of Sir Edward Marshall Hall* (London: Victor Gollancz Ltd 1929) 409–20.

[33] *Rex v Armstrong* [1922] 2 KB 555 (CA), before the Chief Justice (Lord Hewart), Mr Justice Avory and Mr Justice Shearman.

[34] Op cit note 31 at vi.

[35] See Wilson & Pitman *Encyclopaedia of Murder* op cit note 31 at 271; Gaute & Odell *Murder Whereabouts* op cit note 23 at 44.

[36] Published in 1960 by Constable & Co Ltd, London.

[37] Op cit note 36 at 24.

[38] Act 51 of 1977.

[39] *State v Lekaota* 1978 (4) SA 684 (A).

[40] At page 12 of the typed judgment the judgments in the cases of *Rex v Difford* 1937 AD 370 at 373 and *State v Kubeka* 1982 (1) SA 534 (W) at 537F–G were quoted to this effect.

[41] At page 45 of the typed judgment, citing Davis AJA's judgment in *Rex v De Villiers* 1944 AD 493 at 508–9.

[42] *Regina v Mlambo* 1957 (4) SA 727 (A) at 738 and *Rex v Blom* 1939 AD 188 at 202–3

[43] At page 14 of the typed judgment of the decision of the appeal court reference is made to the cases of *Rex v Dhlumayo* 1948 (2) SA 677 (A) at 705 and *State v Robinson* 1968 (1) SA 666 (A) at 675.

[44] 1957 (4) SA 727 (A) at 737. It should be pointed out that it was a dissenting judgment, but not specifically on this point; there is no reason to think that the majority judges would have disagreed with what was said.

[45] At page 29 of the typed judgment: 'the temptation to exchange his wife for the proceeds of the life policies must have been enormous.'

[46] I have reproduced part of my Adcock-Ingram address to the University of Cape Town Medical History Unit on 3 October 1988.

[47] See Robert Furneaux *The Medical Murderer* (London: Elek Books 1957) 9–16.

[48] *Forty Years of Murder* op cit note 6 above at 253–4.

[49] See *Trial of William Palmer* edited by George H Knott, revised by Eric R Watson (Notable British Trials Series) third edition (London: William Hodge & Co Ltd 1952); Wilson & Pitman op cit note 31 at 497. The earlier work by George Fletcher, *The Life and Career of Dr William Palmer of Rugeley* (London: T Fisher Unwin Ltd 1925), is very well illustrated and of much interest.

[50] *Trial of Dr Smethurst* edited by Leonard A Parry MD BS FRCS London (London: William Hodge & Co Ltd).

[51] 'Doctor's Dilemma — 1858' *Justice of the Peace* 18 June 1988 p 393.

[52] *The Reminiscences of Sir Henry Hawkins* (London: Thomas Nelson & Sons 1904) 306. The case is discussed by him at 306–10. A more detailed analysis is by the leader of the defence team, Montagu Williams QC, in *Leaves of a Life* op cit note 23 at 294–300, with a reproduction of his lengthy speech to the jury on pages 348–63. (At the time of the trial he was not a silk; he was appointed a QC only in 1886 when, owing to his having had an operation on his throat to save his life, he had to cease being counsel and took a post of metropolitan magistrate.) Two other accounts are to be found in Wilson & Pitman *Encyclopaedia of Murder* op cit note 31 at 398–400 and Furneaux *The Medical Murderer* op cit note 47 at 42–7. I have had recourse to all four sources.

[53] Op cit note 23 at 300. On that page he pays a touching tribute to Lamson's wife, who stood faithfully by him to the end, though she knew well he was guilty of murdering her brother.

[54] On Castaing, see Furneaux *The Medical Murderer* op cit note 47 at 93–7; Wilson & Pitman *Encyclopaedia of Murder* op cit note 31 at 156.

[55] Patrick Devlin *Easing the Passing: The Trial of Dr John Bodkin Adams* (London: The Bodley Head 1985) 8.

[56] Op cit note 55 at 8.

[57] Op cit note 55 at 10.

[58] Op cit note 55 at 89.

[59] Devlin op cit note 55 at 38.

[60] He married Lady Mary Lindsay, daughter of the 27th Earl of Crawford.

[61] Op cit note 55 at 39.

[62] Op cit note 55 at 69.

[63] Op cit note 55 at 57.

[64] Op cit note 55 at 125.

[65] Op cit note 55 at 146.

[66] Op cit note 55 at 180–1.

[67] Op cit note 55 at 183.

[68] See *Sunday Tribune* 11 September 1983 p 8.

[69] For example, Rodney Hallworth & Mark Williams *There's a Will* (London 1983); Theo Ruoff in (1985) 59 *Australian Law Journal* 632; Leslie Sellers in the *Sunday Times* (Johannesburg) 5 August 1984.

[70] See Percy Hoskins *Two Men Were Acquitted: The Trial and Acquittal of John Bodkin Adams* (London: Seeker & Warburg 1984). The two were Adams and Hoskins himself, for he was the only journalist consistently to contend that Adams was not guilty of murder.

[71] Op cit note 55 at 199.

[72] Op cit note 55 at 91.

[73] Op cit note 55 at 92.

[74] *Political Adventure: The Memoirs of the Earl of Kilmuir* (London: Weidenfeld and Nicolson 1964) 323–4. The publication was a very much toned-down version of the original draft, which was vitriolic in expression. The toning-down was at the insistence of the Cabinet office. See the fascinating article by Sir Robert Rhodes James, who did the editing, in *The Spectator* of 11 July 1992 p 19.

[75] On the foregoing I have had the advantage of consulting R F Heuston *Lives of the Lord Chancellors 1940–1970* (Oxford: The Clarendon Press 1987) 183, especially at 189.

[76] Op cit note 75 at 199.

[77] *Law and Politics: The House of Lords as a Judicial Body, 1800–1976* (London: Weidenfeld and Nicolson 1979) 426–7.

[78] Stevens op cit note 77 at 459. Professor J A Griffiths in his leading book *The Politics of the Judiciary* 3 ed (London: Fontana Press 1985) 184 said that for Devlin the social service a judge rendered was the removal of a cause of injustice, requiring both impartiality and the appearance of impartiality. To him, a judge should not be a dynamic lawmaker, but an activist lawmaker, keeping pace with the consensus in the community.

[79] Op cit note 77 at 469.

[80] *The Guardian Weekly* 21–7 August 1992 p 25.

[81] Op cit note 55 at 198.

[82] Op cit note 55 at 226.

[83] I am especially indebted for what follows for the information provided in *The First Report of the Shipman Inquiry: Chairman Dame Janet Smith DBE: Volume One: Death Disguised* HMSO Crown Copyright 2002, published 19 July 2002, and also available on http://www.the_shipman_inquiry.org.uk/reports.asp; and it will be referred to as *Death Disguised*; and in Brian Whittle and Jean Ritchie *Prescription for Murder: The True Story of Mass Murderer Dr Harold Frederick Shipman* (London: Warner Books 2000). Also most helpful were Ted Ottley 'Dark Side of Dr. S: The World's Most Prolific Serial Killer' www.crimelibrary.com/serial8/shipman and Gerald England 'Harold Fred Shipman: An account of the murderous GP of Hyde' www.nhi.clara.net/shipman.htm. I have consulted in addition press reports in *The Daily Telegraph* (London), the *Independent* (London), *The Guardian* (London) and *The Times* (London).

[84] See *Death Disguised* § 1.30.

[85] There is a far more detailed account in Appendix E to *Death Disguised*.

[86] There is a summary in Appendix A of *Death Disguised.*
[87] In § 5.54 of *Death Disguised.*
[88] *Death Disguised* §§ 6.62–6.64.
[89] See *Death Disguised* § 7.28.
[90] *Death Disguised* § 7.45.
[91] *Death Disguised* chapter nine.
[92] *Death Disguised* § 9.4.
[93] *Death Disguised* § 9.19.
[94] *Death Disguised* § 9.58.
[95] *Death Disguised* §§ 13.12–13.16 and 13.75–13.80.
[96] § 13.15.
[97] *Death Disguised* § 13.79.
[98] *Death Disguised* § 13.17ff.
[99] *Death Disguised* § 13.21ff.
[100] *Death Disguised* § 13.26.
[101] *Death Disguised* § 13.30.
[102] *Death Disguised* §§ 14.41 and 13.43.
[103] *Death Disguised* §§ 13.50ff.
[104] *Death Disguised* § 14.8.
[105] They included a national clinical authority to assess poorly performing doctors; annual appraisals by the General Medical Council; new procedures for records by GPs; and tighter control over drugs. See the leader in *The Guardian* 20 July 2002.
[106] On Petiot, see Wilson & Pitman *Encyclopaedia of Murder* op cit note 31 at 511–15. He was guillotined on 26 May 1946.
[107] *Death Disguised* § 14.21.
[108] 'The Woman Who Talked Too Much' in his book *Murder Will Speak* (Cape Town: Howard Timmins 1962) chapter I.
[109] See *Trial of Eugene Marie Chantrelle* edited by A Duncan Smith (Notable British Trials Series) Edinburgh: William Hodge & Co Ltd 1928.
[110] See *Trial of Sidney H Fox* edited by F Tennyson Jesse (Notable British Trials Series) London: William Hodge & Co Ltd 1930; Browne & Tullett *Bernard Spilsbury* op cit note 25 at 336–43.
[111] See Jonathan Goodman (ed) *The Lady Killers: Some Famous Women Murderers* (London: Sphere Books Ltd 1990) 159, reproducing extracts from the *Stockport Advertiser* (Cheshire) 11 December 1863.
[112] See Wilson & Pitman *Encyclopaedia of Murder* op cit note 31 at 266; Gaute & Odell *Murder Whereabouts* op cit note 23 at 141.
[113] There is a detailed account of her life and doings in Ernest Bowen-Rowlands *In the Light of the Law* (London: Grant Richards 1931) 228–38. Montagu Williams in his *Leaves of a Life* op cit note 23 at 44–6 deals with his defence of her in two of her trials. I have relied on both works.
[114] Williams op cit note 23 at 45.
[115] Williams loc cit. Bowen-Rowlands (op cit note 113 at 204), though, did not regard the verdict as extraordinary or perverse.
[116] Op cit note 23 at 47.
[117] See Wilson & Pitman *Encyclopaedia of Murder* op cit note 31 at 454–5.
[118] See Wilson & Pitman *Encyclopaedia of Murder* op cit note 31 at 620–2; Furneaux *The Medical Murderer* op cit note 47 at 134–7; H Montgomery Hyde *Norman Birkett: The Life of Lord Birkett of Ulverston* (London: Hamish Hamilton 1964) 449–51.
[119] I am indebted to Hugh Miller for his account of the case in his *Forensic Fingerprints* (London: Headline Book Publishing 1998) 137–49. A photo of the skin is at 83.
[120] The Rt Hon Sir Ellis Hume-Williams Bart PC KBE KC *The World, the House and the Bar* (London: John Murray 1930) 20–3.
[121] Op cit note 120 at 22.
[122] Op cit note 120 at 22.
[123] Op cit note 120 at 22–3.

[124] In *Other Men's Millions* (Cape Town: Howard B Timmins nd) chapter XVI and *The Best of Eric Rosenthal* (CapeTown: Howard Timmins 1975) chapter XVII. The accounts are identical.

[125] By Michael Joseph Ltd, London.

[126] On pages 182–3.

[127] London: Stevens & Sons Ltd 1973 p 299.

[128] *In The Goods of Sharman* (1869) LR 1 P & D 661; *In the Goods of Smith* (1889) 15 PD 2; *Kitcat v King* [1930] P 266.

[129] By the Law of Succession Amendment Act 43 of 1992.

[130] Act 66 of 1965.

[131] Act 24 of 1913. Prior to this statute, Ordinance 104 of 1833 (Cape) section 4 made it an offence, during or after the lifetime of a testator or testatrix, to steal or for any fraudulent purpose destroy or conceal any will, codicil or other testamentary instrument. There does not appear to have been any such legislation in Natal. In the Transvaal, section 10 of the Administration of Estates Proclamation 28 of 1902 made it an offence during or after the life of the testator to steal or wilfully destroy or conceal any will, codicil or other testamentary instrument. In the Orange Free State, section 7 of the Administration of Estates Ordinance 18 of 1905 read the same, except that it spoke only of a will.

[132] 1985 (3) SA 25 (A).

[133] The underhand will was created in the Cape by Ordinance 15 of 1845, in Natal by Law 2 of 1868, in the Transvaal by Ordinance 14 of 1903 and in the Orange Free State by Ordinance 11 of 1904. Today the governing statute in South Africa is the Wills Act 7 of 1953.

[134] 1924 AD 618 at 701. That it was a dissenting judgment does not signify.

[135] I venture to allude to my article 'The Will that Won't — Formalities Gone Bananas' in *Huldigingsbundel Paul van Warmelo* (Pretoria: University of South Africa 1984) 128.

[136] See Working Paper IX Project 22 *Review of the Law of Succession: Formalities of a Will* (June 1986); and *Report* (June 1991).

[137] Working Paper 14 Project 22 § 7.85.

[138] 1908 EDC 32, the sequel to which is to be found in Bisset and Smith's *Digest of South African Case Law* (Consolidated edition) to the end of 1921 vol 5 col 1160.

[139] 1924 AD 618.

[140] At 683.

[141] Pietermaritzburg: University of Natal Press 1962 pp 113–14.

[142] Thus, for instance, *De Lange v Rudman* 1928 EDL 439 (where the plaintiff failed to establish that the testator's signature had been forged); *Dukada v Dukada's Estate* 1937 EDL 372 (where the will was set aside on the ground that a signature of one witness was not genuine).

[143] 1938 EDL 199.

[144] Quoted in *Faber Book of Aphorisms* (1962), edited by W H Auden and Louis Kronenberger. I have refrained from quoting Byron's lines in *Don Juan* canto ci: ' 'Tis strange — but true; for truth is always strange; Stranger than fiction.'

[145] Johannesburg: Jonathan Ball Publishers 1998 pp 110–16. Cecil called the testator Morris Liondore, but this was incorrect. I have elaborated on Cecil's account with my notes on 22 December 1962 of what I heard at a dinner at Cecil's house then from Maurice Porter, the attorney involved in the dénouement of the case. Unfortunately, my notes cannot be reconciled entirely with what Cecil wrote.

[146] The preliminary proceedings are set out in *Johannesburg Bar Council v Stein* 1946 TPD 115.

[147] Central News Agency Ltd 1953 pp 33–4.

[148] 1952 (1) SA 423 (SR). The decision was followed in *R v Basson* 1965 (1) SA 697 (C).

[149] 1985 (3) SA 25 (A).

[150] 2001 (1) SA 410 (D). As with so many cases of forgeries or alleged forgeries of wills, the court had great difficulty in determining who did what and what exactly happened.

[151] See *Sunday Star* 24 October 1993 pp 1 and 5.

[152] Transvaal High Court 3 May 1999, unreported. The judgment was kindly furnished by Mr Cecil Greenfield, handwriting and document examiner. He told me that the expert witnesses were actually Brigadier Fourie and Captain Bam, both retired members of the police forensic department.

[153] London: Stevens & Sons Ltd 1973 pp 304–6.

[154] (1860) 2 F & F 24, 175 ER 942; (1864) 4 F & F 1, 176 ER 440.

[155] London: Edward Arnold 1914 pp 119–26.

[156] London: Hutchinson & Co Ltd 1930 pp 176–7.

[157] I am indebted to the detailed account of Hobbs's life by James Morton in *New Law Journal* 25 May 2001 p 794.

[158] London: Frederick Muller Ltd 1980 pp 56–7.

[159] London: Weidenfeld and Nicolson 1983 pp 119–20.

[160] On the search for a will and on claimants up to 1983, see Menchin *Where There's a Will* op cit note 158 at 28–30; Bresler *Second-Best Bed* op cit note 159 at 124–30. For the story up to 1996, see James R Phelan and Lewis Chester *The Money: The Battle for Howard Hughes's Billions* (New York: Random House 1997).

[161] See Jerry Moskal *Houston Business Journal* 19 December 1997

[162] Op cit note 160.

[163] 640 SW 2d 942 (Court of Appeals of Texas, Houston (14th District) 5 August 1982).

[164] *Moore v Neff* 629 SW 2d 827 (Court of Appeals of Texas, Houston (14th District) 4 February 1982). See, too, Phelan & Chester op cit note 160 at 178–88.

[165] This would be the position, too, under s 1 (1) *(a)* of the Intestate Succession Act 81 of 1987 of South Africa, which states that where a person dies intestate, either wholly or in part, and is survived by a spouse, but not by a descendant, such spouse inherits the intestate estate. It would make no difference that the deceased left a parent or a sibling, let alone an aunt or uncle.

[166] See Phelan & Chester op cit note 160 at 59–69.

[167] Recounted by Lucinda Bredin & Kate Wharton in *Evening Standard Magazine* May 1990, reproduced in Bruce Palling (ed) *The Book of Modern Scandal* (London: Orion Books Ltd 1996) 312–17.

[168] I have consulted *The Daily Telegraph* (London) of 27 July 1999 and various subsequent accounts on the Internet.

[169] I have derived much help from the account of the judgment in *Financial Times Weekend* 23–24 November 2002 p 5; also from the account in *Saturday Star* (Johannesburg) 23 November 2002 p 13.

[170] The Authorized (King James) version reads: 'Surely every man walketh in a vain shew: surely they are disquieted in vain: he heapeth up riches, and knoweth not who shall gather them.'